D1055409

Subverting the System:
D'Aubigné and Calvinism

Habent sua fata libelli

Volume XIV
of
Sixteenth Century Essays & Studies
Charles G. Nauert, Jr., General Editor

Composed by NMSU typographer, Trey Hoffman, Kirksville, Missouri
Cover Design by Teresa Wheeler, NMSU Designer
Printed by Edwards Brothers, Ann Arbor, Michigan
Text is set in Bembo II 10/12

Subverting the System:
D'Aubigné and Calvinism

by Catharine Randall Coats

Volume XIV
Sixteenth Century Essays & Studies

PQ
1603
.C63
1990

This book has been brought to publication with the
generous support of
Northeast Missouri State University

Library of Congress Cataloging-in-Publication Data

Subverting the system: D'Aubigné and Calvinism / Catharine Randall
Coats
    p. cm. – (Sixteenth century essays & studies ; v. 14)
    Includes bibliographical references and index.
    ISBN 0-940474-16-6 (alk. paper)
    1. Aubigné, Agrippa d', 1552-1630–Religion. 2. Christian literature,
French–History and criticism. 3. Calvin, Jean, 1509-1564–Influence. 4.
Calvinism–France–History. 5. Calvinism in literature. I. Title II. Series.
PQ1603.C63   1990
841′, 3–dc20   90-47487
                                                       CIP

Copyright© 1990 by Sixteenth Century Journal Publishers, Inc., Kirksville, Missouri.
All rights reserved. No part of this work may be reproduced or transmitted in any format
by any means, electronic or mechanical, including photocopying and recording, or by any
information storage or retrieval system, without permission in writing from the publisher.
Printed in the United States of America.
    The paper used in this publication meets the minimum requirements of the American
National Standard for Permanence of Paper for Printed Library Materials Z39.48, 1984.

224420863

Contents

Foreword

Much is said in contemporary scholarship about the value of interdisciplinary research–much is said, but little is done. A special attraction of this study of the French Calvinist author Agrippa d'Aubigné by Catharine Randall Coats is that she has dared to undertake a truly interdisciplinary study, combining her specialty of French Renaissance literature with attention to the way in which Calvinist theology affected the literary endeavors of Calvinist writers, not only her own subject, Agrippa d'Aubigné, but all French Protestant authors of the later sixteenth century. Here she argues that Calvinist theology created special problems of conscience because its emphasis on the authority of Scripture made believers regard their proper task as exposition and presentation of the truth already revealed, while any effort to create an imaginary world of creative fiction seemed a rejection of the truth and a self-glorification of the author that amounted to rebellion against the authority of God. John Calvin himself, with his thorough grounding in the classical tradition of Renaissance humanism, could still engage in literary creation with a relatively free conscience; but the following generation of *epigoni,* dominated by his successor at Geneva, Theodore de Bèze, felt a deep hostility to the prideful literary creator. In fact, with few exceptions, French Calvinist writers of the later sixteenth century avoided poetic fiction and did in fact confine their efforts to cautious exegesis of revealed truth.

This is the basic assumption of the present book, presented chiefly in an introductory chapter. But according to the present author, Agrippa d'Aubigné represents a clear and conscious rebellion against such constraints; and the balance of the book demonstrates how d'Aubigné through his career more and more openly dared to engage in independent literary creation and to assert his right as a sincerely reformed Christian to do so. Thus theology and literature come together in this study to illuminate a major problem in the literary history of the French Reformed tradition.

Charles G. Nauert, Jr.
General Editor
Sixteenth Century Essays & Studies

1

Literary Constructs for Theological Conventions: Authorizing the Word of the Self

THE LITERARY IMPLICATIONS OF CALVINISM have never been elucidated. And while Agrippa d'Aubigné is commmonly held to have been influenced, religiously and politically, by Calvinism, his literary reaction to this theological framework has never been fully analyzed. I propose to examine Calvinism through explicit reference to Théodore de Bèze, epigone of John Calvin and contemporary of Agrippa d'Aubigné. We shall determine the reservations de Bèze expressed concerning non-scripturally motivated literature, that is, the writing of the self. I will then comment upon the conflict d'Aubigné experienced between his theological interdiction of fictional creation and his desire to write. It is my contention that, despite or perhaps because of his religious beliefs, in the course of his literary career d'Aubigné progressed from the stage of paraphrase, through exegesis, exposition and epic, to develop ultimately his own fictional model. His work was expressed in theo-literary language, in which theological terms acquired new literary applications, while literary constructs conveyed theological convictions. This was innovative for a Calvinist, for whom literature–a focus on the self rather than on the Creator–was perceived as part of the fallen world. It is within the confines of the dialectic of sin and salvation, of language as fall and mediation, that d'Aubigné conceived of himself as a sinful creator.

The Calvinist Paradigm

The Calvinist distrust of fiction was a major stumbling-block which d'Aubigné had to overcome in order to write non-exegetical works. Indeed, with the exception of d'Aubigné, we find no *literary* works by Calvinist writers. The *absence* of these works demonstrates an implicit constraint in Calvinism.[1] For Calvinists, the revealed Word of God was always preeminent

---

[1] The fact that some Calvinists actually abjured, and returned to the Catholic church (simultaneous with their inauguration, or resumption, of a literary form of expression) can only strengthen the case for some problematic in Calvinist writing. For in the case of such writers, a greater liberty of expression can be discerned subsequent to their return to the Catholic faith. Examples of such recidivists are Jean de Sponde and Béroalde de Verville.

1

over the word of an author: "the [Calvinist writer] was oriented toward *logos* rather than *mythos* as the fit vessel of truth."[2] John Calvin's "stile invisible"[3] effectively translated Calvin's intention that the purpose of writing be that of magnifying God's Word. The epigoni intensified this view, emphasizing in particular the criterion of *utilitas,* and Théodore de Bèze, in particular, mandated scripturally-based writings.[4] De Bèze interpreted portions of Calvin's work more narrowly and rigorously, specifically opposing fiction as a construction of the self. The greater flexibility in writing that we can find in the expository technique of Calvin's *Commentaries,* as contrasted with the strict exegetical production of de Bèze, would indicate that d'Aubigné, in his audacious series of literary works (several of which are obviously self-exalting), may have returned to Calvin, against the Calvinists who were d'Aubigné's contemporaries, to legitimate a sense of the self in his works.[5] While Calvin never specifically wrote an anti-literary program, de Bèze did. His preface to *Abraham sacrifiant* reacts against the strong mythological component of the Pléiade. De Bèze calls for a rigorous fidelity to the biblical text. An example of his standard for self-effacement is his play *Abraham sacrifiant,* essentially no more than a reiteration, in notably sparse and "unartistic" terms, of the Abraham and Isaac story. *Abraham sacrifiant* was a manifesto against the proliferation of writing unmotivated by, or deviant from, the Word. Despite the dramatic genre, the title page of de Bèze's play resembled an exegetical tract. After the title and author appeared a biblical reference, "Gen XV Rom III," and then

[2]Thomas Torrance, *Calvin's Hermeneutics* (Edinburgh: Scottish Academy Press, 1988), 142. Regarding Calvin's view of nonscriptural writing, Torrance says, "the human arts and sciences are rightly pursued within the world where they have their divinely appointed place and their proper validity . . . but they cannot extend their methods of investigation and discernment beyond the world, for then they would transgress their proper limits and lapse into superstition. On the other hand, knowledge must not be torn away from religion. The dangers to be thus avoided are presumption and naturalism."

[3]Mario Richter, "La Poetica de Théodore de Bèze e le *Chrestiennes méditations,*" *Aevum* 38 (1964): 494.

[4]When positing Calvinism as a force over against which an author with any pretensions to self-expression would have to react, it is important to note, therefore, that Calvin and Calvinism are not exact equivalents. Calvin's perspective is distorted and rigidified by De Bèze and the epigoni.

[5]An interesting line of inquiry, which I do not have space to pursue here, would be to adopt the position that Calvin himself (and not de Bèze alone), in fact, while many have deemed him a humanist, was first and foremost a theologian and that, in this light, he too would have had a good deal of trouble with d'Aubigné's secular, self-exalting literary works. I have explored such a reading of Calvin elsewhere, in relation to d'Aubigné's works; cf. "Representing and Re-presenting the Self: Fact and Fiction in d'Aubigné's *Sa Vie* and the *Histoire universelle,*" *South Atlantic Review* (Spring, 1989): 23-40; "The Devil's Phallus: Notions of Writing in Béroalde de Verville and Agrippa d'Aubigné," *Stanford French Review* 16, no. 1 (Spring, 1989): 37-48; "Dialectic and Literary Creation: A Protestant Poetics," *Neophilogus* 72 (1988): 168-79. However, for the purposes of this study, the points of contact between

the play's didactic message, which was practically inextricable from the biblical pre-text: "Abraham a creu à Dieu, et il luy a esté réputé à justice." The final word of the play disclosed de Bèze's goal, the potential author's mutism (as well as that of his audience): "Voilà, messieurs, l'heureuse recompense / Que Dieu vous doint pour votre bon silence." This final silence was the ultimate aim, as de Bèze saw it, of the faithful Calvinist writer. For him, even exegesis was extraneous, since it commented upon language intended to be univalent.[6] His role in writing, de Bèze claimed in the preface, was to praise God. He opposed this aim to what he perceived as the self-glorification of his primary literary competitors, the Pléiade. Consequently, the content of his work was limited to "histoires sainctes," and was purged of the profane and mythological element upon which the Pléiade relied. The significance of de Bèze's program is heightened by the reader's knowledge that de Bèze was once an advocate of the Pléiade's program.[7] De Bèze intentionally precluded any relationship between sacred and profane writing. This resulted in the codification of a stringent series of limitations on textual production and the expression of the self.

De Bèze's writing did not tend in the direction of self-expression, but rather in that of standardization in order to better explain the Word and to regularize its interpretation for the *culte*. It is for this reason, then, that during his tenure in Geneva, de Bèze "surveill[ait] tout et tous, interdi[sait] le théâtre profane, blam[ait] quiconque [avait] chez lui la *Légende dorée* ou l'*Amadis de Gaule*."[8] De Bèze's concern over literary work (in the preceding example, the *Légende* is mythological, and *Amadis* is romance) exemplified his desire to clarify and regularize religious experience and expression. De Bèze denied the self in an attempt to reinstate the prelapsarian equivalence of Word and word, the utter incorporation of the latter by the former.

---

de Bèze and d'Aubigné, contemporaries, are so explicit that it seems best to focus on those in defining the Calvinist paradigm against which d'Aubigné must write. Stephen Ozment, *The Age of Reform* (New Haven: Yale University Press, 1980), 315, suggests that "the similarity between humanist and Protestant interest in rhetoric and eloquence may be more structural than material. Both saw man as a complex unity, driven by will and passion, but Protestants remained far more skeptical about his rational, moral, and religious abilities than most humanists . . . doctrine was always the rider and the humanities the horse. . . . the rhetorical arts served the more basic task of communicating true doctrine."

[6]Thédore de Bèze, *Icones,* intro. by Alain Du Four (Geneva, 1673, reprint, 1973). Elsewhere in his writing, this self-silencing tendency of de Bèze's remains consistent. In the *Histoire ecclésiastique,* for instance, he collects "les escrits d'une foule de témoins et . . . leur but était trop élevé et sainct pour supporter la moindre vanité d'auteur." Accordingly, he published this work anonymously.

[7]Regarding de Bèze's strong reaction against a school whose philosophy he had formerly espoused, see his preface to *Abraham sacrifiant* (Geneva: Rycher, 1560).

[8]Jean Delumeau, *Naissance et affirmation de la Réforme* (Paris: Gallimard, 1965), 115.

Writing is tantamount to a second Fall; a literary assertion of self is construed as the self in opposition to God. This may be why an examination of the list of books published in Geneva in the mid and late 1500s shows that, at least for the early Calvinists,

> la théologie garde la première place avec les textes sacrés, les commentaires, la dogmatique, la controverse, la morale, l'homilétique, l'édification . . . [et quant à] la littérature française et en musique . . . il est vray il [ne] s'agit [que] . . . de poèmes et de chants religieux. Hormis les livres utilitaires, les ouvrages tout à fait profanes restent une infime minorité.[9]

De Bèze permitted only exegetical writing, a repetition of the Bible which followed the contours of the Word so closely that no schism between the model and its representation in restatement might be discerned. Only words warranted by the Word are encouraged. The explicit linking of human writing and filth connects creativity and sin. So Théodore de Bèze indicted fallen writing, likening himself to David, who murdered Uriah in order to possess Bathsheba:

> Je voy le lict souillé et infect, où j'ay embrassé le péché et la mort. . . . Je te voy, main traisteresse, par qui ces deux lettres meurtrières ont esté escrites.[10]

David's letters to Joab were "lettres meurtrières" because it was through the medium of those letters that David ordered Uriah the Hittite killed. Those letters were so closely associated with David's sin, therefore, as to be virtually identical with it. Writing was here emblematic of sin.

So it was that with de Bèze, "les images du Psalmiste sont souvent affaiblies pour servir mieux à des fins didactiques."[11] Thus, de Bèze performed a selective–indeed, reductive–reading of the Bible. De Bèze intentionally spoke in rough, neutral tones, subordinating himself to the functional rendering of the biblical text. His self was negated, except as it might function as an exemplum: "chez Bèze, tout lyrisme, toute passion se mêlent à une sorte de prière anonyme collective."[12] De Bèze prescribed the "plain style," an unadorned, anti-allegorical style which adhered to the Word. Faithfulness to the Word required annihilating the self, in the sense that one's prior proud sense of self would be erased by one's awareness of one's

---

[9]Pierre Chaix et G. Moeckli, *Les Livres imprimés à Genève 1550-1600* (Geneva: Droz, 1966), 10.

[10]Théodore de Bèze, *Chrestiennes méditations,* ed. Mario Richter (Geneva: Droz, 1964), 73.

[11]Richter, "Introduction," *Chrestiennes,* 24.

[12]Marguérite Soulié, "L'Utilisation de la Bible dans les *Méditations* de Jean de Sponde," *Mélanges sur la littérature de la Renaissance à la mémoire de V.-L. Saulnier* (Geneva: Droz, 1986), 296.

sinful nature. As the later Calvinists Favre and Mathieu Pybrac asserted in 1640,

> Pour vivre à Dieu, l'homme doit en Dieu vivre,
> Qui vit à soy meurt soudain à son Dieu.[13]

Calvinist writers, influenced by de Bèze's example, looked to the imperative of self-effacement, thanking God that "la grace donc vient de Toy jusques à moy pour me chasser de moy affin de me trouver et tout mon bien en Toy."[14] Calvinist writing, with the exception of that of d'Aubigné, was strictly biblically oriented. Its characteristics were a distrust of the potentially deceitful world, as well as an obsessive awareness of the writer's infinite distance from God. Jean de Sponde, for instance, wrote that it was only by experiencing stricture (here described in terms of spatial enclosure) that he could come closer to God: "Seigneur, je me restreins en cest enclos, et comme me resserrant en moy-mesme hors du Monde, je sors plus librement vers toy, et te magnifie."[15] Only by making himself smaller and by restraining his speech could he write. In other instances, the author's prose on the printed page dwindled in form and in space, beginning as a full page and ending in silence as the inverted apex of a triangle. Such a figure displayed the closure of the attempt to write and symbolized the quelling of the human voice. Simon Goulart's *Le Sage vieillart* ended with this configuration. The last words of his text replaced the author's signature with the name "Jésus Christ."[16] D'Aubigné, too, was subsumed into the Divine Presence at the end of the *Tragiques*. However, unlike other Calvinist writers, he did not in this way seek to represent the silencing of his individual speech, or the end to his literary creation. Rather, his text remained, a solid block dominating the page, while that of Goulart was literally and figuratively pared down to nothing. In another demonstration of Calvinist writers' unease, Philippe du Plessis-Mornay likened God to a "censeur."[17] D'Aubigné's literary creations, however, disregarded the criterion of accountability to God, achieving a progressively independent status,[18]

---

[13]Mathieu et Pybrac, *Les Quatrains du Sieur Pybrac* (Paris: Robinot, 1640), 33.

[14]De Bèze, *Chrestiennes*, 57.

[15]Jean de Sponde, *Méditations*, ed. Alan Boase (Geneva: Droz, 1972), 151.

[16]Although this is a printer's convention in use at the time, there are many other presentations which might have been selected instead. I believe this choice has symbolic value, therefore.

[17]Philippe du Plessis-Mornay, *De la Vérité de la religion chrestienne* (Paris, Richter, 1582), fol. I.i^r. And it was true that all books printed in Geneva had to receive the official sanction of the church authorities: "Pour obvier qu'il ne soit imprimé nul livre auquel l'honneur et la gloire de Dieu ne fusse rejetés, a esté arresté et conclu que tous imprimeurs doivent apporter le premier livre qu'ils auront imprimé, lequel devra demeurer dans la maison de la ville."

[18]D'Aubigné, "Lettres sur diverses sciences," *Oeuvres*, ed. Henri Weber (Paris: Gallimard, 1969), 860.

particularly as he increasingly took up secular concerns. Refusing to allow the criterion of *utilitas* or merit in writing to limit textual creation, d'Aubigné also insisted on a *literary* evaluation of those of his theological *confrères* who wrote, though their work was scripturally-derived in its entirety. He likened de Bèze to Ronsard and Marot stylistically, for example, and discussed only the presentation of de Bèze's work, omitting any mention of religious content or orientation.[19]

Would-be Calvinist writers therefore had to examine their consciences, and their endeavors at expression, to determine whether or not they were conforming to the strict exegetical standard de Bèze set. We can see the inner tensions this produced to varying degrees in writers such as Henri Estienne, Jean de Sponde, Philippe du Plessis-Mornay, and Guillaume Salluste Du Bartas. They knew that the word "fiction" was often construed negatively in the Renaissance, and that this concern over fiction as lying or false creation was exacerbated by the Reformation. *Fingere* can be understood as the poetic act of "making," but in the Reformation this act was more commonly labelled *feindre,* the fashioning of lies.[20] The Huguenot Jean de la Taille protested in *Saül le furieux* that "je n'ay des histoires fabuleuses mendié icy . . . mais celles que le vérité mesme a dictées."[21] For the Calvinist, "vérité" is "dictée" because it is God's communication. "Vérité," therefore, may never be an individual fabrication. Calvinist writers acknowledged this truth by writing *no* nonbiblical literature.

Thus, the strongest example of the resulting pull between fidelity to Calvinism and the desire for individual expression was the work of Agrippa d'Aubigné. D'Aubigné progressively diverged from the Calvinist restrictions on writing. While other Calvinist writers conformed to the Protestant paradigm, finding the only licensed outlet for literary expression to be the reorganization of biblical material,[22] d'Aubigné wandered far from the established text. This was even the case with his *Méditations,* which, due to their format, are often misread as rigorous Calvinist exegesis. Critics have "essay[é] de voir comment [la] qualité de réformés, c'est-à-dire d'hommes qui 'désirent de servir purement sans se polluer aux superstitions de la papauté,' modifie la teneur et la couleur de [leurs] escrits,"[23] but no one has attempted to detach d'Aubigné from this stereotype to examine the tensions in his work which, while faithful to *his* conception of the Bible, amounted in some respects to a subversion of Calvinism. According to

[19]D'Aubigné, "Lettres," 862-63.

[20]Cf. Grahame Castor, *Pléiade Poetics* (Cambridge: Cambridge University Press, 1964), chap. 1.

[21]Jean de la Taille, "Saül le furieux," *Oeuvres* (repr. Geneva: Slatkine, 1968).

[22]Richter, *Jean de Sponde e la lingua poetica dei protestanti nel cinquecento* (Milan: Cisalpino-Goliardica, 1973), 201.

[23]Ibid., 191.

Jacques Aymon, d'Aubigné must *already* have been trying to do that which Calvinism forbade:

> Ceux qui mettent la main à la plume pour écrire les histoires de l'Escriture Saincte en vers, seront advertis de n'y mesler pas de Fables poétiques et de n'attribuer pas à Dieu les noms de fausses Divinités, et d'adjouster ni retrancher aucune chose de l'Escriture, mais de s'en tenir aux propres termes du Texte sacré.[24]

Only exegesis, a voice of no authorship, was recognized by de Bèze.[25] How, then, did d'Aubigné dare to diverge from actual, biblical, revealed-historical truth into the realms of fiction?

For d'Aubigné, who wrote and did not deny himself, who considered himself instead to be an active agent of God's Word while still retaining his own autonomy, the result was an extreme form of literary self-consciousness. For him, the primacy of the Calvinist model of the Bible was not a "stimulus to the imagination" or "normative for poetic art as well as for spiritual truth,"[26] but rather a formidable obstacle to literary creation. D'Aubigné had to develop a sense of self sufficiently strong to do homage to the Word despite his competitive relationship with it. D'Aubigné valued Scripture too much to circumvent it. Instead, he went in and through it, sublimating his sinful nature, saving himself through his writing.

Much of d'Aubigné's work was not in line with scriptural motivation. It deviated because d'Aubigné licensed a discussion of the *self* that distracted from the focus on Scripture. Calvinism asserted that in seeking to create literarily, man swerved from the essential, salvific focus on God. D'Aubigné, however, focused on his literary endeavors, consciously using them to work in, and through, his sin[27] to an ultimate certainty of his election. Hence,

---

[24]Jacques Aymon, *Tous les synodes nationaux des églises réformées en France* (The Hague, 1710), 210.

[25]While Calvin admits, and employs, exposition as a scripturally-derived form of writing, de Bèze severely limits the use of exposition in his own works, preferring a close exegesis subordinated to the text at hand. Exposition seeks to translate a scriptural story into a relevant, contemporary mode, using exegetical techniques. Exposition may transpose a text into exempla or even story form, whereas exegesis does not apply any elements of the Bible to anything else, but simply parses a text word by word in a sort of critical dissection. Exposition introduces relevant passages from *other* locations in the Bible, and may relate the material under discussion to contemporary existence, thus *adding on to* the biblical word. Calvinist exposition is in no way intended to facilitate human expression (or exalt human experience); rather, it seeks to provide a model or exemplum for right-thinking or right-living. And certainly, for both Calvin and Bèze, it would be unthinkable that the text might be an excuse or jumping-off point for the expositor to make personal revelations or editorialize, as may indeed be the case with d'Aubigné.

[26]Soulié, "L'Utilisation," 137.

[27]A telling example is found in the examination of textual variants for *Les Tragiques*. D'Aubigné substitutes "son péché" for "son proche" in the verse "pour vivre il faut fuir de son péché la veuë."

d'Aubigné's definition of his writing as testimony of a chosen status conflicted with the Calvinist turn away from the self.

While all of d'Aubigné's works warrant examination in light of the problem of the appearance of the literary self, the most significant is probably the *Avantures du Baron de Faeneste.* All the major d'Aubigné critics fail to discern the crucial location of the *Avantures* within d'Aubigné's literary network, preferring to deal with the more easily accounted for (because apparently self-evidently Calvinist) *Tragiques* and *Méditations.* Consequently, they overlook the issue of how d'Aubigné could remain a faithful Calvinist and yet write fiction–fiction that was occasionally salacious.[28] This is certainly a dilemma with which d'Aubigné wrestled. In a letter to "Simon Goulard, ministre à Genève, l'an 1616," for instance, he vituperated Goulart for permitting censorship of d'Aubigné's works: "C'est qu'ayant esté refusé d'un privilege par la hayne seule de ma personne. . . ." D'Aubigné took this as a personal affront. He was, indeed, self-aware in a way that Calvinism did not encourage.[29] D'Aubigné was also acutely aware of the mandates he was flouting; for instance, in the *Avantures,* the character who represents Calvinism, Enay, comments on the rigorous standards to which Calvinists were expected to adhere in both oral and written expression:

On ne permet pas ces gayetés [allégories . . . parabolles . . . fables . . .] à nos Ministres, mesme on leur défend les Allégories tant qu'on peut, pour *les attacher à leur texte* sans eschapper (my emphasis).[30]

The Word of God, "leur texte," was an unsurpassable prototype; no creation could supersede that of God. Creation, in the sense of an original, autonomous "making" of form, was God's absolute prerogative.

---

[28]We know that, at the very least, d'Aubigné had read Calvin, *The Institutes, Commentary on the Psalms* and the *Romans,* as well as *Des Scandales.* De Bèze was a contemporary of d'Aubigné, and d'Aubigné had read de Bèze's *Abraham sacrifiant* and probably also, later, the *Chrestiennes méditations.* I purposefully use "de Bèze" rather than "Bèze" throughout, for his contemporaries referred to him in this way. Cf. d'Aubigné, *Sa Vie,* 389, for instance, or the numerous references to de Bèze in Ronsard's "Discours sur les misères." D'Aubigné also corresponded with Simon Goulart. He was familiar with the work of Du Plessis-Mornay; Du Bartas, especially *La Sepmaine*; and cites Henri Estienne and Jean Crespin. Occasionally d'Aubigné's inflection of Calvinist doctrine is marked by obscenity. Upholding Calvin's denial of transubstantiation in "Conte de la présence réelle" in *Pièces épigrammatiques,* he writes,
Tout ce que tien le Prestre en sa poche, en sa manche,
En sa braguette est sainct et de plus je vous dy,
Qu'en aiant desjeuné de son Dieu le dimanche,
Vous devez adorer son estron le lundy.
(D'Aubigné, *Oeuvres complètes,* 346)

[29]D'Aubigné, "Lettres," 872.

[30]Idem, *Les Avantures du Baron de Faeneste,* ed. Baron de Caussade (Geneva, 1630; Slatkine, 1967), 41.

D'Aubigné knew how dangerously far afield he was ranging in this transgression. In the *Histoire universelle* he transcribed and commented upon the Calvinist credo: "et d'autant que [la Parole de Dieu] est reigle de toute vérité . . . il n'est loisible aux hommes ni mesmes aux anges d'y adiouster, diminuer, ou changer."[31]

It is for such reasons that the Calvinists condemned the *Avantures,* burned it in the square in Geneva, and publicly rebuked d'Aubigné.[32] Thus, by writing the *Avantures,* d'Aubigné braved the authorities of the religion he professed, demonstrating a heightened consciousness of his actions in the world and as a writer.[33]

The problematic inherent in d'Aubigné's work was, then, perceived by his contemporaries. Yet modern criticism has failed to recognize the tension between d'Aubigné the Calvinist and d'Aubigné the writer. The critic Albert-Marie Schmidt has discussed Calvinist strictures on writing such as those I am suggesting. In his opinion, d'Aubigné is a failed writer, a *non*-creator.[34] I maintain, however, that d'Aubigné worked toward a conception of autonomous, self-legitimized fictional prose created within an inevitable theological and literary tension. He had to valorize somehow his word literarily without detracting from the Word theologically. Calvinism paradoxically contributed to this development in that d'Aubigné had to re-read and revise the theological system within which he wrote. As d'Aubigné framed his revision, the self formed in literature through, and in opposition to, Calvinist constraints derived its strength from the absolute respect accorded to Scripture as the revelation of the Word. D'Aubigné's *oeuvre* suggested that once the self was posited as a creator, its word, too, might claim a similar status. Selfhood is stamped with the corruption of this world.[35] Yet, dialectically, a recognition of selfhood is necessary so that the sinner may, as in a mirror, regard his sin and himself. Therefore, independent authorship might, as d'Aubigné saw it, be permitted to exist. Calvinist aesthetics is an anti-aesthetics which mandates a focus solely on God. A writer should be the instrument and transmitter of the Word, but in no way an autonomous creator. D'Aubigné's singularity is immediately evident when we contrast it with the standards to which, in the theological system he espoused, he should have held. His texts always pointed beyond themselves to him as their creator; they confirmed his selfhood.

[31]Idem, *Histoire universelle,* 1:148.

[32]Idem, "Notice," *Les Avantures,* 200. "Cette édition, publiée à Genève, fut supprimée dès son apparition, comme renfermant des blasphèmes, et impiétés."

[33]His boldness increases with his literary career. Due to a fear of censorship, the first edition of *Les Tragiques* appeared anonymously.

[34]Albert-Marie Schmidt, "Quelques Aspects de la poésie baroque protestante," *Revue des sciences humaines* 76 (October-December 1954): 55.

[35]Calvin, *Institution,* I, 1, 1.

D'Aubigné's *Méditations* is a case in point. It appears to be a standard Calvinist exegetical tract, commenting on biblical texts, with no individual's underivative development. In fact, however, there are numerous instances in the *Méditations* in which appears a predominant authorial *persona* that is hardly consistent with the Calvinist imperative of the diminishment of the self. By writing meditations that contain at one and the same time scriptural commentary and also fictional developments, d'Aubigné explicitly defied Calvinist cautions. Yet, as a believer, d'Aubigné valued Scripture too much to bypass it. Instead, in order to write, he rewrote Scripture into his personal sense.

I have spent some time establishing the basis for a Calvinist aesthetics or, more to the point, anti-aesthetics in order to demonstrate more clearly the manner in which Agrippa d'Aubigné conformed to, and, more importantly, deviated from, this model. I will attempt to explore the manner in which d'Aubigné's narrative fiction was a logical culmination of the strategies he devised to circumvent the Calvinist prohibition of literature. I will also hope to show in what way d'Aubigné allowed the mingling of sacred and profane needed to develop such a genre.[36] His conception of the self was a crucial factor in this operation.

The elucidation of d'Aubigné's self-concept requires an innovative, problematic vocabulary,[37] for the sixteenth century did not have a sense of self comparable to modern self-consciousness, and was only beginning to demarcate such borders as, for instance, those between public and private self-expression. D'Aubigné's often arrogant literary self-expression also contravened the Calvinist intention to eradicate pridefulness in the self. With this in mind, de Bèze and the Calvinist hierarchy composed manuals designed to place the believer on the right path. Yet the dialectic movement between interior (self) and exterior Other (God) undermined such a project, for the Other had always to be the unsurpassable point of reference. Thus, Calvinist didacticism actually provided an avenue for the subversion of its own system, for Calvinist manuals required at least a provisional focus on

---

[36]Terence Cave, *Devotional Poetry in France c. 1570-1613* (Cambridge: Cambridge University Press, 1969), 78.

[37]Distinctions exist between Catholic and Calvinist terminologies as well, with the latter progressing even further toward abstraction, relying on a vocabulary heavily freighted with religious concepts rather than images. Mario Richter compares the work of Henri Estienne with that of the *Pléiade,* noting the following differences, among others, in word choice. Estienne always calls "Dieu" what the Pléiade members term "le Ciel, les Cieux" or "les astres." For Estienne, "fortune" is "Providence." Unlike the *Pléiade, divin* is for him a more appropriate attribute of God than *majesteux.* The shift away from mythology toward a specifically Christian terminolgy, as well as a less representational vocabulary, reflects the Calvinist desire to minimize human experience or interpretation in order to focus on God. Cf. Richter, "La Poetica di Théodore de Bèze e *les Chrestiennes méditations,*" *Aevum* 38 (1964): 192.

the self in order subsequently to denigrate and disperse the self.[38] But the toleration of any–even a negative–conception of the self opened the door to individual expression and self-examination. Such a permissive aperture constituted one of the strategies of which d'Aubigné availed himself when rationalizing his writing.[39]

D'Aubigné's sense of the imperatives of his individual expression lead him to devise a route of self-justification that asserted the writer's privilege within the theology he espoused. D'Aubigné sought to differ from other Calvinists who, overwhelmed by the prohibition on biblical imitation, wrote derivatively. Calvinist poets recognized the temptations of literature. For instance, concerned to purify writing of any mingling of sacred and profane, Guillaume Salluste Du Bartas developed the concept of the *muse chrestienne*. By this formula, writing, like prayer, was accountable to the Word. Concerned about this same issue, Henri Estienne in his *Apologie pour Hérodote* described the possibilities of distortion inherent in writing. Estienne established poetry and the Bible as antithetical:

> Je commenceray donc par la description de l'estat du premier siècle, la prenant toutesfois non de la Bible, mais des *poètes*, lesquels générale-ment au regard de leur profession luy sont contraires, c'est-à-dire autant menteurs comme elle est véritable.[40]

Estienne listed specific ways in which the biblical text might be corrupted either by preaching or by writing; all derived from an undue mixture of the human with the divine, an assertion of the right to alter tendentiously

---

[38]Self-examination actually facilitates fictional creation. Fiction is a challenge; it asserts its difference from theological concerns. A new narrating voice is created through the concentration on the self. Creation occurs through such separation (as God distinguishes light from dark) and through the author's violation of norms. We might note that language is first used by Adam for the purposes of self-narrating (rather than naming) when he experiences the Fall. That is, although God grants Adam onomastic powers to name all other creatures, the Bible does not record any spoken words by Adam until the point at which he attempts to justify himself to God (by blaming Eve) after eating the apple. Adam thus creates a misuse of language, a schism between himself and his creator, and a consequent self-consciousness that inaugurates human time (as well as a purely human, flawed use of language). God himself is outside of time. Literature is, therefore, always postlapsarian. For, as Michael Edwards, *Christian Poetics* (Grand Rapids: Eerdmans, 1984), 73, observes, "one could not imagine story in Eden. Since evil and death [were] unkown, one presumes that being was undivided." Yet, division, separation, and self-distinction are all necessary to literary creation.

[39]Another example of a creative rereading of Calvinist doctrine that d'Aubigné effects is found in the reverse side of predestination. Man's nature, the doctrine holds, remains ambiguous, but the elect are nonetheless justified in Christ. However, d'Aubigné notes, in this way man's work–or d'Aubigné's writing–may similarly be justified. "La justification ne concerne pas seulement la personne humaine, mais elle englobe également toutes ses oeuvres si injustes que puissent être celles-ci." André Biéler, *La Pensée économique et sociale de Jean Calvin* (Geneva: Librairie de l'Université, 1959), 202. The quality, or idiom, of his *oeuvre* may be questionable to main-line Calvinists, yet d'Aubigné's intention in writing may derive from, as well as confirm, his sense of his election.

[40]Henri Estienne, *Apologie pour Hérodote, "Avis"* II, xxvii.

the sense or configuration of the text. He asserted that Catholics often distort scriptural passages "pour en faire des risées . . . en faisoy[ant] venir les passages [d'ailleurs] à propos des spéculations qu'ils songoyent." By fabricating phrases of their own, Estienne claimed Catholics "allègu[ent] des sentences sous le titre de la Bible qui ne se trouvent en aucun livre d'icelle," and thereby reduced theology to a matter of fiction. Indeed, a nefarious literary admixture resulted from the borrowing of sermon texts from popular compendia of fables: "ils ajoutent des contes et des légendes aux sermons tirées de la *Légende dorée.*"[41] Such prohibited practices were only too similar to those used in works such as d'Aubigné's *Avantures du Baron de Faeneste* and the *Confession du Sieur de Sancy.* Writers like Philippe Du Plessis-Mornay and Jean de Sponde were ill-at-ease with their own expression, preferring that God actually write their works for them. Mornay confesses, "il me semble impossible d'estre Poëte et Théologien"[42] (which is precisely the synthesis that d'Aubigné effected through theo-literary language). Sponde denied all autonomy to his verses; he warned himself, "toutesfois rien de toy: c'est les Cieux qui produisent . . . ces effaicts."[43] Du Bartas demurred that "cet Esprit . . . / Est le sainct Orateur qui dicte ma harangue."[44] Similarly, Des Masures' David in *Tragédies sainctes* was a non-actor, a human cipher temporarily empowered by God to slay Goliath. David acknowledged: "A Toy, Seigneur, . . . c'est à Toy seul, non à moy, qui rien suis."[45] De Bèze uttered a similar disclaimer: "mon Dieu, ce bien n'est point de mon oeuvre . . . la grace donc vient de toy jusques à moy pour me chasser de moy."[46] And de Bèze insisted on conformity to the Word and a way of reading modeled upon the revealed text. The self was subordinated to religious and historical exigencies, increasingly constricted and suffocated as art was turned toward life to act as an exemplum.[47] Rather than daring to be the subject of his work, the Calvinist writer spoke in passive formulations that rendered him the object of his work. Sponde and Du Bartas both at times described processes whereby they themselves "become" the paper upon which God's text was written and read.

With the exception of d'Aubigné, Calvinist writers meticulously avoided deviation from a univalent biblical reading. Most Calvinists pursued legitimation by quilting their writings extensively with biblical borrowing so that

---

[41]Estienne, *Apologie,* II:76-80.

[42]Mornay, *Vérité,* 159.

[43]Sponde, "Essai," *Méditations,* 236.

[44]Du Bartas, "La Judit," *La Muse chrestienne,* ed. André Baiche (Toulouse: Association des publications de la faculté des lettres et sciences humaines, 1971), II:21.

[45]Louis Des Masures, "David combattant," *Tragédies sainctes* (repr. Geneva: Droz, 1932), 15.

[46]De Bèze, cited in Soulié, "L'Utilisation," 301.

[47]This is similar to the feeling of constriction but subsequent spiritual awakening John Bunyan experiences at intervals in his autobiography, *Grace Abounding.*

their work may in no way serve as a vehicle for personal expression. D'Aubigné, however, marked biblical elements with his stamp, giving them a new configuration.[48] For example, in writing *Les Tragiques,* d'Aubigné borrowed biblical elements in an unprecedented mingling of sacred and profane precisely because the use of biblical fact in a secular or semi-secular fiction worked to redeem the profane element, permitting its existence but moving beyond it. By anchoring his fiction to a theological base, he achieved the portrayal of a thoughtful, multifaceted self as writer and worshipper. In conceiving of sin as a dialectic sign of soteric possibility,[49] d'Aubigné's texts both magnified and stood separate from the Bible. His works all, to varying degrees, contained unprecedented creative permissions in their treatment of subject matter. In an age during which one might be put to death for mis-saying one's theological beliefs, and in a Calvinist theological climate in which, as Des Masures acknowledged in the "Epistre" preceding his *Tragédies sainctes,* "qui invente . . . ment,"[50] d'Aubigné's body of work demonstrated a progressive, intentional liberation from such strictures.

D'Aubigné and Contemporary Critics

It is for this reason that I take exception to Michel Jeanneret's statement in *Poésie et tradition biblique au seizième siècle* that d'Aubigné, while demonstrating a limited degree of literary invention, remained in the Calvinist camp. Jeanneret, like most d'Aubigné critics, recognizes d'Aubigné's Calvinist theology but does not acknowledge the revisionist literary perspective in which d'Aubigné interpreted that religious framework. In my reading of

[48]These concerns resurface approximately fifty years later in England. The issues of representational vs. abstract language, immanence vs. transcendence, and the nature of writing are dealt with in ways that mirror the ambivalence French Calvinist authors feel toward literary creation. In *The Eloquent "I": Style and Self in Seventeenth Century Prose* (Madison: University of Wisconsin Press, 1968), Joan Webber distinguishes between the Anglican, whose sensibility in seventeenth-century England typifies that which we have been labelling as Catholic and which is exemplified in sixteenth-century France by Ronsard, and the Puritan, who corresponds to, and is in fact a direct descendant of, the Calvinist. She finds literary self-consciousness in both cases, but notes that it is oriented differently and occurs in varying degrees. In the Anglican model, the self is characterized by playfulness, a valorizing of art, the author's perceived freedom to metamorphose at will and the perception of the self as a microcosm. Consequently, like that of Ronsard, the Anglican style is highly metaphoric and symbolic. The world is artificial but because the artifice shaping it is that of God, further artifice–and fiction–is legitimized. The Puritan paradigm, on the other hand, is one of tight control.

[49]Karl Barth finds evidence that Calvin's stance on predestination is more lenient than that of de Bèze, is in fact impossible, and leads to universal salvation, in such dialectic statements in Calvin's work. For instance, he notes the dialectical manner in which Calvin shows that the elect and the damned belong together: the elect can only be defined in terms of that from which they are reprobate. Hence, to whatever degree that they participate in the definition of what is elect, they, too, are saved. Cf. Karl Barth, *Church Dogmatics,* II, 2 (Edinburgh: T. and T. Clark, 1959), 346-47.

[50]Des Masures, "Epistre," *Tragédie saincte,* II, 136.

d'Aubigné's texts, his stance is one of extreme self-consciousness,[51] a more "modern" notion of textuality in which he wove his "self" integrally into his work as guarantor of it.[52] In this way the text itself became the mechanism for the author's redemption. Jeanneret notes that

> la méditation invite au contraire à toute espèce d'interventions; c'est donc ici que la diversité et la profondeur des significations prêtées par les calvinistes au psautier vont apparaître le plus clairement.[53]

Contradicting his previous statements, Jeanneret here suggests one of the ways in which d'Aubigné was able to incorporate and refigure the parent text, creating his own model text. D'Aubigné gradually extended this strategy and wrote fiction. He took his point of departure in the *Méditations* from the text of the Psalm, but moved beyond exegesis to express his subjective, apocalyptic view of human/divine separation. In addition, since in the meditation the soul reflects on God's works within the soul, the genre of the meditation had the potential to be conceived as a more personal and emotive form. D'Aubigné availed himself of this flexibility, writing himself ever more pervasively into the text. We recall that de Bèze, on the other hand, expressly worked to void the text of himself so that it might function as a universal exemplum, in which he represented Everyman.[54] Unlike de Bèze, d'Aubigné dared to compare himself with the divinely-inspired Psalmist, so that "le 'je' [peut] ser[vir] ici de sujet à ses propres expériences."[55] Also, d'Aubigné's terminology was not as abstract or as didactic as the vocabulary of other Calvinist writers.

It is my belief that in the *Tragiques,* the relationship between author and text differed greatly from the norm of the Calvinist exegetical tract which the Bible informed and authorized. D'Aubigné asserted the value of his creative act without regard for external endorsement. We shall examine in detail such artifices as those of word-images, multiple points

---

[51]Individuality is a term that may only be applied anachronistically to the Renaissance and Reformation. In this era, the self was still a mere schema, an outline to be filled by a transcendent, external source. We shall see that this is not wholly the case for d'Aubigné, who posits a strong, in some measure self-determining, construct.

[52]It is intriguing to speculate that d'Aubigné may actually derive this inter-referentiality—commenting on one of his works in another to strengthen the perception of a literary universe of his own construction—from Calvin. E. Harris Harbison, *The Christian Scholar in the Age of the Reformation*, observes that "the *Institutes* came to be the central axis round which Calvin's biblical *Commentaries* revolved. Here in the *Institutes* was the theology upon which Christians could agree, there the various sources or illustrations of the central doctrine of God's Word. For fuller discussions of doctrinal points, the author of the *Commentaries* began to refer his readers to the *Institutes*." As we shall see, this is similar to relationship between d'Aubigné's *Sa Vie à ses enfants* and his *Histoire universelle.*

[53]Michel Jeanneret, *Poésie et tradition biblique au xviiᵉ siècle: Recherches stylistiques sur les Psaumes* (Paris: Jose Corti, 1969), 404.

[54]Cf. chap. 2 below on the Meditational Genre.

[55]Jeanneret, *Poésie et tradition*, 405.

of view, a ludic tendency to switch narrating pronouns, and the surprising number of times d'Aubigné as author emerges, inscribed in his own texts. All such strategies were innovative and cannot be found in the works of contemporary Calvinist writers. Another strategy is that of a *mis en abyme* structure, in which d'Aubigné referred to his individual texts within the overall body of his works. This sort of subjective intertextuality emphasized that his text arose from, and referred to, him alone. For d'Aubigné, text and author were coterminous in a relationship reminiscent of that of God with the Bible.

D'Aubigné was, therefore, unique in developing and implementing an idiosyncratic, individual approach, a theo-literary methodology, which reconciled sacred and profane elements within the context of the scriptural tradition. One of d'Aubigné's most important innovations was the association of salvation with writing. This directly contrasted with de Bèze's indictment, previously mentioned, of writing as sin. In an example drawn, significantly, from his literary and self-reflective autobiography, d'Aubigné described his fear that he would experience defeat in battle. He prayed to God for deliverance, and his prayer was granted. In response, he composed a literary work, an epigram memorializing the experience: "se voyant délivré, il tourna en un épigramme que vous verrez entre les siens."[56] He thereby claimed for his writing the explicit status of act of faith as well as implicitly asserting it as the medium of salvation. His writing triumphantly proclaimed the efficacy of his belief, for he recorded in it "l'effet de [ses] prières."[57] At the same time, while motivated theologically, he expressed himself literarily, in choosing to write an epigram, an explicitly courtly genre, rather than, for instance, writing a psalm. These strategies contradict Albert-Marie Schmidt's statement that "aucun des poètes [calvinistes] n'a disposé d'une originalité suffisante pour obtenir une notoriété durable . . . considerant Dieu comme une espèce de gloire offusquante, il réduit à rien ce qui ne participe pas directement à ce tout."[58] Schmidt further asserts that none of the Calvinist poets, including d'Aubigné, attempted to revise the conventions of genres. Schmidt omits a discussion of the *Avantures,* which in fact did rework generic format.[59] Indicating the factor he feels most likely to hamper poetic creation, Schmidt inadvertently signals the very manner in which d'Aubigné justified his writing dialectically, achieving salvation through sin: "la vie du poète chrétien est une vie anti-logique: il se débat dans une perpétuelle alternance de damnation actuelle et de salut en

[56]D'Aubigné, *Sa Vie,* 224.

[57]Ibid., 409.

[58]Schmidt, "Quelques Aspects," 383.

[59]D'Aubigné's poetry is, indeed, less innovative than his prose, prose perhaps being a vehicle better suited to the articulation of the self due to its fewer formalistic constraints.

espérance."[60] Schmidt proposes a morphology of Calvinist writing. First, he says, the believer became aware of God's absolute injunctions. He then attempted to conform his life and works to those commands, but failed because he was sinful, thus confirming to himself his own eventual damnation. Finally, he surrendered himself to God's grace.[61] D'Aubigné, unlike other Calvinist writers, did not, through a "mérite négatif," offer "le plus souillée de toutes les offrandes: lui-même."[62] Rather, in a dialectic circle, d'Aubigné offered his writing as the actual profession of faith by which he was assured of his election, salvation and, consequently, his license to write.

Mario Richter, in his analysis of Calvinist poetics, treats this problem of the relationship between sin and writing. He speaks of the "subordinazione dell'arte al problema della salvezza, completamente risolto soltanto dalle Scritture."[63] Richter indicates that the only way for Calvinists to write was by reducing their own potential creativity, by becoming a channel or transmitter, not even an interpreter. Ignoring the epic quality of the *Tragiques* (unusual and innovative in that the Bible, the supreme model for Calvinist writers, did not employ the genre among the many it used), disregarding the tension between writer and text in and through which d'Aubigné's self-concept was elaborated there, and relying solely on the *Tragiques* rather than examining the totality of d'Aubigné's rich and varied *oeuvre*, Richter concludes that d'Aubigné was completely subordinated to the Calvinist norm of exegetical writing:

> non si potrebbe spiegare la particolare poesia dei *Tragiques* senza il presupposto della più rigorosa poetica calvinista, che prescriveva al poeta la massima fedeltà della Bibbia e che non si stancava di propporre un linguaggio immediato, quelle che Calvino chiamava *rudis stylus* . . . lontana quindi da ogni inerte compiacimento naturalistico, strumento necessario per concedere al poeta un impegno morale e interiore.[64]

Richter later contradicts himself, saying that, as opposed to Henri Estienne, who "non ammettava che la parola di Dio fosse profanata de finzioni e da immagini proprie della poesia pagana,"[65] d'Aubigné permitted himself liberty in his choice of literary tools:

---

[60]Albert-Marie Schmidt, "Calvinisme et poésie au seizième siècle en France," *Bulletin de la société de l'histoire du protestantisme français* (1935): 224.

[61]Ibid., 222.

[62]Idem, *Catalogue du colloque Calvin: Catalogue pour une exposition à la Bibliothèque nationale* (Paris: PUF, 1965), 215.

[63]Richter, *Jean de Sponde*, 197.

[64]Ibid., 201.

[65]Ibid., 191.

Pur essendo un appasionato uomo di religione e irriducible combattente, d'Aubigné si prese dunque la libertà di utilizzare, senza proccupazioni extraletterarie, tutta l'esperienza poetica del suo seculo.[66]

Richter does not, however, demonstrate how a Calvinist came to legitimize such liberty of self-expression. This is a significant omission. I contend that d'Aubigné's self-devised prerogative of selection of the material for literary creation was directly dependent upon his certainty of his own election.

Marguérite Soulié focuses on Calvinist exegeses in her reading of the *Tragiques.* She does not extrapolate a specific literary aesthetics from her examination, although she does note the principle of subordination to the Word. Calvinist exegesis negated individualism. Soulié's thesis is that d'Aubigné saw himself as a prophet,[67] one who would announce the truth as God's mouthpiece. "Dans *Les Tragiques* d'Aubigné déclare que ce poème nouveau a été inspiré par Dieu . . . il ne cesse d'assumer le rôle du Prophète biblique que le souffle de Dieu possède et contraint." I believe that this is an incomplete reading of d'Aubigné's literary program, for d'Aubigné eventually revealed himself *as* self, rather than in a role (e.g. a prophetic persona), and was conscious of so doing. Soulié, however, claims that d'Aubigné did no more than follow Calvin's expository technique. She notes that d'Aubigné "suit de près le commentaire de Calvin" and that "souvent d'Aubigné obtient cette image à partir d'un commentaire de Calvin." She does not elaborate on the significance of the occasions when d'Aubigné stepped beyond his mentor's treatment of texts.[68] De Bèze certainly would not have condoned an individual worshipper's arbitrarily proclaiming himself a prophet. Soulié similarly fails to account for the liberties d'Aubigné took in the *Avantures* and for the self-congratulatory tenor of *Sa Vie à ses enfants.* Soulié concludes that the "créateur formé par Calvin n'est pas un Prométhée." Yet in the preface of the *Tragiques,* d'Aubigné explicitly claimed to be acting like Prometheus, stealing his powers of invention from God.[69] Soulié observes that d'Aubigné had been chosen to be a witness to God's work in history. D'Aubigné did more: he chose this role *for* himself, and witnessed *to* himself: "mes yeux sont tesmoings du sujet de mes vers."[70] D'Aubigné dared to present his texts (*signes visibles*) to be endorsed by the divine Word (*l'invisible*), even when these texts did not deal with religious topics.

---

[66]Ibid., 201.

[67]Soulié, "L'Utilisation," 137.

[68]Ibid. She notes one example of d'Aubigné's self-assertion without commenting on why it occurs: "[il] va plus loin que Calvin, car il fait des Anges les intercesseurs, les avocats des martyrs auprès du Père, rôle qui est réservé par les Evangiles au Saint-Esprit."

[69]Ibid. Also, d'Aubigné asserts on the title page that this book is "*Les Tragiques*/ ci devant/ donnez au public/ par le larcin de Prométhée."

[70]Ibid., 240-90; and d'Aubigné, "Les Tragiques," v. 29.

Soulié takes note of d'Aubigné's "apophéties." These were proleptic predictions, such as d'Aubigné's warning that Henri de Navarre's lips would be pierced for his infidelity to the Word. Soulié does not examine the creative quality of these predictions, viewing them simply as real-life evidence of d'Aubigné's prophetic role. Like God, he might alter time. But Soulié misses the crucial point that d'Aubigné did not function as a prophetic transmitter; rather, he crafted these "prophecies" in an artistic manner and with self-serving aims. He intentionally distorted the prophecies so as to enhance his powers of invention. Rather than act as an interpreter of God's prophecies, d'Aubigné devised his own. For the "apophéties" were all textually recorded; they had actually already occured yet were deliberately–and deceptively–portrayed as being still to come. Such a portrayal set up a temporal variability similar to the narrational point-of-view switches which d'Aubigné effected in *Sa Vie* when he referred to himself variously in the first and third person, thus claiming the power of multiple perspectives for his authorial persona. Such strategies suggest that the "apophéties" may be read as instances of encapsulated fiction in embryonic form, to the extent that fiction is an assertion of the self beyond the limits of temporal and spatial reality. They, and fiction, are independent, self-validating constructs that demand the credence of the reader.

Soulié is, therefore, mistaken in asserting that "ce que [d'Aubigné] demande au seigneur, c'est la mort à soi-même . . . lui-même était totalement soumis à [la Bible]."[71] To this effect, she cites those books of the Bible from which d'Aubigné borrowed as well as the frequency of citation. The greatest number of references is to the Psalms. This Soulié interprets as substantiating her case against any poetic invention or creative disposition on d'Aubigné's part.[72] I feel, rather, that the significance of d'Aubigné's recourse to the Psalms was his search for a way to legitimize literary creativity by recalling the Davidic model of divine inspiration. He claimed affinities with the psalmist. By placing himself within the dialectic of sin and salvation–such as David himself experienced[73]–d'Aubigné recognized the role his writing might play as participant in, and mediator between, both states of being.

Henry Sauerwein stresses d'Aubigné's similarities with standard Calvinist exegetes. He claims that "d'Aubigné does not want to write; he is forced to write. He does not contemplate his work before putting it on paper. . . . The work is already existent and bursts forth."[74] In my view, such an

---

[71]Ibid., 43-44.

[72]Ibid., 299-320.

[73]Regarding the theme of sin and salvation, it may be interesting to compare de Bèze's treatment of the David and Bathsheba story with that of Antoine Montchrestien, *David* (1621), in which it appears that only an utter surrender of the self can result in salvation.

[74]Henry Sauerwein, *Agrippa d'Aubigné's Les Tragiques: A Study in Structure and Poetic Method* (Baltimore: Johns Hopkins Press, 1953), 170.

assertion fails to account for the self-conscious strategies of stylistic reworking, the carefully-constructed "tableaux," and the dialogic relationship d'Aubigné established between reader and d'Aubigné's textualized self. Like Soulié, Sauerwein maintains that, as with the *Méditations,* d'Aubigné composed the *Tragiques* exegetically, the sole difference being that in the former, he glossed an already created text, while in the latter d'Aubigné created a new work.[75] And, in Sauerwein's view, the latter was equally uninnovative in its reliance on biblical source material. In his view, these works duplicated the Bible without deviating from it. We shall see that the contrary was the case, and that major shifts from the biblical text in fact characterized the *Tragiques.* Such shifts empowered the rudiments of individual literary creation.

Sauerwein's structural study of poetic developments in the *Tragiques* focuses on word-clusters that enabled d'Aubigné to create a "supra-literal" or emotional line of development atop the linear narrative. These functioned associatively, as did the typically Calvinist antitheses which appeared in the *Tragiques.* The emotional or sensorial overlay created by the word-clusters did not merely act as a structuring device, however.

It also constituted a strategy for the permission of personal expression. In this regard, Sauerwein's examination of the book *Vengeances* is helpful. He demonstrates that, of the seven books composing the *Tragiques, Vengeances* was the only one to which, in the preface, d'Aubigné did not assign a customarily recognizable stylistic label. Rather, he described it in his own terms, calling it "théologien et historial." Sauerwein suggests that such a style is made up of an expanded "style tragique" equated with "style sainct." This sort of combination recalls the theo-literary aspect of d'Aubigné's work that I have posited. Similarly, the book *Feux* was unusual in that it was set in the frame of, and designated as a "dream," a classical convention indicating poetic fiction and personalized literary musings.[76] Such a device underlies the self-conscious character of d'Aubigné's literary creation.

Richard Regosin explores in more detail the generic ramifications of the term "tragique." Although, like Sauerwein, Regosin repeatedly refers to d'Aubigné as the "Huguenot exegete," Regosin nonetheless makes room for d'Aubigné's innovations, noting that since the sixteenth century was yet in the process of defining the tragic genre, d'Aubigné remained "free to assume his personal poetic stance" within the contemporary elasticity of that convention. Unspecified boundaries enabled a conscious stylistic manipulation of literary elements, thereby preparing the path for the type of theo-literary mingling d'Aubigné effected. By choosing such a genre, d'Aubigné elected an arena that encouraged self-expression. Regosin does not explain what such freedom might mean within the confines of Calvinist

[75]Sauerwein, *Agrippa,* 124.
[76]Ibid., 30.

thought, nor does he explore the possible motivations that might have led d'Aubigné to choose such a fluid genre. While Regosin finds that "there appears to be no major sixteenth-century literary antecedent which influence[s] the composition of the *Tragiques*," he does not explain what it meant for d'Aubigné, as a Calvinist, to display such unprecedented creativity. He does make the point that, in employing the ruse of the purloined manuscript described in "Aux lecteurs," d'Aubigné separated himself from his work "to focus attention on the poem and the poet within: it underscores *Les Tragiques* as fiction."[77] Distance, then, was a component of d'Aubigné's repertoire of literary strategies. This argument reinforces the literary self-consciousness I have suggested was integral to d'Aubigné's permission of writing, and further substantiates my assertion that d'Aubigné had a panoptic perspective on his works. By writing himself into the text, he gained greater control over it as well as over his reader. He became an effective agent within his text as actor, and outside his text as author. At the same time, a conflict of roles ensued: "the tension between the narrator as a man and as a divinely inspired poet and prophet is maintained throughout the *Tragiques.*"[78] The schism between human and divine language which de Bèze postulated became more problematic for d'Aubigné at this point. One way this rift might be reconciled is through a different orientation of the reading act; Regosin concludes that the task of d'Aubigné's audience was to learn how "to *view* and understand the word-pictures he paints in order to learn God's oft-concealed meaning."[79] I would phrase the imperative somewhat differently: Protestant salvation (i.e. correct interpretation of divine material), d'Aubigné's works suggested, might be achieved through careful *reading*. In that sense, d'Aubigné's text functioned sacramentally. It was a locus for the intersection of divine intention and human reception.

I would further suggest that d'Aubigné proposed to open up possibilities for literary creation by resorting to a quasi-sacramental notion of the efficacy of the text. D'Aubigné showed that, despite its earthly stamp, a text might lead beyond the human state to God. D'Aubigné did not purport to re-speak the Word, but to redeem human speech so that it might speak in its own idiom about the divine, as well as secular matters. As I shall demonstrate, this was not a representational model, but rather an iconic formulation.[80] All lines of direction in an icon disrupt point-of-view and

---

[77]Richard Regosin, *Agrippa d'Aubigné's Les Tragiques: The Poetry of Inspiration* (Chapel Hill: University of North Carolina Press, 1970), 62.

[78]Regosin, *Agrippa,* 85-86, notes, "within the world of *Les Tragiques* there is no constant vantage-point; rather, there is a moving perspective which ranges back and forth between the terrestrial and celestial realm. We stand . . . between two worlds . . . experiencing the transition of the terrestrial universe as it evolves into the kingdom of heaven."

[79]Ibid., 97; my emphasis.

[80]I rely here on the Orthodox Church's definition of the word "icon." See chap. 5 on the *Avantures* for a more detailed discussion.

perspective, moving the interpreter away from concentration on the image itself.[81] A painting, on the other hand, is "framed," and can be contained and analyzed as a static object[82]; the result is that immanence is inappropriately emphasized over transcendence.

Regosin senses the crucial role in d'Aubigné's creativity that the sin-and-salvation dialectic played; he notes that "the poet moves even closer to God as he and his poem become the actual instrument by which ultimate justice is carried out," but Regosin does not explain how d'Aubigné overcame his perception of his sinfulness in order to become God's instrument. He also asserts an enhanced status for d'Aubigné's work as an *addition* to the Bible: "it now stands as a new book of the Bible . . . within the world of art."[83] He does not recognize, however, the autonomy d'Aubigné claimed for his work. Indeed, it is hard to see how, for a Calvinist, participation in the "world of art"–or, at least, a primary focus on it–could be desirable.

Ulrich Langer approaches textuality in the *Tragiques* as being that zone of inter-subjectivity which is generated by the rhetorical discourse. I would go further, to say that within the text d'Aubigné dialogued not only with his reader but also with his multiple, temporally varying, figurations of himself. Langer describes d'Aubigné's text as the product of a heist; it has been stolen from the Bible. He constructs a model in which d'Aubigné's theft instituted a dialectic between author and audience. The stolen book epitomized discourse mirroring the legitimized Word. In order to vivify the word, Langer maintains that the emotive reaction d'Aubigné called for ("donnons-nous-en pour esmouvoir") had to be enacted through the reader's "lecture à haute voix." Rhetoric thus represented the efficacy of divine grace, the Pauline Word which animated the letter. Like other d'Aubigné critics, however, Langer maintains that d'Aubigné's word utterly annihilated itself in divine voice at the end of the *Tragiques*. Such a reading fails to account for d'Aubigné's later works, in which nothing of the kind took place. Rather, the *Avantures,* through the use of occasional obscenity among other strategies, epitomized the author's ability to stand distinct from the biblical model. Similarly, in *Sa Vie à ses enfants,* multiple textualized images of the self, explicitly associated with literary production, conveyed the autobiographical project. While Langer concedes that d'Aubigné reworked his sources, Langer views such action not as original creation, but as recreation or reiteration of the divine Word which the reader was led to perform: "la création artistique . . . s'efface par la lecture jusqu'à l'oeuvre soit transparente à la perception finale de Dieu." Langer suggests a sort of "reader-response" theory of the sign. Just as the sign is both presence and

[81]Kurt Weitzmann, *The Icon* (New York: George Braziller, 1978), 23.

[82]Concerning the iconic tendency to point to an interpreter beyond the actual matter portrayed, see Weitzmann, *The Icon,* 223.

[83]Regosin, *Agrippa,* 62.

absence, so, in the text, meaning was both present through authorial intervention, and absent until the reader re-established it. Langer misreads Calvinist doctrine when he says that in the *Tragiques*, "la poésie se donne à lire comme le pain qui devient le corps de Christ." Langer proposes thereby a Catholic model of enclosed Presence that d'Aubigné would find unacceptable. Further, in declaring that d'Aubigné wants "un texte qui soit consubstantiel à l'événement," Langer overlooks the fact that the *Tragiques*, composed over a lengthy period beginning in the 1570s, were not published until 1616.[84] In the meantime, d'Aubigné reworked and incorporated segments into other parts of his literary works by way of illustration.[85] Thus, the work evolved in time concomitant with d'Aubigné's gradual textual self-shaping. The history of publication hints at a dialectic of past, present, and present-in-the-past which is emblematic of the nature of the text itself.

Langer acknowledges that the text seemed to possess a mediatory function which made d'Aubigné unique among Calvinist writers; his "text est . . . un deuxième Saint-Esprit [pratique une deuxième élection]."[86] I would suggest that the text's mediatory role was effective for d'Aubigné himself: d'Aubigné was not only literarily self-conscious, he was also convinced of his salvation. In this regard, we note that although for Calvin works were inefficacious in obtaining salvation, one's election might neverthe-less be manifest in one's works.[87] If writing may be viewed as a possible product of one's belief in one's election, then authorial assertion was not only an important literary tool for d'Aubigné, it was also a significant theological statement. His writing arose from his conviction that he was acting in an orthodox manner, despite appearances to the contrary.

While some d'Aubigné critics acknowledge Calvinism as the superstruc-ture within which d'Aubigné wrote, none appear to recognize the literary manner within that theological system by which d'Aubigné simultaneously incorporated and revised such concepts. Criticism has been limited to the explicitly exegetical productions of Calvinists. I seek here to define precisely how Calvinism constrained one author, who nevertheless persisted in his self-expression and literary creation.

To summarize the Protestant paradigm, literature is without legitimation. The signified, God, preempts all human expression. Univalence prevails over multivocity. Stylistic ornamentation is threatening, for it makes of man's work an idol. Writing is only sanctioned when, as in the case of

---

[84]Ulrich Langer, *Les Tragiques d'Agrippa d'Aubigné: Rhétorique et intersubjectivité* (Paris, 1983), 84-92.

[85]Cf. for instance the *Méditations*, 534, "Or ce dur estat," and *La Confession du Sieur de Sancy*, 580, "Le Pape peut facere infecta facta."

[86]Langer, *Les Tragiques*, 21.

[87]Calvin, *Institutes*, III.xvii.5, ed. F. L. Battles, 808; J. Wayne Baker, *Heinrich Bullinger and the Covenant: The Other Reformed Tradition* (Athens: Ohio University Press, 1980), 195.

exegesis, it conforms so closely to the text that it cannot exist separately from it. The Protestant aesthetics is not one of beauty or personal statement, but of appropriateness, aiming at cultic uniformity. It is an aesthetics of negation; literature's existence is only condoned through its dispersal. This Calvinist model obtained throughout the tenure of de Bèze, until the leadership of Simon Goulart.[88] Before Goulart's tenure, the Council of Trent enacted reforms, such as increased preaching, prompting a Calvinist counter-adjustment. Finding that their abstract writings did not have the persuasive power that the elaborate, sensorial Catholic tracts did, Calvinist writers under Goulart adopted a more descriptive, "incarnational" approach in which images were relied upon to closely figure reality or presence. D'Aubigné's work, for the most part, remained chronologically within the strict Calvinist prohibition solidified by de Bèze, so d'Aubigné demonstrated unprecedented literary audacity in stretching that model without endorsing, as did Goulart, Catholic representationality. D'Aubigné therefore stood as a *plaque tournante* between hard-line Calvinism and post-Tridentine modifications. D'Aubigné wrote texts that surpassed exegesis in their emphasis on the self and in the scope of their literary awareness; he also wrote fiction.

In order to comprehend fully the role of d'Aubigné's texts, it is essential to read them from his self-definition as sinful creator. We need to determine how writing, a suspect activity, and self-expression, for de Bèze a sort of introspective idolatry, might conjoin in d'Aubigné's work to license a writing "I." Finally, we need to place the textual product in perspective for the time period, both literarily and theologically.

D'Aubigné worked within a biblical background that became more subjective as his literary career evolved. His work required new ways of reading and conceiving literary and theological language. His *écriture* came to be the representation of a debased secular *parole* meant to enact its own legitimation through its incorporation in a new construct: an *écriture-parole* that was both theological (*parole*) and literary (*écriture*); it was, in itself, a dialectic.

D'Aubigné stretched the definition of truth. For him, truth was dialogic rather than monologic: the author interacted with God, just as the reader responds to the writer. D'Aubigné's literary self-consciousness led him to recognize the imperative of appearing in his own texts. He excavated the self through authorial affirmation. This is why he so frequently appeared as a character, an actor, or as a textual inscription, citing his own words as they appeared in other of his works: he was an artistically-permitted trace of his humanity in his writing.[89] D'Aubigné realized that even exegesis

---

[88]Cave, *Devotional Poetry*, 43.

[89]Léon Wencelius, *L'Esthétique de Calvin* (Paris: Belles Lettres, 1937), states that Calvin permitted the representation of the "created" but not of the "Creator." In representing himself, then, d'Aubigné employed Calvin's permission: d'Aubigné himself is an element of the created order.

was not a "pure" form of writing, for it in some ways required the at least partial involvement of the author's self, if only in that the explicator delved for and displayed latent content rather than merely that which was specifically manifest. The biblical expositor reorganized biblical elements in a subjective pattern of meaning. So did d'Aubigné create fiction from his own life. Once we determine the manner and shapes in which he is present in his text, we may learn much about the literary and theological dimensions of d'Aubigné's fiction.

We shall trace the evolution in d'Aubigné's conception of writing from exegesis to exposition in the *Méditations,* where we will also find prefigurations of the freedom for fiction. Here, d'Aubigné expanded the expository convention of importing related biblical passages, reasoning that exposition's intent was to render the biblical example more immediate by illustrating its truth through contemporary occasions. Therefore, he determined to allow his personal experiences into his text as corroboration of the biblical assertion. (This was a return to Calvin, against de Bèze, for Calvin extensively employed such exposition in his *Commentaries.* In many ways, d'Aubigné seemed to seek to renew the original formulation of Calvinist theology.) We will next examine the dialectic between speech and writing in the *Tragiques.* Such a relationship is that found between *Verbum* and *verba,* God as creator and man as writer. The use of polemic in the *Confession du Sieur de Sancy* provided an outlet for satirical expression of the self in the world. It also problematized the interaction between self and other, as d'Aubigné deliberately adopted an adversarial persona in order to, paradoxically, propagate his own views. By finally rendering this character a risible fiction, he exalted the polemic fictional strategy he successfully employed to this end. The extraordinary fictional invention of the *Avantures du Baron de Faeneste* constituted d'Aubigné's answer, still as a Calvinist, to the problem of the legitimation of non-exegetical writing and reading. It did so by examining the relationship between image and word, by creating a pattern to enable the reader to distinguish between the two, while reading them jointly, or emblematically. Finally, *Sa Vie à ses enfants* contains a complex articulation of multiple selves, attesting to the strong sense of self d'Aubigné evolved throughout his works. This *mise en abyme* structure also recalls the manner in which his texts reflected upon or referred back to other of his works, thereby confirming the omniscient authorial identity.

This examination of d'Aubigné's self-consciously contructed literary universe confirms him as an author of unusual scope; one who subverted and rewrote the theological system within which he existed; one who dared to exalt the self over and through Scripture; one whose extreme self-awareness sculpted the world over again, in textual form.

2

The Reconciliation of Sin and Writing in d'Aubigné's
Méditations sur les pseaumes

INSTEAD OF CLOSELY FOLLOWING THE EXEGETICAL TECHNIQUE of close explication of the biblical passage at hand, suddenly and inexplicably in the *Méditations* d'Aubigné bursts forth into highly personalized mini-narratives which, upon comparison with the Psalm they puportedly devolve from, show little or no apparent foundation in that Psalm. I believe that d'Aubigné is applying the greater elasticity of Calvin's expository technique, in which extended exegesis is effected through the incorporation of biblical passages from other locations having to bear on the theme being treated. Through this extension, d'Aubigné cleverly articulates the beginnings of a *permission for fiction* that deviates from the Calvinist content to the extent that fiction is a freer, non-derivative expression of a "self" *beyond* the model to be explicated.

In order to grasp fully the innovations d'Aubigné is developing, it is helpful to understand the "typical" Calvinist meditational format from which he deviates. In many respects, d'Aubigné demonstrates affinities with this exemplar which are responsible for the label of "Calvinist writer" customarily accorded him. However, he makes strides towards the recognition of the Calvinist writer as a specific, individual voice in the *Méditations,* and this can be seen as the first step in a series of progressive strategies designed to emancipate him from the Calvinist strictures on writing and, especially, on fiction as reviewed in Chapter One.

The Meditational Genre

Meditations, for Calvinists, are "an adaptation to private devotion of *sermon*-technique–text, debate, apostrophe, and prayer."[1] Hence, Word, not human writing, is valued. Medieval exegesis called for a four-fold unveiling of the text. Calvin restricts exegesis to a simpler literal and spiritual examination. He rejects the allegorical method of the Catholic church because it facilitates varying interpretations deriving more from man's creativity than from the productivity of the text. The meditational genre, as Calvin encourages its development, derives from the tradition of commentaries, in which each line is scrupulously analyzed in a strict progression

---

[1]Cave, *Devotional Poetry*, 39.

25

that exactly duplicates the contours of the parent text. By condoning exposition, Calvin does allow some freedom in the treatment of the text: "ainsi l'auteur se propose d'enrichir un texte à l'aide d'autres passages bibliques qui le prolongent ou l'explicitent en vue d'une obéissance précise, de l'engagement concret qui fait sienne la méditation."[2] Exposition is a useful implement in heightening the reader's comprehension of the scriptural message, for exposition expands the model situation into something that may be more familiar or more immediately applicable to the reader. Exposition can situate the passage contextually and, through judicious reference to contemporary issues, help the reader to locate himself historically within the truth of the *exemplum*. Exposition is always didactic and specific; it never licenses a gratuitous personal observation on the part of the reader or writer, and is in no way intended to spotlight the explicator, who should efface himself before the unsurpassed perfection of the text he is explicating. Exegesis is only necessary because God's truth, transmitted through a human medium, is translated in corrupt terms. The explicator must render such communication transparent and accessible through his faithful conformity to, and development upon, the biblical passage. The Calvinist meditational genre is not designed to encourage individual rumination on, and critical examination of, the Bible, but rather to provide a universal pattern for religious experience, within the confines of the Word, which is applicable without alteration to all men.

For Calvinists, the meditation is, therefore, a theological rather than a literary genre. It can only be seen as artistic to the extent that Calvin concurs with Augustine, who "attempt[s] . . . to work out a theory of literary beauty which [will] penetrate below the level of sound and style in the external sense, to the level of truth, that is, to the fidelity of the author's language in interpreting [divine] reality."[3] Aesthetics, then, is in some way valorized, but only as it makes divine beauty evident. Secular reality does not participate in this legitimation.

Meditations are not popular among Calvinists until fairly late in the sixteenth century.[4] This may be attributable to the Calvinist doctrinal bias

[2]Soulié, "L'Utilisation," 298.

[3]Joseph Mazzeo, "St. Augustine's Rhetoric of Silence: Truth vs. Eloquence and Things vs. Signs," *Renaissance and Seventeenth Century Studies* (New York: Columbia University Press, 1964), 15.

[4]Jean de Sponde, "Introduction," *Méditations*, cv. Alan Boase notes that in 1586, Du Plessis-Mornay attempts to situate his *Méditations* within a spiritual tradition by including a text from Savaronola, a Dominican! Boase finds that it is unusual for a Calvinist to write meditations, which utilize the relative permissiveness of the expository technique, instead of exegesis. Du Plessis-Mornay therefore feels the need to legitimize his writing by placing it in a historical relationship with other such writing. The only predecessor he is able to find, however, is a Catholic.

against the concept of "works" as instrumental in attaining salvation.[5] The composition of the meditations, so similar in many respects to manuals for self-improvement, might lead the reader to believe that he accrues spiritual merit merely by reading appropriate tracts. Writing may thereby be misconstrued as works. Louis Martz notes a similar phenomenon in Puritan poetry: "Not only [does] Calvinistic theology discourage the Puritan from engaging in methodical meditation; it [leads] him to turn his energies in quite a different direction."[6] Structured like medieval mnemonic devices, the meditations imply a human capacity for perfectibility, through the absorption of the divine qualities outlined in the tracts. Catholic meditations amount to spiritual *summas* and, Calvinists feel, appeal to human pride. Calvinist meditational writing such as that of de Bèze is characterized by abstraction. This is explained by his distrust of sensorial aids in devotion. Incarnational description, he feels, stresses worldly analogies with the divine, and is not effective in focusing the attention on the things of the spirit. Such Catholic imagery traps divine essence in base matter. Consequently, the Calvinists forbid any description of God, for any human attempt at such depiction will never be truthful, but rather will display the artistic delusions of flawed humanity.

D'Aubigné's *Méditations,* on the other hand, are vividly imaged.[7] To achieve this, he employs a strategy similar to that Richard Baxter suggests in *The Saints Everlasting Rest* (1650). Baxter advises other writers of meditations:

> I would not have thee, as the Papists, draw [images] in Pictures, nor use mysterious, significant Ceremonies to represent them . . . [But you may] get the liveliest Picture of them *in thy mind* that thou possibly canst (my emphasis).[8]

Since both image and word are juxtaposed, the potential for error in interpretation is minimized, as opposed to the possibilities for misreading posed by one component, unaccompanied. We may compare this to the effectiveness of an emblem, which results from the joining of word and

---

[5]D'Aubigné, "Sa Vie," *Oeuvres,* 438. D'Aubigné shares Calvin's disparagement of works. In a passage from *Sa Vie,* he relates that, confronted after one of the peace-making sessions during the Wars of Religion by a hypocritical Catholic prelate who is bemoaning the religious hostilities and inquiring what he can do to help the problem, d'Aubigné abruptly informs him that he can do *nothing* "parce que nous ne sommes pas bons."

[6]Louis Martz, *The Poetry of Meditation* (New Haven: Yale University Press, 1954), 158.

[7]Cf., among others, the image of the priest in d'Aubigné's *Méditations sur les pseaumes,* ed. Henri Weber (Paris: Gallimard, 1969), 497-98; the "beau pourtraict" on p. 524; the "pourtraict des ames aveuglees" on p. 572. All subsequent references will be to this edition of the *Méditations.*

[8]Martz, *Poetry of Meditation,* 173.

image.[9] Written representation, contained and clearly explained by the word which conforms to the Word, may not be as threatening as vivid and explicit imagic depiction. For d'Aubigné, this is a way to rationalize the exceptional episodes of freedom from constraint that we may discern in his *Méditations.*

Théodore de Bèze's *Chrestiennes méditations,* a work which first appears in 1582 shortly after de Bèze translated the *Psalms* into the vernacular, best epitomizes Calvinist constraints. The constant subordination of lyrical language to a more familiar, colloquial sensibility is his standard throughout his biblical translation, and it carries over into the subsequent meditations. The *Chrestiennes méditations* is designed to encourage common folk to focus on the Psalms as universal *exempla,* applicable in every way to their lives as paradigms of a proper prayer life. They are to function as "quelque formulaire de prières."[10] To this end, de Bèze meticulously extirpates any self-expression. The "self" in the text would, by its idiosyncratic individuality, hamper the meditations' potential for general applicability. Everyman must not be too intricately detailed or he will lose his efficacity as a universal model. Mario Richter observes in his study of the *Chrestiennes méditations* that de Bèze emulates Calvin in pursuing a literal reading of the text. No subjective conjecture is permitted. While he is more free than Calvin in that he does not force his analysis to proceed line-by-line, de Bèze is much like his mentor in the emphasis he places on "una necessità stretamente didattica e liturca"[11] in his writing.

Considerations of language figure prominently for d'Aubigné, however. In his preface to the *Méditations* he stresses the merits of the simple and unadorned biblical style, yet the language he uses for his exposition is dramatic, densely imaged, and highly personal. This is much unlike de Bèze, who more exactly fulfills the Calvinist ideal that

> la Bible enseigne la vertu de la simplicité, et de nombreux protestants
> se persuadent qu'une matière sacrée appelle réserve et modestie . . .
> Ce goût du dépouillement . . . est . . . poussé si loin, chez . . .
> un Bèze . . . que les prosaïsmes s'accumulent . . . Nos auteurs
> semblent décidés à observer la mise en garde de Calvin.[12]

---

[9]Daniel Russell, *The Emblem and the Device in Renaissance France* (Lexington, Ky.: French Forum, 1985), 87-88. Russell observes that "[Pierre] Joly believed that one important reason for the persuasive force of the emblem form is its capacity to simulate a revelation or an intuition through . . . the choice and composition of text and illustration. The reader . . . refer[s] back and forth between the text and the illustration. . . . The advantage of this revelation is that it forces an immediate and total acceptance of the message in a way that a logical argument cannot."

[10]De Bèze, *Chrestiennes méditations,* 38.

[11]Richter, "La Poetica di Théodore de Bèze e le *Chrestiennes méditations,*" *Aevum* 37 (1964): 514.

[12]Michel Jeanneret, "Style de l'humanisme religieux," *Poésie et tradition biblique au seizième siècle* (Paris: Jose Corti, 1969), 169.

De Bèze formulates his purpose in composing the *Chrestiennes méditations* in a fashion that is oriented away from the self, toward the other as reader and the Other who is God. He declares that he writes "afin que je serve de miroir ou de patron aux autres."[13] This specular image of the self is, for the writer, truly an anti-selfhood, or an emptying of personality. It aims at an opacity of the self so that it may be purely functional: not an individual entity, but a thing, a mirror or a pattern in which *another* may perceive himself, his flaws, and his need for undoing. De Bèze parrots Calvin in this regard, for in his preface praising Guillaume Budé's translation of the Psalms (1560), Calvin lauds Budé for rendering the Psalms in a clear fashion so that they may be a "miroir où nous peussions contempler tout ce qui nous doit induire à bien prier."[14] The result is a series of contemplations carefully crafted so as to appear anonymous. The sinner proffers a prayer, but his voice is not meant to be recognized: it is not authorized. Rather, the authority of the Bible is magnified, for through customary Calvinist accumulation of repetition, antithesis, and biblical parallelism, de Bèze avoids the construction of any independent writing self in the *Chrestiennes méditations.*[15] He does not deviate from the stylistic guidelines of his mentor, nor does he swerve from him doctrinally. He employs consistently impersonal rhetorical figures. D'Aubigné differs from de Bèze in this respect, also, for he mandates a new form of literary expression commensurate with unprecedented theological assertions: "ce siècle, autre en ses moeurs, demande un autre style. / Cueillons des fruits amers, desquels il est fertile."[16]

The title of de Bèze's work contrasts with d'Aubigné's less doctrinally-directed title, *Méditations sur les pseaumes.* De Bèze is demanding a *liturgical* conception and application of the Psalms. That is, the *Chrestiennes méditations* are expressly designed for use at public services of the cult, and do not encourage individual perusal. D'Aubigné, however, writes *Méditations* that move within the standard framework of meditations (in format, they are apparently similar) but that also evidence a more lyrical, personal strain: his are *truly* meditations, upon which the imprint of the reflecting self remains. The self is the indispensable filter for all experience, even theological. As such, the formulation of the self sways the reader's interpretation of

---

[13]De Bèze, *Chrestiennes méditations,* 38.

[14]Peter Rudolphe, "Calvin et la traduction," 187.

[15]As Robert Cottrell notes, this denial of the self is a fairly commonplace medieval notion. Contrasted with d'Aubigné's innovative assertion of the self, it attests to Calvin and de Bèze's essential similarities with medieval thought rather than with Reformation and post-Reformation thought (which many deem "modern"). Cottrell, *Grammar,* 82, observes that "the rejection of narrative is of a piece with the denial of the distinction between 'I' and 'Thou,' man and Christ."

[16]D'Aubigné, *Les Tragiques,* vv. 77-80.

content. In fact, literarily, the self becomes the form to which all content must conform and over which, ultimately, it prevails.

The liminary meditation in de Bèze's collection immediately establishes the anonymity of writer and reader, and highlights man's ineptitude and blindness. The self is shattered, rendered by two antiphonal voices rather than one coherent speaker. The dialogue between "je" and "tu" is a hierarchy, a judgmental power relationship: a voice berates "tu" for his misguided ways. "Tu" represents Everyman, while "je" then epitomizes, as well as forces, "tu's" oral confession of his sins. "Tu" is not self-motivated, but is compelled to formulate his confession as "je" through the insistence of the divine voice. "Tu" is impotent; he has no efficacy in obtaining salvation. "Je" may be granted salvation once he shows contrition, but it is only through his "undoing" that he may be saved.

> De là es-tu entrée, mal-heureuse? Hélas en ce desert de jeunesse, desert, di-je, bien frayé et à travers, auquel toutesfois il n'y a droit chemin ne sente . . . là ay-je trouvé vanité. . . . Mais povre desvoyé qu'as-tu trouvé au bout de ce tant mauvais chemin? Certainement tout le rebours de ton intention.[17]

"Tu/je" has no autonomous voice. Similarly, de Bèze has no independent status as a writer, for he only speaks through God's grace and as an uncreative re-saying of God's Word: "que ta merci, Seigneur, m'ouvre la bouche, laquelle mes pechez m'ont close: car appartient-il aux pecheurs de parler de toy? Mais oste cet empeschement. . . ."[18] Were he required to rely on his own volition or capabilities, no writing would materialize.

De Bèze slashes at the prideful conception of self; his *Chrestiennes méditations* intend to re-shape the human in a form which will deny humanity: "Hélas, povre misérable, et plus que chétive créature, qui n'es jamais plus des-raisonnable, qu'alors que ta propre raison aveugle te mene, et ta volonté du tout desreiglee te pousse."[19] D'Aubigné, on the other hand, boldly proclaims humanity's redeeming qualities, choosing to begin the *Méditations* with a paean to fraternal love: "Voici le souverain bien de la vie humaine, ce qui seul en elle peut estre nommé agreable . . . c'est . . . de voir comme frères ceux qui cognoissent un mesme père" (496). Note that the valorization of the self with which his literary enterprise commences is still situated theologically: it is because men show love for God that they are permitted to exist as individuals. De Bèze fashions tendentious compositions and, in a subversive sense, so does d'Aubigné. Therefore, the final Psalm each author chooses should mirror his initial attitude and reinforce his authorial

---

[17]De Bèze, *Chrestiennes*, 42-44.
[18]Ibid., 77.
[19]Ibid., 42.

program for the reader, returning in a chiasmus to the beginning, and causing a re-reading of the book. Salvation proceeds in the same way: man is brought to recognize his death in sin, then through grace is returned to his origins to account for, and thus efface with God's help, his misdeeds.[20] De Bèze concludes with a predictable emphasis on man's sinful nature, yet holds out the consolation that man may be redeemed in Christ. This may only transpire, however, if man loses his humanity through concentration on the Godhead:

> La corruption de la nature t'estonne-elle? Le fils de Dieu se faisant homme l'a plainment sanctifiee pour toy. Tes pechez qui sont fruits de ceste corruption t'espouvantent-ils? il les a portés tous sur le bois, et a payé à ton acquit.[21]

D'Aubigné, however, affirms man *across* his sin, joining him physically with God in a triumphant vein:

> Or voici le comble de joye et de liesse: c'est que cette felicité estant departie en diverses mansions, remplira chacun selon sa mesure, afin que chacun soit heureux parfaitement . . . c'est là où nous attend cette beatitude (571).

The positing of *multiple* recipients of grace combats univalent literalism and indicates a possible permission for the individual's assertion. D'Aubigné also emphasizes that each man shall be filled according to his needs. He uses "chascun" in an individual sense. De Bèze, contrarily, addresses his interlocutor "tu" in a way that clearly defines him as Everyman.

Differences in the presentation of the two meditations thus point to the contrasting conceptions of the role of the self and of sin in writing. While de Bèze cries, "O mon Dieu, tu sçais le désir que j'ay d'estre instrument de ta gloire [mais] . . . hélas . . . mes péchez m'envoyant à la mort . . . voilà mon dessein rompu,"[22] d'Aubigné seems undaunted by sin, rising above it to concentrate on God:

---

[20]The chiasmus figures completion, harmony, and perfection for Renaissance writers. Such circular images proliferate in d'Aubigné's *Les Tragiques*. In one instance, he laments that evil deforms the earth and "lui ôte son rond." The circular motion of reading called for by the *Méditations* thus figures the cycle of return to grace after the Fall and illustrates the soteric role of reading in activating this process anew.

[21]De Bèze, *Chrestiennes*, 95.

[22]Ibid., 5.

> Vous ne treuverez ici aucune picoterie de nos controverses. A une
> seule différence vous cognoistrez de quelle Religion je fais profession.
> C'est que je parle par unité à Dieu qui est un et seul (494).

D'Aubigné seems to flaunt deliberately the points at which his exegesis is
disloyal to exegetical principles by juxtaposing his text with the entire
Psalm upon which he is commenting. By quoting the Psalm *in toto*, he
invites comparison with his work and renders possible an immediate apprehension of the differences between the two. De Bèze's *Chrestiennes méditations*
do not even incorporate the Psalm through quotations of any length, but
rather assume a generalized knowledge against which his less specific, more
didactic reading takes place. This means that de Bèze's writing shows less
tension between model and exegetical interpretation; he conceives of his
meditations as encapsulations of segments of the eternal truth the Psalm
contains. De Bèze does not swerve from the explicit sense of the Psalm
he glosses. He effects purely denotative reading, maneuvering within the
textual closure of the revealed Word. There is no schism between his
writing and the Word. This, however, in no way valorizes his writing as
co-equal with the Word; rather, it empties out "his" possession of the
writing, acknowledging that all expression has always been God's. D'Aubigné,
however, moves with elastic tension between the text of the Psalms and
his own text, occasionally adhering to, occasionally deviating from, the
model, playing his own creation off polemically against its precursor. For
instance, in his treatment of Psalm 84, he personalizes its first verse. The
Psalm reads, "Éternel des armees, combien sont aimables tes tabernacles."
D'Aubigné's development is much more substantial and more intimate,
evoking a familiar and accessible Father. His first phrase mimics that of
the Psalm, but the remainder of the sentence and what follows take the
Psalm in a different direction, showing d'Aubigné's personal intervention
in, and interpretation of, the Psalm:

> Eternel Dieu des armees, c'est à toy à qui nous adressons nos voeux
> et nos plaintes, par ce qu'il y a propitiation en ton sein, equité en
> tes jugements, force et victoire en ton bras, comme estant le Dieu
> trés fort, qui retiens en ta puissance les issues de la mort. Que beaux
> sont tes tabernacles (509)!

In another example, d'Aubigné elects to end his meditation with a brief
literary endeavor, a poem, rather than a message in prose. He revises the
Psalm's assertion "ô que bienheureux est l'homme qui s'asseure en toy" in
a pithy poetic formulation:

> Bref Dieu trés fort, heureux je croi
> L'homme qui s'appuye sur toi (520).

It is significant that he inserts "je's" belief as an essential factor in this assertion, the actual syntactic conjunction between "Dieu" in the first verse and "l'homme" in the second, while the model remains neutral and impersonal in its declaration. The incessant *va-et-vient* between the biblical text and his own results in d'Aubigné's incorporation of the biblical message, but with very different emphases. Throughout his literary career he articulates an *inter-referential system* among his works and the Bible, in which he is constantly glossing, correcting, adding to or differing from the *already written*. This requires a high degree of self-consciousness and distance from the Bible. He must be aware of his differences in order to devise his own work. He must similarly respond to texts *he* has already written, conceiving of himself as a being who, along with his language, evolves and changes in time. The self he inscribes in an early book may alter later in his career. De Bèze's work in this regard is one-dimensional, while d'Aubigné's begins to demonstrate a strategy of overcoming previous influence through the superposition of his discourse, and through the dynamic interplay of his text in opposition to another. His palimpsest strategy is not derivative, but rather revisionist.[23] The care with which he consciously *frames* his *Méditations,* constructing a historical "occasion" for the choice of each Psalm as well as an "argument," conveying his individual interpretation of the Psalm, shows his desire to distinguish his text from the model, to play the active role de Bèze relinquishes in guiding the reader to an awareness of distinct authorship in the text. De Bèze, on the contrary, launches into his meditations with no prefatory preparation, engulfing himself and the reader in the *exempla* the Psalm displays.

As de Bèze acknowledges, God utterly invades him, annihilating his individual self: "la grace vient donc de toy jusques à moy pour me chasser de moy." De Bèze experiences a fractured, fragmented self on the way to destruction; parts of his devastated self speak to other, estranged parts: "tu" is queried by an interlocutor who is another segment of the separated and scattered self. He is asked, "meschante bouche d'un meschant homme, oses-tu nommer ce nom tant sainct? . . . langue traiteresse. . . ."[24] This intensifies the image of shattered unity, contrasting with the totality of God. The hands with which de Bèze writes are indelibly stained with sin, and taint his writing irremediably:

---

[23]We may contrast his treatment of the palimpsest image with that of Du Bartas. Du Bartas intends that the palimpsest image express the overlaying, and ultimate subjugation, of the human text by the biblical Word/text. Human writing, Du Bartas contends, must give itself over to God to become the "written-upon," just as God's Word "discourt sur son discours [celui de l'auteur] et nage sur son livre." Guillaume Salluste Du Bartas, "La Judit," *The Works of Guillaume Salluste Du Bartas,* ed. Urban Holmes, Jr. (Chapel Hill: University of North Carolina Press, 1938), vv. 169-72.

[24]De Bèze, *Chrestiennes,* 57, 71.

Hélas, il n'est pas icy question d'effacer une tache telle quelle, mes ordures et pollutions sont si vilaines, si puantes, si avant *encrees* en moy jusques en l'ame de mon ame (my emphasis).[25]

Writing is de Bèze's mechanism for confessing sin. Through their association with impurity, therefore, "lettres" are "meurtrières."[26]

If de Bèze, head of Geneva after Calvin, fashions a paradigm of how the genre of meditations is liturgically applicable, it is interesting that other Calvinist writers do not deviate from the model he establishes. His intent is forthright: "pour remplir la lacune laissée par l'abolition du confessionnel."[27] And, indeed, Jean de Sponde's *Méditations sur les pseaumes* (1588), unlike d'Aubigné's *Méditations,* conforms to the prescription of the *Chrestiennes méditations.* Sponde's preface immediately disavows any personal efficacy in his writing: "quelque incapacité qu'il soit en moy . . . quelque indignité que mon insuffisance . . . ayt acquise . . . la legerté de mes mérites."[28] His work yields to "la Théologie . . . [qui] m'a captivé à ceste estude plus particulièrement."[29] His primary concern is to distinguish it from less worthy literary endeavors:

Il y a cinq années que je vous présentay le travail de ma jeunesse sur Homère, auquel vous fistes un si favorable accueil, que j'en espère tant plus à cestuy-ci, dont le sujet a beaucoup plus de beaux advantages.[30]

Like de Bèze, Sponde does not invite a comparison of his exegesis with the Psalm, for unlike d'Aubigné he does not print the two together. Rather, with Sponde, "le texte du psaume est englobé par la méditation elle-même et débité verset par verset."[31] The meditation is a gloss, not an original creation. Sponde's meditational explication clings like a parasite to portions of the Psalm, deriving its only inspiration from it, while d'Aubigné's diptych-like formulation of the Psalm as a complete entity associated with his meditation as a separate construction highlights the autonomy of d'Aubigné's writing. Sponde begins on a note similar to de Bèze's insistence

[25]Ibid., 72.

[26]Ibid., 73.

[27]Sponde, *Méditations,* 3-4. In discussing Marguerite de Navarre's *Miroir de l'ame pécheresse* in *The Grammar of Silence,* 120, Robert Cottrell notes a phenomenon similar to that demonstrated by both Sponde and de Bèze: "Christian reality can never be narrated; it can only be reflected. The poet and the reader merely trace out—one with the pen, the other with the eye—a pattern or paradigm that stood complete before they came to it."

[28]Sponde, *Méditations,* 3.

[29]Ibid., 4.

[30]Idem, "Introduction," *Méditations,* cviii.

[31]Idem, *Méditations,* 5.

on sin and human inadequacy: "rien de si misérable que l'homme. . . ."[32] However, Sponde, more a poet[33] than a preacher, demonstrates

> sa méthode [qui] est celle du poète, qui enrichit sa poèsie de chaque image gratuite susceptible de s'y incorporer, plutôt que celle d'un commentateur, qui se contente d'une amplification ou d'une explication.[34]

Yet, as a Calvinist, Sponde believes that poetic license can be a dangerous dissipation, a sinful failure to focus fully on God. D'Aubigné overcomes a similar distrust of fiction. Sponde states, "je ne te [Dieu] contemple point, mais seulement le Monde . . . je suis trop au large, et ma fantaisie s'écarte et se dissipe."[35] When Sponde does attempt some personal intervention, he sabotages his effort through his writing. For instance, Alan Boase remarks concerning Sponde's third meditation that "loin d'être, comme l'auteur l'avait voulu, une expression plus personnelle de sa foi, ce chapitre semble posséder ce caractère moins nettement que les autres." Sponde does not demonstrate the incidents of extraordinary, self-obtained liberty from the Psalms that are found in d'Aubigné's *Méditations*. In Sponde's *Méditations*

> c'est que tout développement, qui prend uniquement son point de départ dans le texte, ne peut, quelle que soit sa valeur littéraire ou religieuse, être regardé sans hésitation comme l'expression d'un point de vue nettement personnel.[36]

De Bèze's meditator is compelled to silence by his sin and thus is denied an autonomous speaking/writing self. Sponde's meditator follows de Bèze's example: the writer is utterly dependent on God for the origin and survival of his voice. He cries, "O Dieu ouvre la bouche seulement. Ta parole anéantira ce qu'elle mesme a basti."[37] Sponde enunciates a dialogue similar to that of "tu/je" in the *Chrestiennes méditations*. His discussion takes place with a type called "Prophane." Like de Bèze, Sponde recognizes salvation

---

[32]This may have something to do with the prevalence of a more Catholic "incarnational" imagery which, if one works backwards from Sponde's later reconversion to Catholicism, may be seen to run throughout Sponde's work. In addition, doctrinally Sponde remains a Catholic (even before his reconversion) through his insistence on the importance of the *visual church*. Cf. his "Déclaration," *Méditations,* 354. This emphasis parallels his use of visual imagery in a more "poetic" fashion than other Catholic writers. Cf. "L'Ange révolté, ceste chair, et ce monde . . ." in poem XII; "Sonnet sur le mesme subject," in Jean de Sponde, *Stances de la mort,* ed. A. Boase.

[33]Sponde, "Introduction," *Méditations,* cxvi.

[34]Mario Richter, *Jean de Sponde e le lingue poetiche dei protestanti nel cinquecento* (Milan: Cisalpino Golliardica, 1973), 150.

[35]Sponde, "Introduction," *Méditations,* cxxiv.

[36]See comments by A. Boase in Sponde, *Méditations,* xxiv.

[37]Richter, *Jean de Sponde,* 97.

only through the undoing and devaluation of the self: "l'homme . . . lamente le mal qu'il trouve en soy-mesme."[38] Self-denigration, rather than self-assertion, is the only stance for a human writer to take. As with the fractured being de Bèze evokes, Sponde's speaker is a man who witnesses his own disintegration:

> Ces os dont les jointures et la dureté soutenoient ce corps, sont brisez comme la poussière. Je les ay veus assemblez . . . mais ceste cire s'est écoulée auprès de ce feu, et tout s'est espars devant mes yeux.[39]

Finally, as is the case with de Bèze, Sponde claims no authorship: his "je" is merely a locus for the re-assemblage of biblical elements and adds no creative factor.[40] All writing is subordinated to the Word: "nos mains sont en sa main . . . nos authoritez en sa restriction, les mises de nos oeuvres en son controlle."[41]

D'Aubigné is innovative for a Calvinist in that he perceives writing as a possible vessel of divinity as well as the scaffolding for a self-construction which, textualized and expressed in the language of salvation, may be permitted and even, itself, saved. He says,

> c'est assés que par cette Epistre je convie mon Lecteur à eslever (en simplicité du langage de Canaan) ses pensees à Dieu, au sein duquel il y a propitiation.[42]

"Je" is a distinct *persona* who possesses authority; the "Lecteur" is a coherent entity who is capable of action and whose "pensees" are acknowledged.

---

[38]Ibid., 124.

[39]Sponde, quoted in Marguerite Soulié, "L'Utilisation," 304. Soulié states that "si le contenu des *Méditations* reste fidèle dans l'ensemble à la doctrine de Calvin, l'attitude intellectuelle de Sponde le distingue nettement des autres théologiens auteurs des méditations. Sponde, nourri de la Bible mais aussi des philosophes et des poètes antiques, ne sacrifie rien de sa culture d'humaniste en composant cette oeuvre théologique." However, she fails to account for how, as a Calvinist, Sponde can rationalize the mingling of sacred and profane that occurs in his poetry. Also, humanist imitation and biblical imitation do not innovate; they are "original" only in the sense of *re-organization*. Elsewhere, Soulié undermines her thesis by calling Sponde's work a "marquetterie," implying thereby a lack of cohesion and the absence of a self-conscious, directive authorial personality.

[40]Richter, *Jean de Sponde,* 158.

[41]Ibid.

[42]D'Aubigné here conveys the essential role of his writing in compelling theological observance in his reader (the beginning of his strategy of theo-literary combination) for it is "par cet Epistre" that his reader is called to "eslever ses pensees à Dieu."

D'Aubigné reverses the downward movement by which God customarily graces humanity.[43] He implies that humanity may overcome its sinful nature dialectically, by recognizing it and offering it up to God. Unlike Calvin, he does not wait for grace to proceed, but rather solicits it.[44] In this way, the self comes to have value.

The exegesis of Sponde and de Bèze is geared toward securing the salvation of the reader through a denial of the self. It results in the replacement of the self's inner preoccupations with directed meditations on the divine. D'Aubigné's exposition of the Psalms differs markedly; he inverts this procedure and, by focusing on the divine, finds an arena in which that which is human may be sanctioned. De Bèze, Sponde, and d'Aubigné all write of salvation, but only d'Aubigné's text speaks of the process through which it is possible to attend to the divine and to be saved.[45] He writes, "si l'homme charnel qui est en nous répugne à ces hautes pensees, voici les leçons qu'il lui faut donner, les verges en la main" (535). D'Aubigné uses his meditational writing to surpass the conventional, passive figuration of the meditator, and speaks of himself in an active mode. Through his writing, the Word may be made manifest. By transmitting the Word, d'Aubigné's word is legitimized. This apparently explicit causation opens up new vistas for literary creation, for if, as d'Aubigné does, one reverses the process of interpretation and works back *from* effects *to* causes, the effects (his writing) become essential to the revelation of their cause, and hence are valorized.[46]

---

[43]While the use of an apparently contradictory term such as "eslever" may be found in other Protestant writers, it is used there in a *passive* sense: God's grace may "eslever" men to him, but men may never attain God on their own. Calvin asserts, "nos esprits sont trop rudes et trop pesans pour monter si haut." Calvin, "139e Sermon sur Job," cited in Stauffer, *Dieu, la création,* 262.

[44]Calvin, *L'Institution,* I.i.51.

[45]While the *Méditations* are actually written later than many of d'Aubigné's works, I have chosen to discuss them first, because they do not demonstrate to the same extent the strategies of overcoming which we shall perceive in his other texts. There are rudimentary indications that he seeks to move beyond the Calvinist norm, but, perhaps because of the constraints of the genre, he does not wholly succeed in doing so. Indeed, d'Aubigné's works do not always necessarily show a clear-cut chronological progression, for many of his works overlap and literary considerations double back on each other. It is true, on the whole, that not until the perceived need after the Council of Trent to "borrow some of the equipment of profane poetry" did the example of Simon [Goulart] cause a general breakaway from the Calvinist austerity within which d'Aubigné's formation [is] historically situated." Cave, *Devotional Poetry,* 48.

[46]"*Les Méditations sur les pseaumes* d'Agrippa d'Aubigné offrent ces moments décisifs de conversion spirituelle lorsque l'esprit et la volonté de l'homme en prière se voient . . . éclairés . . . par l'action de l'Esprit saint." Soulié, "L'Utilisation," 300.

Instances of Permission in the Méditations sur les pseaumes

There is a literary conflict inherent in the composition of the *Méditations* that can be discerned as early as the preface. D'Aubigné excoriates those writers "de ce siècle" who revert to a state of Babel-like confusion. He desires to speak as does the Bible, in a plain style of perfect equivalence between words and things. Language will thus refigure the harmony between man and God ("je parle par unité à Dieu" [494]) before the schism of the Fall which instigated miscommunication. Writer and reader will also thereby be made one.

Yet in contradistinction to the desire to efface themselves that the Calvinist writers demonstrate, and the corollary of the silencing and replacing the human utterance by the divine,[47] d'Aubigné manifests a conception of himself as distinct from God, and thriving in that separation. Dialectically, it is his *sin* which enables him to do so. While sin is evil, it also causes an "apartness," the distance necessary for the self to perceive itself. The self may then choose to express a need for salvation. This desire brings him closer to God and validates the self as mediator in a sort of contractual salvation covenant. D'Aubigné distinguishes himself out of a certainty of his merit as a writer: the writing is his, the reader is his ("mon lecteur"), he makes the decision to discuss the breakdown in language which parallels man/God separation, proposing to unify the different facets ("styles") into the univalence of the biblical model:

> J'ay estimé estre à propos de faire voir comment parmi les styles les plus élabourés . . . les passages de l'Escriture . . . preuvent par arrest du Ciel, illustrent par exemples, et recreent les esprits qui aiment Dieu (493).

D'Aubigné is not an instrument, but rather an agent in his own right. His "je" proliferates in the preface, while God is only mentioned five times. D'Aubigné also maintains his self distinct from the reader, engaging the reader dialogically (113) while directing the pattern of his reading. On the other hand, de Bèze does not even acknowledge that he has an individual reader, and avoids thereby the admission of any specific authorial intention. By not addressing his reader as "Lecteur," as does d'Aubigné, de Bèze remains anonymous within his text, and facilitates the merging of "tu" and "je" necessary to activate an *exemplum*. D'Aubigné is not attempting to

---

[47]Robert Cottrell discusses a similar phenomenon in *The Grammar of Silence*, 104; Marguerite's evangelical piety takes an exegetical form like that of de Bèze and Sponde in its erasure of the human speaker: "As more and more biblical citations and paraphrases appear in the poem, images of light replace those of darkness and gloom. Effacing itself before the presence of the Word; Marguerite's text becomes a clear, polished mirror that reflects God's text. The voice we hear in the poem is no longer that of the distraught Marguerite but that of God speaking to man through Scripture."

achieve the mutual anonymity of reader and writer at which de Bèze aims in his biblical *exempla*.

I see the *Méditations* as a work preliminary to the fictional permissions d'Aubigné later employs in the *Avantures*. It embodies a thoughtful literary strategy through which d'Aubigné reconciles the Calvinist writer's pre-emption by the Word with his standing as a literary creator. He does so by pursuing expository techniques to their logical conclusion: in order for exposition to be effected, a conscious selection must be made of appropriate passages. The activity of distinguishing useful from useless passages depends on a unique mentality. This assumption of responsibility valorizes the author's critical capacities and ultimately, in d'Aubigné, leads beyond re-structuring and reconfiguring elements to the creation of new material. We may discern isolated instances in the *Méditations* which, I believe, display in miniature the permission of writing; they are embedded in the larger scaffolding of the text and are easily overlooked. They constitute the beginning of d'Aubigné's revision of Calvinism to attain his own theo-literary goals. We shall examine the frame, or conventional generic format, as well as the permissive eruptions that it cloaks. We shall see that d'Aubigné diverges significantly from the Calvinist model, enabling him to formulate a unique view of the purpose of writing as an expression of the saved self.

D'Aubigné chooses for himself the structure of "argument" and "occasion"[48] to test his ability to write yet remain faithful to God's Word within the dialectical opposition of freedom and fidelity: "cette-ci fut choisie, où il y a des choses qui sentent la contrainte, et quelque différence en l'usage de la liberté" (495). In so doing, he deliberately ignores Calvin's injunction that

> puisque l'Escriture nous explique . . . dilegemment . . . nous devons plustost nous arrester à ceste interprétation qu'à nos fantaisies.[49]

By building his meditation within the structure of "occasion" and "argument," he shows his explication of the Psalm to be generated by external, often secular situations. While the dual division is a didactic technique (he says he writes "bien plus utilement que les poètes et les peintres" [496]) and as such conforms to the Calvinist qualification of useful

---

[48]At the beginning of each Psalm, d'Aubigné first writes an "occasion," a description of the actual, historical situation in his life which gave rise to the meditation he writes. He follows this with an "argument," a brief outline of the main points he hopes to make in the meditation.

[49]Calvin, *L'Institution*, II.v.105-6.

writing,[50] this can also be viewed as innovative, for it shows the *free* desire of the human to attend to the divine rather than demonstrating a *requirement* (motivated by God, an external force) that he do so. For instance, d'Aubigné tells us that he meditates on Psalm 133 in response to a criticism the King voices of his writing style. Finding that d'Aubigné's style epitomizes a too negative and contentious spirit, the King challenges him to try his hand at something not as sarcastic as his usual polemic (117-18). Other similarly non-theological scenes motivate d'Aubigné's writing. His meditation on Psalm 51 appears to be an early instance of political ghost-writing, in which he supplies the King of Navarre with the words to express "une repentance [qu'il] fit . . . à la Rochelle" (536). The meditation on Psalm 88 arises from the death of d'Aubigné's wife, a thoroughly personal motivation rooted in d'Aubigné's sentimental existence rather than in his aspirations toward theological instruction. By selecting the Psalms under such circumstances, and by composing his meditations for a specific purpose, d'Aubigné's *Méditations* approach the genre of the "frame story" as practiced by Jacques Yver's *Printemps* and Marguérite de Navarre's *Heptaméron*.[51] As such, d'Aubigné moves toward greater narrativity, recounting what amounts to an anecdote situated in human time, rather than relating human existence as episodic and incomplete without God (as do the other Calvinist writers).

Yet, the Calvinist framework is still evident. God's voice delineates the margins to which d'Aubigné's speech is to be limited: "Eternel mets garde à ma bouche, garde le guichet de mes levres, de peur qu'elles prononcent en l'amertume. . ." (523). And, in typical obeisance to the Word, d'Aubigné crafts the *Méditations* so that God's voice is the one that is heard first: "celui de qui vient toute bonne donation, qui a tousjours present et le pouvoir et le vouloir, a rendu nos désirs abrégez, nous contente et dit, 'Voici'" (496). However, a subtle reversal occurs: God's voice is contained *by* and communicated *through* d'Aubigné's narrating voice that introduces it and thereby enables it to speak. D'Aubigné alters the Calvinist format by daring to suggest that God may depend on man for his own completion. In addition, d'Aubigné alerts his reader that he dares to write without God's explicit permission: "mon lecteur prene en bonne part un partage que je fai icy *sans authorité expresse* de l'Escriture" (499; my emphasis).

---

[50]Such guidelines are much like the Ramist practice of schematization. On Ramism, Selinger notes in *Calvin Against Himself*, 178, that it "[is] especially popular in areas that favor Calvinism." Castor, in *Pléiade Poetics*, 133, observes that Ramus, like Calvin "posit[s] a pre-existent body of true knowledge, already complete and perfect, which require[s] only to be uncovered and revealed to the intellectual sight of men."

[51]Both Marguérite and Jacques Yver situate their stories in the tradition established by Boccaccio's *Decameron*. They write a story in which their characters become narrators of stories-within-the-story.

One constraint against which d'Aubigné moves is the Calvinist condemnation of the use of allegory. Calvin distrusts allegory because it introduces the possibility of individual error in interpretation; it is a system of mediation that intervenes between the articulation of divine truth and its reception. He states,

> les allégories ne doivent estre receues sinon d'autant qu'elles sont fondées en l'Escriture; tant s'en faut qu'elles puissent approuver aucune doctrine. Davantage, les raisons ne nous défaillent point par lesquelles nous pouvons réfuter ce qu'ils disent. . . . N'auroyent ils point de honte de mettre en avant ie ne sçay quelle allégorie légère contre tant de tesmoignages si clairs? [Mais] . . . l'entendement de l'homme est tellement du tout aliéné de la iustice de Dieu, qu'il ne peut rien imaginer, concevoir ne comprendre, sinon toute meschanceté, iniquité et corruption.[52]

D'Aubigné's application of allegory in his meditation on Psalm 133

> (Telle bénédiction a esté accomparee au bausme de haut prix qui d'espandoit sur la teste du grand Sacrificateur [Aaron], distillant des cheveux sur la face, d'elle espandu sur l'estomac, . . . sur l'Ephod et en fin passant de la ceinture jusques aux extremitez de la tunique. Ce type et sacrement de la grace du S. Esprit . . .) (497)

is a flagrant violation of Calvin's injunction against allegory. D'Aubigné's use of allegory thereby highlights the equivocal status of his work and situates it in a zone of tension between the desire toward the expression of the personal religious experience and the command to observe the Calvinist boundaries on writing. He deliberately creates the confrontation between the Calvinist model and his writing: Psalm 133 does *not* contain an allegory, but rather a straightforward recounting of the historical sacralizing of the priest, Aaron. D'Aubigné chooses to see it allegorically, as a representation of the action of grace in ameliorating the divisive religious climate in France. His only criterion for any restrictions on his use of allegory is stylistic rather than theological; he doesn't want to overdo it: "ce champ nous fourniroit plus d'allegories agreables si la moderation ne nous commandoit d'en user sans abus" (506).

While d'Aubigné's style has affinities–such as the use of antithesis–with that of other Calvinist writers, he atypically occasionally mingles song and verse with prose. This is unusual for the genre of the meditations. In this he is like the Psalmist, and follows the Davidic model of lyric expression. Rather than rely on concrete imagery, as does the Bible, d'Aubigné prefers abstraction, stating that "les choses à espérer, sont celles que nul oeil n'a

[52]Calvin, *L'Institution*, V.li.90.

veues . . . qu'aucun esprit n'a esté suffisant de comprendre. . ." (535). He struggles with intangibility within his work for, as Simon Goulart recognizes, the impalpability of Protestant style does not carry sufficient appeal to the readership, while the Catholic reliance on sensory images has far greater influence. The conflict d'Aubigné experiences concerning the merits of representation over abstraction is important for his entire literary project. Abstraction conforms to the Calvinist refusal to represent things for fear that they may be distorted as idols. However, while he apparently yields here to the Calvinist model, the dearth of concrete images is, rather, a mechanism d'Aubigné employs in order to valorize ultimately (for a limited purpose) concrete imagery. That is, his refusal in the greater part of the *Méditations* to provide the reader with specific images upon which to meditate may not be seen as a concession to Calvinist doctrine but rather as a decision on his part to wield power: he, as author, withholds information the reader desires. He thereby asserts his capacity for textual manipulation. Later, and in isolated episodes, when he does employ concrete imagery he does so to attest to the strength of his discourse. In the *Avantures,* for instance, d'Aubigné describes Faeneste to establish him as an image, only to reveal the image's inadequacy before the onslaught of Enay's criticism of him. Enay, of course, represents d'Aubigné himself. D'Aubigné is a polemicist; in all his works, his aim is to persuade and convince. He progresses from the tentative forays toward concrete expression that are intermittently visible in the *Méditations* to a more explicit use of imagery. In the *Méditations,* therefore, d'Aubigné works against Calvinist univalence by presenting the reader with two opposing interpretations juxtaposed in the same text: the reader then determines and elects the valid one. This is unlike Calvinist meditational manuals, wherein rules and regulations are sternly spelled out without equivocation or room for modification. D'Aubigné eschews didacticism, setting up an *arena of choice* within his work:

> Ayant esté [dict] par deux tableaux quelles sont les bénédictions celestes sur le bénits, . . . remarquer les maledictions qui pendent sur la teste des coeurs rebelles à Dieu (504).

As d'Aubigné is a more active, self-conscious writer than other Calvinists, he expects the reader to be involved in the text–albeit in a role that d'Aubigné specifically directs. The reader is asked to superimpose through his act of reading his own interpretation upon d'Aubigné's text. Both inscriptions, finally, are layered over God's Word which, in turn, is itself *written upon* us to guarantee our salvation: "ces seins qui estoyent sanctuaires, ces coeurs tables de la Loi, et sur lesquels elle estoit escrite du doigt de Dieu" (511). In such a way, the text of d'Aubigné's *Méditations* becomes a sort of palimpsest formed by the interaction between text and pre-text (the

Bible), writer and reader: "il faut passer de l'ombre au corps, et de l'image à la chose" (506), from the text to God and an awareness of one's salvation.

When the *Méditations* pass beyond universal pertinence to a specific reader-writer dialogue, d'Aubigné demonstrates a desire to have a personal effect on the manner in which his work is read, as well as on the possibility of pointing the reader toward salvation. Through occasional direct addresses to God, d'Aubigné appears, if not God's equal, at least as one meriting His attention. D'Aubigné's writing serves as God's *aide-mémoire:* he reminds the Lord, "c'est nous que tu as choisis et sanctifiez, tu nous as separé pour ton peuple acquis" (515). The heightened status he accords himself causes a tension with the customary genre of the meditations, in which God alone is to be that which is spoken of and thought upon. D'Aubigné recognizes this, asserting that "toutes nos doctrines doivent tendre directement à ce qui est de la gloire de Dieu, nous tournerons toutes ces similitudes à leur vrai but," but goes on to stipulate that the human recipient of the Word is to be valued in that it is within his heart that the Word acts: "que l'origine des faveurs de Ciel qui descoulent sur nos testes agit premièrement en nos coeurs" (503).

In this way d'Aubigné begins to devise strategies of overcoming the Calvinist distrust of the world and of non-exegetical writing. By initially defining himself against Catholics, he evolves a coherent polemic self. He can then pivot to confront Calvinists with this *persona*. Through his writing, his self becomes multivalent and is expressed in different genres. This self-conception possesses theological and literary aspects which it desires to harmonize. Thus, through the interplay of evolving and enriched senses of self, d'Aubigné comes to perceive his writing act as justified, since it is writing which confirms his terrestrial existence and heavenly salvation.

The instances of such strategies which we shall now examine possess characteristics in common with the episodes in *Les Tragiques, La Confession du sieur de Sancy* and *Sa Vie à ses enfants* which d'Aubigné dubs "apophéties." They all show an extreme self-consciousness, an almost vaunting confidence in the self as possessing the key to truth, and a formulaic structure which points to, and beyond, the biblical prophetic model. In their orientation towards the writer rather than his subject, these may be called embryonic permissions for fiction, for they are assertions of the writing self independent from the framed material with which he has been dealing heretofore. While they do not label themselves as "untruthful" and, in the case of the "apophéties," in fact aim at a Truth beyond that which other humans apprehend, they touch on matters that cannot be empirically verified until later (in the "apophéties") or which surpass the subject matter at hand (in the meditational examples). They appear to be fantastical constructions originating only in the author's brain and unauthorized by any Other. That they may later turn out to reveal truth rather than fiction appears incidental.

Imagination is permitted to exist autonomous of any endorsement in reality or in a parent text.

Thus, in the case of the *Méditations,* eruptions in the explicating text suddenly occur where the Psalms no longer give impetus to the writing, where the generic conventions are exceeded. D'Aubigné's individual voice can be heard, and true invention takes place. D'Aubigné uses the Calvinist-endorsed tactics of exposition as his point of departure in such instances, only to move beyond it, bringing in material from his own life or his own imaginings, rather than from other biblical incidents alone. Incorporated within the legitimate framework of a meditation, this personal expression is given a status equal to that of the sacred subject elsewhere under discussion. In fact, it might pass unnoticed and unchallenged were it not for d'Aubigné's insistence, through the physical juxtaposition of Psalm and meditation, that the two texts be read comparatively. One can only conclude that d'Aubigné *wants* his voice to be acknowledged, unlike de Bèze, who prefers that it be annihilated. D'Aubigné takes a big risk in so doing, for as in his decision to employ allegory, he is aware that such breaches in a text's continuous fabric invite the possibility of error. They do, however, create *intertextual space,* a theater in which the emergence of the self may take place.[53]

D'Aubigné had a similar intent when he audaciously compared writing that arises from his personal experience with a book Satan writes: "Satan nous dicte de plus furieuses leçons et apprend des textes à l'affligé. . ." (526). Such writing can be redeemed by a concentration on the writer's sin which, paradoxically, ensures him of his salvation: "à telz exces de douleur, il est bien besoin que l'esprit conservateur s'oppose en destruisant, et dicte aux esleus nouvelles pensees. . ." (527). Also, the content of d'Aubigné's writing can only be endorsed when it mirrors, and participates in, the nature of the Word through *form:* painting is explicitly denigrated, linked as it is with sin:

> mes transgressions . . . se presentent . . . la laide image de ma mort: le pis est que ce sont pas vaines fumees de songe, mais vifs tableaux des actions . . . le subtil fait le mestier de peindre quand il veut: son pinceau . . . fait voir . . . [des] horreurs (538).

The image is forceful and must be contained by the word which thus acts as the instrument for the eradication of sin. As the divine Verbum exerts authority by causing a discontinuity in human existence, d'Aubigné may seek to view his own work as the possibility of valorizing human writing

---

[53]Milton later employs a similar strategy, using allegory dialectically: "The authority of allegory is established by its guarded and self-qualified relation to the truth. Allegory cannot err, because it represents error itself, endlessly circumscribing the domain of truth." John Guilleroy, *Poetic Authority* (Chicago: University of Chicago Press, 1985), 139.

through the enactment of a similar disruption in the divine text. His writing does not destroy or diminish the divine, but opens interstices for the textual expression of the self, just as the self is separate from (because it is devalued by its sin) yet reconciled to (through salvation, sin's necessary correlate) God in Calvinist theology. This establishes a "problematical relationship of sacred voice to sacred text,"[54] but, as noted, by including the distinct secular text within the sacred meditation, the two are reconciled dialectically.

D'Aubigné is courageous in his decision to "beget himself," for he knows and utters the Calvinist imperative: "le premier degré [de combat] est de vaincre contre soi mesme" (513). Yet, certain that he is one of the elect, and emphasizing predestination in a positive sense, d'Aubigné links this assurance of salvation with the testimony of his writing so that the two form an equation that permits the self. As John Guilleroy observes regarding Milton's poetic creation,

> to elect oneself . . . is at least a scandal in the religious life. . . . Poets do not easily give up the immemmorial association of poetry with vision and prophecy, with sacred origins and . . . such resistance is fundamentally a consequence of anxiety about authority.[55]

D'Aubigné, by endowing himself with both a theological and a literary role, surmounts this dilemma.

Thus, a careful examination of d'Aubigné's meditations on the Psalms highlights key techniques which conform to the Calvinist model and constitute the religious framework of the *Méditations*. His meditations also embody "instances of permission" for the authorial self within the text.

In Psalm 73, the logical progression of the exposition is interrupted by a long development that is not licensed by the Psalm and that seems to derive its origin from the one word "sanctuaires" in the Psalm verse: "jusques à ce que je sois entré aux sanctuaires de Dieu fort, et que j'aye consideré la fin de telles gens" (522). From this d'Aubigné extrapolates the following drama, and an entire scene unfolds, with the roles of Comforter Angel and Suffering Church as actors, the cherubim and the "elect" as spectators. Multiple points of view are provided so that the reader may identify variously with the different speakers. The actors are ranked from least to most holy (the Church and God), so that as the reading progresses, the reader figuratively ascends a spiritual ladder toward his own incorporation in the band of the elect.

[54]Ibid.
[55]Ibid., 174.

En ces saisons de desolation l'Ange consolateur mene les esleus
frapper à la porte du Sanctuaire, à ce grand cabinet des secrets de
l'Eternité. Adam voulant s'acquerir la science de bien et de mal, pour
se faire pareil à Dieu, trouva un Cherubin, officier du Paradis terrestre,
qui le mit dehors honteusement . . . mais les coeurs humiliés sont
reçeus doucement à la recognoissance de leur salut . . . quand ils
demandent les paroles de vie . . . les enfans de Dieu, estans à l'huys
du Sainct des Saincts, voyent arriver une femme . . . d'une parfaite
beauté, qui avoit ses vestmens deschirés, ses cheveux brunis, couverts
d'un sac et parfumés de cendre; ses deux yeux noyoyent son visage
de larmes . . . quelqué desolee qu'elle fust, et tormentee en son
courage, elle n'avoit rien diminué e sa majesteuse gravité, le respect
de laquelle empesche la trouppe de passer le seuil; et elle seule l'ayant
franchi prononça la harangue qui s'ensuit, de laquelle elle fit les
virgules de souspirs, et les points de sanglots redoublés (528).

Several pages of the Femme's complaint follow, during which the reader
realizes that she represents the church. She fears that God has abandoned
her, without resources, to the secular century. Finally, she experiences, as
it were behind the scene, an unmediated theophany:

A ces mots les ailes des Cherubins qui couvrent la Propitiatoire
commencerent à s'eslever; de là sortit une nuee de parfums et baumes
excellents qui encensa et remplit le lieu, si bien que nous perdismes
la Fille du Ciel pour un temps; . . . nous ouysmes une harmonie
angelique qui nous ravit en extase jusques à ce que l'air esclairci, et
nos esprits estans serenés, nous vismes ressortir la triumphante avec
un visage aussi gay que desolé auparavant . . . [elle] parla ainsi à
tous: O combien est grand à merveilles le bien que Dieu a preparé
à ceux qui l'ont reveré (531).

In this digression, d'Aubigné employs tactics not customary with Calvinist
exegetes. He adds elements not included in the Psalm itself, such as the
"cabinet des secrets de l'Eternité," which seem to be produced by a highly
personal, individualistic "mind's eye" view of heaven. Also, while like other
Calvinist writers, d'Aubigné continues to insist on the superiority of Word
(and even human word) to image, he nevertheless includes a fully-delineated
image which might be entitled "the Church complains to God in heaven."
Through such an elaborate portrayal, he is able to develop a *prosopopeia,* a
dramatic form of allegory. The visual description becomes secondary; it is
a mere point of departure, and what matters is not the setting, but the
script. D'Aubigné chooses to develop a drama rather than a description;
this choice has some importance for him and for the reader. Its significance
lies in the strategy of incorporation: as the text of the episode subsumes

but does not destroy the image-description of it, so the Word may incorporate d'Aubigné's own writing, just as "nous lisons en quelque escrit de ce temps une peincture de l'estat des damnez" (534).

How does one explain this lengthy development? D'Aubigné might simply reiterate the Psalm's assurance that God will care for his Holy One. Instead, he stages a drama of reconciliation that may be interpreted as paradigmatic of the potential permission for writing by the sinful creator. D'Aubigné makes explicit the focus on the self. First, his attention to matters of language stands out in this episode. While portraying the incident, he takes care to parse the grammatical structure of the Church's discourse: her sighs are commas, and periods are formed by her sobs. Her self-expression adopts the idiom of writing. Similarly, d'Aubigné concentrates on the self through writing. He suggests, "c'est là où il faut dire en soi-mesme: . . . Je prendrai garde . . . que je ne peche [pas]. . ." (523). This statement is an important addition, for there is no such internal dialogue with the self in the Psalm. We know that d'Aubigné links writing with selfhood, and we may infer that the following exposition will deal with a similar concern. This is supported by several indications in the text. D'Aubigné's use of rhetorical devices clashes with the Calvinist tendency to subordinate eloquence to didacticism.[56] A second textual clue is the lengthy scene in which the Ange Consolateur leads the Elect to the door of the sanctuary (528-35). This is found nowhere in the Psalm d'Aubigné claims to explicate, signalling a purposive personal intervention. D'Aubigné develops a drama of inquiry, in which the Elect are ultimately compelled to focus on themselves and on their sins, as he does in his writing. Thirdly, the theme of presence and absence implicit in the initial empty stage, the Church's arrival and then her sudden disappearance and equally abrupt reappearance, parallels d'Aubigné's awareness of, and concern over, his own presence in the text. As though suddenly reminded of his Calvinist adherence, d'Aubigné reprimands himself that earthly fabrications, such as his, can never attain the status or efficacy of the Word:

> voilà les enseignements de la fille du Ciel, des oracles du sacré lieu, qu'il vaut mieux recevoir par les mains de l'Eglise que par les contes que nous faisons de nos doigts (532).

---

[56]Calvin, *L'Institution,* II.viii.141. "Il nous faut observer que les préceptes de Dieu contiennent quelque chose plus que nous n'y voyons exprimé par parolles. Ce qu'il faut néanmoins tellement modérer, que nous ne leur donnions point tel sens que bon nous semblera, les tournant ça et là à nostre plaisir. Car il y en a d'aucuns qui par telle license font que l'authorité de la Loy est vilipendiée, comme si elle estoit incertaine. . . . Il faut donc, s'il est possible, trouver quelque voye, laquelle nous conduise seurement et sans doute à la volonté de Dieu. C'est à dire il faut regarder combien l'exposition se doit estendre outre les parolles, tellement qu'il apparoisse que ce ne soit point une addition adjoustee à la Loy de Dieu, des gloses humaines, mais que ce soit le pur sens naturel du législateur, fidèlement déclaré."

D'Aubigné must make his statement, as the Church makes her complaint, then undergo a process of affiliation to the divinity in order to reappear, joyous with the confirmation of salvation, capable of transmitting divine truth as well as human expression in his word. The "je" in the Church's complaint, at first framed clearly so that the reader knows "je" refers to her, continues such a lengthy lament that it is gradually destabilized; the reader no longer knows for sure whether "je" is the Church or the narrator. The forceful lamentational anaphora has an urgent, personal resonance:

> Jusques à quand m'oublieras-tu continuellement? Jusques à quand cacheras-tu ta face de moi? . . . Jusques à quand s'eslevera mon ennemi contre moi? Eternel mon Dieu, regarde, exauce moi, illumine mes yeux, de peur que je ne dorme la somme de la mort (530).

This perception is strengthened by the "nous" used for the Church's confessional statement in which d'Aubigné also participates:

> Pour reprendre ce bon vouloir, nous ne saurions si tost dire, "Il faut confesser à Dieu nostre mesfait," qu'aussitôt l'Eternel ait osté la peine de nos peschez et voilà le désespoir changé en esperance (142).

D'Aubigné may now profess election, as he does at the conclusion of this "instance of permission": as narrator, he uses the pronoun "nous" to attest to his place in the ranks of the elect, the spectators and auditors of the divine drama devised by human imagining from the divine point of departure accorded by the Psalm: "Nous ouysmes une harmonie angelique qui nous ravit en ectase . . . nous vismes ressortir la triomphante." Henceforth, d'Aubigné affirms, "rien ne me separera de la dilection de Christ" (535). Writing, for him, is no longer the divisive factor Calvinism construed it to be when it equated it solely with sin. In fact, d'Aubigné actually incorporates a fragment from one of his non-exegetical works, *Les Tragiques* (*Jugement,* 1045-54), as an example at the end of the meditation.[57] While it remains anonymous, its inclusion nevertheless attests to the presence of

---

[57]D'Aubigné's works are not always published close to the time in which they are written. *Les Tragiques* is particularly complex in this regard, for it was begun in the 1570s, reworked at different times, and not published until 1616 in Geneva. Segments of verses from the *Tragiques* are often found woven into other of d'Aubigné's texts as supporting examples for statements he makes there; thus, the *Tragiques* itself, through a system of citations, becomes a textual authority. *Sa Vie à ses enfants,* written very near the end of d'Aubigné's life, was not published until 1729 in an edition which also included a reprint of the *Avantures du Baron de Faeneste,* published for the first time in 1617 (the first two parts), 1619 (the third part) and 1630 (the fourth part). The *Avantures* contains many borrowings from *La Confession du sieur de Sancy,* which, however, was not actually published until 1660 in Cologne. Finally, the *Méditations sur les pseaumes* appeared in 1630; the oldest of the meditations (sur Pseaume LI) was written in 1588 while the most recent was composed in 1626, so the *Méditations* show the same process of evolution that can be discerned in the history of the composition of the *Tragiques.*

the authorial self in the text; it is a secretive signature that further equates sin and writing in d'Aubigné's positive dialectic reading of it:

> Nous lisons en quelque escrit de ce temps une peincture de l'estat des damnez, auquel est apporté cette comparaison en ces termes: "Or ce dur estat le poinct plus envieux c'est sçavoir aux enfers ce que l'on faict aux Cieux" (534).[58]

The self now receives the divine imprimatur. The meditation on Psalm 51 shows what therefore seems an astonishing avowal of pride in the extent of his sins: "jai peché sans mesure, si haut est l'amas de mes ordures" (537). While Psalm 51 does speak of sin, it does not quantify it so emphatically. Yet, in the perspective of d'Aubigné's previous permission of the self, we realize that it is only by focusing on one's sin that sin may be converted into salvation: "je reviens à mon crime" (538) "et ainsi toutes les voyes que je tiens me contraignent à venir chercher ta droite" (537). A focus on human writing, d'Aubigné claims, may achieve similar results. If the self (and his textual productions, a part of his existence) moves within a sacred enclosure, redemption may ensue:

> Tu me tiens serré devant et derriere, tu as mis sur moi ta main, si je vai ariere de ton esprit, ou hors de ta face, si je monte aux Cieux, tu y es; si je me trouve dans les abysmes, t'y voilà . . . (539).

The images of straitening are intentionally claustrophobic, compelling the reader to notice not so much the force (God) pressing in on the self, as the self's agitation. God's efficacy must work through man's unwillingness and sin. In the restricted space within which the self moves, he is the actor we observe most closely. He is defined by the very limits that constrain him, yet paradoxically within these boundaries a more clear and vivid conception of the self is created. D'Aubigné similarly sculpts himself within Calvinist constraints that he both welcomes (theologically) and revises (literarily).

The emphasis on enclosure can be seen in another instance in which d'Aubigné wanders far from the biblical pre-text. Reacting to the Psalm verse "car je cognoi mes transgressions, et mon peché est continuellement devant moi" (536), d'Aubigné pursues a personal tangent, deriving from the biblical phrase this unprecedented, baroque development in which the writing self appears reflected *en abyme*:

> . . . un pourtraict effroyable, . . . espouvantable crocodile, qui pleure pour trahir, un loup qui a les dents sanglantes d'un aigneau

---

[58]D'Aubigné uses other fragments from the *Tragiques* elsewhere in the *Méditations;* cf. page 525, for example.

domestique ou du petit chien fidele qui gardoit la maison; et puis
sans pourtraict me fait dans son miroir voir ces mesmes choses en
m'y voyant (538).

The author is framed here, within the confines of the mirror, in a figure
analogous to the manner in which he chooses to structure the *Méditations,*
with the "occasion" containing the "argument." This alerts the reader to
the frame of the genre of the meditations, which houses the textually-
embedded "instances of permission." The utterly unmotivated interpolation,
with its horrifying imagery and symbols of incorporation and destruction,
reverses the writer into the written-upon:

Ainsi les yeux m'attirent m'effrayent, et qui furent organes de peché
sont devenus instrument de punition: desloyal peintre, qui a nos
esprits pour papier, et pour tablettes nos coeurs (538).

D'Aubigné reverts to his theme of the untrustworthy image, of the decep-
tiveness of seeing instead of hearing, which is typically Calvinist, but carries
it further: in a portrait he sees iniquitous things, emblems of sin. Worse,
in a mirror, the author sees himself *as* those evil objects framed in the
painting. It is significant that the self, although ugly and stained with sin,
remains the image that d'Aubigné sees in the mirror. This may be contrasted
with the transmutation Marguérite de Navarre paints in the *Miroir de l'âme
pecheresse* where, anatomizing the image of Christ on the cross, she calls
Christ's face "laid" (for it figures her own sin), but in the final verse she
looks into the mirror where she formerly beheld herself and sees Christ.
The image attests to the conjunction of signifier and signified. In d'Aubigné's
formulation, however, his face remains. This may be interpreted as meaning
that he is eternally unredeemed. However, given the "instances of permission"
we discern in the *Méditations,* it is more likely that it means that the self's
image may remain foul, but his *word* may move dialectically through sin
toward redemption. Such confessional writing will be justified by God's
act of erasure of the sin: "à la fin efface de tes tablettes mon procez pour
retourner à ton oeuvre encommencee assavoir la perfection de mon salut:
puis que ce que tu as une fois commencé et advancé tu ne le delaisses point"
(540). It is impossible for sin to block an all-powerful God. Consequently,
writing is eventually purged of sin and justified. God also permits thereby
the writing self: he returns d'Aubigné to him as a purified being, fulfilling
d'Aubigné's request, again offered through the essential medium of writing:
"rends ce que tu as créé" (540). His writing, an extension of himself,
participates in this ceremony of purification; it is now acceptable to God:
"moi miserable . . . et de voix et de coeur deviendrai un docteur de
repentance" (541). Now, like the figure of the Church, d'Aubigné's expression
is endorsed: "estant authorisé de titre si advantageux, [il] . . . ose plaider

son droict contre son Seigneur" (545). D'Aubigné then sees his death in himself. Yet death is a necessary stage before salvation.

> Quand la mort dissout le corps de l'homme, le separant pour le purifier, elle ne fait point perir le germe immortel qui restitue le tout; la dissolution apporte non la destruction, ni l'extinction, mais le renouvellement (568).

The dialectic between life and death breaks the closure separating human from divine writing. In direct *contradiction* to Psalm 51, d'Aubigné affirms the initial denial of the self which ultimately results in the self's affirmation:

> . . . à l'autel . . . c'est un coeur abbattu . . . toutes ces parties . . . comme bestes qu'on immole, ma chair esgorgee, bruslee devant toi . . . Je me souviens que tu demandes les bestes dans tache: et que sont devenues mes macules? cett' hysope *que j'ai demandé* les a emportees bien loin, si que je me presente nettoyé de ta main (542; my emphasis).

D'Aubigné's decision to request cleansing is an assertion of the self he expresses in his writing. The interplay of God ("tu") and sinner/author ("je") shows that dialogue is possible; this may lead to salvation through the purifying power of the Word. While the Word possesses potency, it is still hard to see how d'Aubigné will ever manage to valorize his writing. In an unexpectedly graphic and coarse image which seems to attest to a strong aversion on d'Aubigné's part, he says that even "les meilleures actions de l'homme sont ordes et puantes comme le flux de la femme" (539). As a Calvinist, he rejects works. Efficacious writing may conceivably be misread as a form of works:

> le tentateur a belle prise sur ceux qui mettent leurs oeuvres en ligne de conte: il desploye en grand marge devant leurs yeux les tableaux abominables de leurs crimes; et quand il faut mettre la main aux bonnes oeuvres, pour les loger à l'autre colonne du registre, ou cercher de quoi payer ses debtes, le trompeur, en riant, leur preste des feuilles desquelles il a coustume de payer ses ouvriers; et ces fueilles sont les bonnes oeuvres, ou les induglences achetees bien cherement (560).

D'Aubigné stresses the *written* tallying of good and evil deeds, establishing an uneasy equation of works with writing. The vocabulary he uses to do so is ambiguous; while "conte" clearly means an "account" here, it may also mean a "tale," and this association is borne out by the mention of "registres" and "fueilles." Such a terminology seems to indicate that d'Aubigné is wrestling, within the *Méditations,* with the problem of the legitimation of literary creation. The *Méditations* may thus be seen to have a second, unavowed agenda: the working-through of the writer's dilemma.

Writing at best appears acceptable only in the form of testimony. What is one to make of the sudden explosions of personal expression that arise within but do not conform to the meditational model? An examination of d'Aubigné's meditation on Psalm 88 provides some clues. Psalm 88 is a Psalm of lamentation that epitomizes the yearning of the soul for God, who seems to have deserted him. D'Aubigné takes this framework and builds onto it an intimate, nearly erotic evocation of his recently deceased wife. In recalling the unity the androgyne experienced ("tu m'as scié par la moitié de moi-mesme; . . . tu as fendu mon coeur en deux" [555]),[59] d'Aubigné conveys the feeling of duality and of schism that results from his wife's death. This sentiment, in the Psalm, duplicates man/God separation. But in d'Aubigné's meditation it takes second place to his discussion of the human ramifications of the death of Suzanne de Lézay. He mournfully reminisces: "nous allions unis à ta maison, et de la nostre, voire de la chambre et du lict faisions un temple à ton honneur" (555). The unanticipated reference to the conjugal bed is extraordinarily suggestive for a Calvinist writer, and signals an intensely personal intervention. In addition, God is not a far-away, inaccessible figure whom he cannot reach, handicapped by his own sin, but rather a confidant, an equal in sorrow, whom d'Aubigné addresses familiarly. This is the elaborate, self-conscious meditation that d'Aubigné grafts on to the simple Psalm verse, "tu as esloigné de moi l'ami, voire l'intime ami" (548). The self assumes an enormous incorporative power in d'Aubigné's writing, appropriating to itself all biblical expression and utterance: "la suite des propos de ton Prophete ne sont-ils pas la description de mon estre, et la leçon de mes funestes propos?" (554) almost as though defying God to deny him his authorial voice in which the personal lamentation must be expressed. We are thus returned to consider-ations of language: man's alienation from God results in linguistic confusion and a breakdown in communication. If, as d'Aubigné construes it, words are legitimized through their intentionality as signs that point to the Godhead, and if the man/God rupture undermines such purposiveness, then how can writing possibly be valued? D'Aubigné resolves this problem by deciding to read the Bible not only as the Word of God, but also as a *text*. (Later, he employs the additional strategy of referring to the *self* as a *textual construct*, as we shall see in *Sa Vie à ses enfants*.)[60] The Word of God, exegetes claim, may only be commented upon. D'Aubigné insists that the Bible may also be *interpreted*. Biblical expression facilitates this approach, for the Hebrew world is not one of theophanies or epiphanies, but rather of *interpretive events*. Narration is interpretation bounded by time. The

---

[59]It is noteworthy that, in his excursus from a biblical description, d'Aubigné chooses a mythic image so indebted to classical and pagan sources.

[60]See the chapter on *Sa Vie à ses enfants*.

temporal interruption of the text to be interpreted (the Bible) creates a spatial aperture into which the self may be inserted and play a creative role. D'Aubigné explicitly *writes himself into* the text of Psalm 88 (and implicitly does so in the other meditations we have examined) with an intent like that of Milton's later revision of Calvinism through his Puritan poetic creation:

> the poet is a lonely creator upon his own abyss. . . . Like a lonely creator of the world, Milton scatters his self-images throughout his poems–the "uncouth Swain"; Adam; . . . Satan, and the epic poet; Christ and Samson. His . . . declaration that the "poet ought himselfe to bee a true poem" finds prophetic fulfillment in the metamorphosis that seems to occur in the composition of his poems: life and art, vocation and invocation merge–and the poet and the poem are one.[61]

D'Aubigné, like Milton, is making a remarkable breach in orthodox Calvinism. He stands on the historical cusp between pure Calvinism and the post-Tridentine Calvinist poets such as Simon Goulart who write more sensory, imaged poetry in order to have greater appeal to the imagination of the faithful. Through the permission for the self that d'Aubigné devises in his prose, he compels the realization that, in order for polemic to persuade, there must be a *self* speaking within it; that abstraction and self-annihilation have little or no power to persuade. Living in the world of soldierly and courtly exigencies, d'Aubigné, unlike Calvin and de Bèze cloistered in Geneva, realizes the need to make religion attractive and personalized.

It is instructive to contrast d'Aubigné's situation and perspective with those of the earlier, evangelical Marguérite de Navarre who, in the Catholic and mystic tradition, wishes to "undo" her work. Her intention and method, although not her reasons, are similar to those of the more conventional Calvinist poets we have mentioned.

> Marguerite recasts the Renaissance theory of imitation in a Christian world. As a reader of Scripture, she absorbs the sacred text, which she then reutters in her poems, imitating or reproducing the Bible. The reader of Marguerite's texts repeats this process. . . . The Word is reuttered in the heart of every reader who submits to the text. The Christian reader does not scrutinize a text in an attempt to extract meaning from it. . . . Nor does he impose meaning on

---

[61]Robert Schindler, *Voice and Crisis: Invocations in Milton's Poetry* (Hamden, Conn.: Archon Books, 1984), 104.

a text. In fact he does not read the text at all, the text penetrates him.[62]

For Marguérite, the imagery of submission is a key to the process of reading. D'Aubigné, however, straddles a period of historical discontinuity. While Marguérite's reading posture is passive, an attitude of waiting for the Holy Spirit to *tell* her the contents of her text-to-be, d'Aubigné is at a turning point where such categories no longer obtain. The construct of the "self" interposes itself, as it were, between text and Holy Spirit. D'Aubigné as a Calvinist, fears to assert the self, but from a literary standpoint *must* acknowledge it. It is out of this very dilemma that his texts are born.

A textualized self within a religious framework calls to the reader for participation and application. It solicits a measure of the reader's creative activity, unlike the passive exemplar mold typical Calvinist exegetes provide.[63] Similarly, the word can restore the *immediacy* that Bible desires (the Hebrew term *dabar* explicitly defines "word" as an event in the world), but which it cannot quite attain due to the Bible's implicit distancing in time from the sphere of contemporary history. D'Aubigné claims, for instance, that "en disant ces choses je pense voir encore sur mes mains et sur mes habits quelque tache du sang innocent que j'ai respandu" (541). The effect is immediate, and elicits a response. For de Bèze, the function of the exegete is, as he interprets David's example, to magnify the Lord. D'Aubigné revises this reading: he sees David's significance in the Psalmist's ability to engage God in dialogue, to argue with him, to find strength in difference, and to affirm the self in the space of that distinction:

> Nous avons un familier exemple de cela au raisonnement de David avec son Dieu, qui argumente ainsi avec lui en plusieurs de ses Cantiques (558).

If, as post-modernists claim, history is the history of self-consciousness,[64] for d'Aubigné, on the eve of the seventeenth century, self-consciousness may be the way to re-establish the relationship between history and divine time, between self and God, text and metatext. Human writing may be

---

[62]Cottrell, *Grammar*, 191.

[63]However, d'Aubigné's textualized self is not posited as an end in itself. D'Aubigné realizes the need to move through the self to speech. The self must not be allowed to become an image or an idol: "L'Esprit de Dieu nous eschauffe contre l'idolâtrie . . . [qui] transfère sa gloire aux choses muettes, sourdes, aveugles, manchottes, et qui sont oeuvres des mains de ceux qui les adorent." D'Aubigné, *Méditations*, 561. D'Aubigné remains within Calvinist boundaries through his reliance on hearing over seeing, and his description of God is, at this stage, anti-representational: "[Dieu] qui n'a pu estre despeinte dignement . . . c'est ce que l'art n'a pu voir." *Méditations*, 523.

[64]Michael Allen Gillespie, *Hegel, Heidegger, and the Ground of History* (Chicago: University of Chicago Press, 1984), 9.

viewed as a facilitator in the dialogue with God. Election sanctifies self-expression. The self speaks the word which constitutes the sign of both permission and purification.

My reading of d'Aubigné's *Méditations sur les pseaumes* takes the work to be not so much a series of meditations as a set of mediations. Here, d'Aubigné dialogues with God and, ultimately, with the self he discloses through the medium of his text, to arrive at a strategy that permits the act of writing and lays the groundwork for the later liberties he will allow himself in more fictional works. In the *Méditations,* "meditational style . . . [paradoxically] records a creation of the self."[65] Literary creation is possible only by moving through and beyond sin. God licenses writing, because God permits and redeems the self dialectically. D'Aubigné witnesses to this phenomenon in a distinctly autobiographical tone:

> Je suis affligé, et comme rendant l'esprit de ma jeunesse: j'ai souffert tes efforts, et ne sçai où j'en suis. Tu sçais, Seigneur, quels orages ont passé sur ma teste dés mon enfance, où j'ai esté comme mort parmi les vivans. . . . Ma vie a esté condamnée en mes tendres ans, et quand j'ai esté sur le sueil de la geole pour marcher au buscher, tu as retiré mon ame du feu des hommes pour l'embraser du tien (533-34).

Writing is no longer a means of alienation from God, but an avenue of *rapprochement.*

---

[65]Martz, *Poetry of Meditation,* 322.

3

Zones of Accomodation between Calvinism and Literary Creation in *Les Tragiques*

REFLECTIONS CONCERNING THE HISTORICIZED SELF seen in the *Méditations sur les pseaumes* are also visible in *Les Tragiques,* a work which significantly evolves through time, with its composition beginning in 1578 and its first printing occuring in 1616. Often deemed the "Calvinist epic," *Les Tragiques* contains instances in which the writer's subordination to the Calvinist interdiction is at times apparent, yet also contains episodes in which the writer's individual expression prevails. Many such instances of temporary liberation are not immediately evident and can only be discerned through comparison with the model for the work, the Bible. It is significant, for example, that the epic genre is not employed by the Bible,[1] for epic seems to presuppose a human prescience that competes with God's omniscience:

> l'épopée suppose un savoir fondamental. C'est parce qu'il a de son destin une idée différente de celle du personnage dramatique ou du chantre lyrique que le héros épique a du temps une notion qui le caractérise: la fin de son aventure non seulement est connue du public, mais lui-même en est averti; songes, apparitions, prémonitions et prophéties font que, pour lui, l'histoire a un sens. . . . le héros avance avec le récitant et ses spectateurs dans une aventure dont la fin échappe à ses prises mais non à sa connaissance. . . . Ce qui lui importe n'est pas le pourquoi essentiel du poète tragique mais le comment.[2]

Reading and Writing the Self

Calvinist predestination, from a surface reading, accords with the epic genre's intentionality. The author knows the ultimate outcome of the text even as he writes it. However, predestination is divinely ordained, and

---

[1] Robert Alter, "Sacred History and the Beginnings of Prose Fiction," *Poetics Today* 39 (1980): 143-62.

[2] Georges Demerson, ed., *La Notion du genre à la Renaissance* (Geneva: Slatkine, 1984), 151.

those who are to be saved can have no sure knowledge of their redemption. By writing epic works, therefore, the author becomes blasphemously similar to God in that he purports to know the meaning of history. In addition, reworking biblical motifs for a specific polemic purpose–the legitimizing of Calvinist over Catholic claims–removes the sacred veneer from the Bible as revealed Word and constitutes it as "text," a source which may be inflected or subtly altered to act as testimony to sectarian ends. Calvin, however, enjoins that "Scriptures [are] sufficient, complete, and necessary. Should anyone think otherwise, he [is] subject to the charge of blasphemy."[3] Yet, *all* Calvinist writing, and not only that of d'Aubigné, may be viewed as ultimately subversive (albeit usually unintentionally) of de Bèze's anti-literary stance, for strict submission to Scripture demands that one

> se refuse à inventer quoi que ce soit d'extérieur à la Bible. Dieu se manifeste . . . par sa parole et ses signes sacrés, et l'on n'a pas le droit de rien imaginer d'autre, sinon sa vérité est convertie en mensonge.[4]

Even Calvinists such as Du Bartas, who, in *La Sepmaine*, subordinates himself to the *Genesis* account by duplicating its form, content, and intentionality, are, in this sense, importing an element alien to the Bible. That element is their *motivation to write.*

The "Calvinist epic" of *Les Tragiques* is thus more problematic than it may at first appear. Even the ambiguity of the deceptively simple title underscores this point: "les tragiques" may be interpreted as referring to the Calvinists as "tragic ones," in which case *Les Tragiques* is a tragic genre, or to the Catholics who will ultimately be punished, in which case *Les Tragiques* is a tragi-comic genre.[5]

In every respect, the reader's attentiveness and involvement are thus required, as he enters history along with the writer, to scrutinize and make sense of it. An oscillation among tenses which can be noted throughout *Les Tragiques* similarly solicits the reader's critical evaluation: the *passé simple* is used to express fundamental, original events, while the *présent,* often in the hortative mode, conveys both actual occurrences and general truths.[6] Biblical *exempla,* unlike those de Bèze designed to be universally applicable, are transported to France: "Gedeon" and "Dalide" become specific examples of Calvinist suffering. The reader, firmly situated historically, is asked to

---

[3]H. Jackson Forstmann, *Word and Spirit: Calvin's Doctrine of Biblical Authority* (Stanford: Stanford University Press, 1962), 22.

[4]Calvin, *Institutes,* I.36.

[5]Regosin, *The Poetry of Inspiration,* 48. He notes that the poem is not called *Les Comiques,* despite the happy ending, because "the poet not Coligny [in the heavens] provides the focus from which the events of the drama are to be interpreted."

[6]Demerson, *La Notion,* 152.

apply his capacities of judgment to the case at hand to discern parallels with, or, more significantly, differences from, the model.

D'Aubigné himself must perform a similar act, because *Les Tragiques* incorporates both a "past" and a "future" image of d'Aubigné and his world. It may well be the work that most localizes the tension between d'Aubigné as worshipper and d'Aubigné as writer. As David Quint comments, "it [is] in literature that the contest between individual innovation and the authority of tradition [is] recast as a struggle for independence from sacred authority."[7] D'Aubigné moves uneasily between his Calvinist allegiance–he cannot expressly authorize himself–and his desire to seize for himself the reins of history, to cause it to conform prematurely to his will, which he necessarily and boldly interprets as God's will.[8] *Les Tragiques* is not fiction, for its substance is extrapolated from real events. However, in some ways it moves toward an autonomy of the writing self. To this point, Richard Regosin observes that

> d'Aubigné exists outside the poetic world of *Les Tragiques*. The topos of the stolen manuscript which opens the prefatory "Aux lecteurs" distances him from the work to focus distinction on the poem and its poet within: [therefore] it underscores *Les Tragiques* as fiction.[9]

Such independence can be perceived in those areas where slippage, intentional or not, attests to deviation from the Calvinist norm. In order to determine those areas, it is necessary to examine, first, ways in which this early composition conforms to Calvinist guidelines, and then ascertain strategies by which d'Aubigné surreptitiously extricates himself to express his own individual, differentiated voice. In this regard, it is useful to contrast *Les Tragiques* with Du Bartas' work *La Sepmaine*.

Such a comparison highlights the extent of d'Aubigné's originality, for "*La Sepmaine* est . . . une ample paraphrase de l'Ecriture sainte."[10] Like Du Bartas, d'Aubigné originally humbles himself utterly before God. Disclaimers, statements of impotence, and emphasis on his own inarticulateness at first proliferate; Du Bartas regrets that "les mots à tous coups périssent

---

[7]David Quint, *Origin and Originality in Renaissance Literature: Versions of the Source* (New Haven, Conn.: Yale University Press, 1983), 219.

[8]Milton experiences a like problem. "He . . . explores the difficulties a divine subject poses for a fallen poet addressing a fallen audience, and seeks solutions to those difficulties both in divine illumination and in literary art." Barbara Lewalski, *"Paradise Lost" and the Rhetoric of Literary Forms* (Princeton: Princeton University Press, 1985), 28.

[9]Richard Regosin, *D'Aubigné's "Les Tragiques": Divine Tragedy* (Geneva: Droz, 1976), 22.

[10]Du Bartas, "Introduction," *La Sepmaine,* ed. Yvonne Bellenger, STFM (Paris: Nizet, 1981), li.

dans ma bouche"[11] due to "ce peu d'art et d'esprit que le ciel m'a donné,"[12] while d'Aubigné is at a loss for words: "Ah! Que dirai-je plus?" (*Misères*, 463). The basis of inspiration also appears to be similar for both writers. As in the Calvinist theory of biblical inspiration, God is the writer, while the author is a mere transmitter. Du Bartas calls the Spirit "le sainct orateur qui dicte [ma] harangue."[13] D'Aubigné acknowledges "Dieu qui d'un style vif . . . escri[t] . . ." (*Misères*, 43), who grants him the tools with which to transcribe the Word: "La plume que je tiens, puis que tu l'as donnee," (*Misères*, 54) while Du Bartas describes the Holy Spirit overshadowing his book in an annunciatory transmission of the divine utterance: "[Dieu] . . . Discourt sur son discours, et nage sur son livre."[14] The two writers seem to view their texts as palimpsests, works composed of the superimposition of many layers of discourse,[15] of which the divine predominates and theirs is only a meager part. True to Calvinist doctrine, human expression can be legitimized only if it is a reiteration of the divine. A sort of organic grafting-on[16] to the divine text must thus transpire, it seems, before d'Aubigné may begin to recount his story. Indeed, the structure of *Les Tragiques* numerically mirrors that of the Bible: its seven books parallel the seven

---

[11]Idem, *La Sepmaine*, I v. 96.

[12]Du Bartas figures his impotence as a writer in the character of Judit in *La Judit*. A devout, retiring and bookish widow, she is an unlikely conduit for divine vengeance, yet her very improbability is essential to the manifestation of God's capabilities. The weak vessel she constitutes has parallels with Du Bartas, who writes only to "undo" his verse and to disclaim his act of authorship, returning his work to God. Judit must surrender herself to God before her discourse can be worthy. At the moment when she seems to vacillate, God sustains and guides her. Du Bartas articulates a similar crisis of writing: "Ma main tremble d'horreur et comme de coûtume / Sur mon sacré feuillet ne sçait guider ma plume" (*La Judit*, ed. André Baiche, III v. 239-40) but when he joins himself with God through his entreaty, the success of his poem is guaranteed: "Guide ma plume lasse, enfle-moy de courage / Et fay qu'à ton honneur j'achève cest ouvrage" (III 250-52).

[13]Du Bartas, *La Sepmaine*, II v. 21-30.

[14]Ibid., II 289-94.

[15]In an image that betokens the superposition of one discourse on another to efface the former, Du Bartas claims, "je veus dessus cuivre graver à jamais . . ." (*La Judit*, III v. 383-86) to eradicate impious utterances and deeds. Through the medium of Judit, this is precisely what he will do in the course of the drama. In this way, Du Bartas' literary creation remains within the constraints of Calvinism: he does not create a wholly new work, but rather magnifies the Bible while erasing the pagan inscription. He is truly the instrument by which God will write salvation narrative. He creates by yielding to God's Word: "Esprit, du tout esprit prend mouvement et vie / . . . espan sur moy ta grace, Affin qu'à ton honneur ceste oeuvre je parface" (*La Judit*, III v. 259-64).

[16]His literary approach is at this stage in line with the theories of the Pléiade, in which the poet is seen not as a creator but rather as an imitator of the already-created world. Ronsard's images in "Hylas" of the poet as a bee express this perspective well. The bee borrows extensively from the substance of others, and then through innutrition produces an amalgam of his essence with theirs. D'Aubigné later sees this procedure as threatening in that it causes what Graham Castor calls a "false mimesis." Borrowing now second-hand from the constructions of other artists rather than from nature, mimetic representation becomes layered and progressively distanced from its true model.

days (six of work and one of rest) of the Creation. Similarly, d'Aubigné occasionally employs formulaic expressions which render any individual voice anonymous. In an imitation of the prophets, for instance, he declares, "Mal-heur, ce dit le Sage, au peuple dont les loix. . ." (*Misères*, 727). And d'Aubigné's prophetic stance, as Marguerite Soulié notes, *seems* derivative of the Old Testament: "il ne cesse d'assumer le rôle du prophète biblique que le souffle de Dieu possède et contraint."[17] The key word is "contraint," attesting to divine inspiration as the only possible justification for writing. For Calvin, "l'Ecriture comme la Foi au Christ incarné est une limite qu'[il] pose fermement, s'opposant ainsi à la création d'une voie supérieure de la connaissance, sa mise en garde contre ceux qui prétendent s'en remettre à une inspiration mystique."[18]

Yet in this very limitation, the rudiments of the strategy d'Aubigné will employ to redeem individual writing may be discerned. He must overcome Calvinism's emphasis on man's sinful nature in order to aspire to "cette vocation surnaturelle."[19] It is only through a paradoxical dialectical *insistence upon* his *sin* as a stain which only the divine will can efface that d'Aubigné may exalt the ink blots sullying his pure white sheets as emblematic of the spots marring the soul of the believer. Since Calvinism is predicated on God's omnipotence, God *must* be able to overcome the sinner's blight. D'Aubigné works through his status as sinner to an utter conviction of his salvation. For him, salvation is both expressed and enacted in writing. His writing is valorized because he chooses to interweave it with biblical material and, more importantly, because *he construes* his ability to manipulate creatively such materials as proof of his election:

> Je . . . ayant esté choisi de Dieu pour instrument . . . j'ai osé generaliser mon Histoire, m'attachant avec expressitude aux choses plus proches de temps et de lieu, aux esloignees plus legerement. Me soit en cela autant permis qu'aux peintres, qui n'oublient aucune proportion de symmetrie dans le coeur de leurs tableaux. . . . Si quelqu'un sent ces discours à la vanterie, je le prie de considérer que *mon livre* [le] *veut* (my emphasis).[20]

His enterprise and polemical purpose are indissociably linked to his sense of *artistic* purpose: "Ami, ces mots que tu reprens / Sont les vocables d'art de ce que j'entreprens" (*Princes*, 63-64). D'Aubigné derives his permission to write from Calvinist doctrine itself. Through his re-reading of it, he concludes that the true act of worship is to move beyond one's sin. Writing–purged of its pejorative connotations–may now take place.

---

[17]Soulié, *L'Inspiration biblique dans la poésie religieuse d'Agrippa d'Aubigné* (Paris: Klinckseick, 1977), 1.

[18]Ibid., 139.

[19]Ibid., 1.

[20]D'Aubigné, *Histoire universelle*, 12-15.

D'Aubigné begins to free himself from the proscription on literary creation.[21] The weight of his Calvinist adherence can nevertheless be sensed in his failure, until the *Avantures,* to emancipate himself fully: his "instances of permission" still retain a biblical flavor, and are found predominantly in his "apophéties." These prophecies, uttered in the present and realized in the future, are in reality inscribed in the present, having taken place in the past. That is, d'Aubigné at the time he *speaks* has no sure way of knowing that his words will be realized in the future. But at the time he *writes,* he presents that which has *already* occured (e.g. the wounding of Henri de Navarre) as though it *has not yet* come to pass, thereby heightening the reader's perceptions of d'Aubigné's potency both as a prophet and as a writer: "Quand ta bouche renoncera / Ton Dieu, ton Dieu la percera / Punissant le membre coulpable: / Quand ton coeur, desloyal mocqueur / Comme elle sera punissable / . . . Alors Dieu percera ton coeur" (*Préface,* 325-30). This intricate interplay of past and present reality[22] attests to a multivalent conception of the self, one which has great power and efficacy in shaping words and the world, and one which overturns the model of the imperative denial of the self which the Calvinist emphasis on sin maintains. D'Aubigné contends that these "apophéties" confer great merit on him as a writer and as a seer:

> il y a . . . quelques episodes comme predictions de choses advenues avant l'oeuvre clos, que l'auteur appeloit en riant ses apophéties. Bien veux je constamment asseurer le lecteur qu'il y en a qui meritent un nom plus haut (*Aux lecteurs,* 7).

In such a way d'Aubigné participates in God's omniscience, and thereby arrogates to himself some of God's role. The laughter (". . . en riant . . .") is a play to keep such an unprecedented assertion from seeming too scandalous.

D'Aubigné's enhanced status is evident in *Les Tragiques.* Daring to employ an image drawn from classical mythology rather than from the Bible, d'Aubigné likens himself to Prometheus, who stole fire from the gods. D'Aubigné is the thief who steals the justification for his self-expression: "Voici le larron Promethee, qui, au lieu de grace, demande gré de son crime, et pense vous pouvoir justement faire present de ce qui n'est pas à luy, comme ayant desrobé pour vous ce que son maistre vous desroboit à

---

[21]This proscription is further defined in Thomas Torrance, *Space, Time and Incarnation* (London: Oxford University Press, 1969), 148. "All true knowledge of God is essentially an acknowledgement not an excogitation. It is the sin of men that they will try to ground their knowledge of God upon the exercise of their own imagination, upon analogies which the human mind can manipulate, and so measure God by its own capacity, but all this, Calvin says, leads to a feigned and new God."

[22]Another example is that in which d'Aubigné predicts the loss of power by the Guise and Médicis families: "Quand l'édifice haut des superbes Lorrains / . . . Par toy [Catherine] eslève t'eccrasera la teste." *Misères,* v. 805-8. All quotations are from d'Aubigné, *Oeuvres,* ed. Henri Weber et al. (Paris: Gallimard, 1969).

soy-mesme" (Aux lecteurs, 3). Uncontrite, because he knows he is absolved, d'Aubigné does not apologize for his sin but rather glorifies it.[23] He rises like a phoenix from sin: "rebrusle-moi encore" (Misères, 49). It is through his recognition of the possibility of a sinful creator that Les Tragiques is written: "mon charitable peché" (Aux lecteurs, 3; my emphasis).[24]

The "crime," and the "peché" d'Aubigné ultimately commits, unexpectedly result in an acknowledgement of his salvation, of which "il traça comme pour testament cet ouvrage" (Aux lecteurs, 4). It is through the paradoxical contamination of sacred by profane that salvation occurs: d'Aubigné signals the unholy intermingling of the two "en un siècle où tout zele chrestien est peri, où la difference du vray et du mensonge est comme abolie" (Aux lecteurs, 3). Yet he cleverly employs the very strategy he denounces in order to create his work, for the matter of Les Tragiques is, in fact, profane, and a significant portion of the book is devoted to discussing the abuses of the century. D'Aubigné's work is actually completed by history: in some respects it functions as a gloss on it, and so must embrace the profane upon which it writes a purportedly sacred commentary: "Et qui sans l'histoire prendra goust aux violences de nostre auteur?" (Aux lecteurs, 4). In this respect, d'Aubigné is like Calvin, who needs sin in order to have a purpose for his writing. Calvin's only possible justification for writing is as a corrective for sin. Unlike Calvin, however, d'Aubigné bursts the confines of the subordination of the self to Scripture; his audacity in his decision to write recalls Promotheus' boldness to deal with the things of the heavens: ". . . si mon esprit audacieux / Veut peindre le secret des cieux" (Préface, 361). D'Aubigné's work, at first apparently composed of elements of, and completed by, history, ultimately subsumes it, subordinating

---

[23]In his little-known epic poem La Création (Collection Tronchin, Geneva) d'Aubigné justifies his writing through his elect status:

Divine Muse, vien espendre dessus moy
Tes graces et tes faveurs . . .
Mais quoy, dira quelqu'un, c'est beaucoup entrepris,
Tes cordes sonnent bas, et l'oeuvre est de grand pris.
. . . Toutesfois comme on voit ès orgues des petitx
Tuyaulx desquels le sont est pourtant inutille
J'en peux dire de mesme au regard de mon stylle
Lequel quoi il soit bas et mène pas de brui . . .
. . . fera quelque frui:
Joint que le tout Puissant qui mes sens ayguillonne
Est le mouvement seul de ma volonté bonne.
C'est ce qui m'enhardist en cela que je fais.
Ce que je dis n'empesche aucunement que Dieu
Ne face sa demeure en quelque certaine lieu
Ainsy qu'il le peut faire en ses esleus.
("Chant premier," vv. 310-33)

[24]D'Aubigné glorifies his sin in that it is only by experiencing sin that one can equally experience the joys of redemption. The certainty he feels that such joy may be his is what enables him to write and even to be grateful for the dialectical end-effect of his sinning.

it to an eschatological schema. His work thereby assumes the status of an independent text that calls for commentary, and in this way attains a position equal to that of the Bible. This new status is seen in d'Aubigné's assertion that his text will be explicated with the same respect and attention as is the Bible: "je vous promets les commentaires de tous les poincts difficiles" (*Aux lecteurs*, 7-8).

D'Aubigné is still not as bold as he will become by the time he composes the *Avantures*. He still resorts to strategies of concealment, whereby he leaves traces of himself in the text but does not yet openly clamor for acknowledgement as a writer other than as a transcriber of the biblical message or as a glosser of a precursor work. The obvious, yet unavowed, identity of *éditeur* and *écrivain* is one such strategy. The *éditeur* claims to have coerced the author into saving his scribblings from the fire: he speaks of "les paperasses crottees et deschirees desquelles j'ay arraché. . ." (*Aux lecteurs*, 4). This description recalls the stains on the sinner's soul and the fire of final judgment from which, by God's grace or by d'Aubigné's dialectical fancy footwork, he is spared. The fiction of a separate editor is even developed into a mini-narrative of its own; we are told that the editor served as d'Aubigné's secretary in the army, and he informs us with a *clin d'oeil*, that "j'en dirois davantage si l'excessive louange de mon Maistre n'estoit en quelque façon la mienne" (*Aux lecteurs*, 5). The fracturing of d'Aubigné's authorial personality into two segments in order to render it more palatable to Calvinists recalls Roland Barthes' distinction between *écrivain* and *écrivant*, suggesting that d'Aubigné is trying to find a way to assert his status, authority, and authorship. He is reconciling the mere "recounter," the exegete, with the "maker," or authorial extension beyond given materials.

By means of such techniques, d'Aubigné perceptibly distances himself from the fold of Calvinist expositors. When in *Aux lecteurs* he states, "nous sommes ennuyés de livres qui enseignent, donnez-nous en pour esmouvoir" (*Aux lecteurs*, 4), he enters into the suspect arena of emotionalism which Calvinist didacticism seeks to avoid when it warns that

> Mesme si quelquefois par la conduite de ces choses et adresse nous sommes atrainez à considérer ce que c'est de Dieu, ce qui advient à tous de nécessité, en la fin après avoir conceu à la volée quelque sentiment de Dieu incontinent nous retournons à noz reveries et nous en laissons transporter, corrompans par nostre vanité propre la vérité de Dieu . . . en nous revoltant d'un seul Dieu pour nous jetter après noz idolatries monstrueuses.[25]

However, as elsewhere in *Les Tragiques*, d'Aubigné seems to retract quickly that which he asserts. The format of his composition is carefully tailored

---

[25]Calvin, *L'Institution*, I.v.80.

so as to appear didactic, and his method demonstrates similarities with the manner of Ramist instruction: "Voilà pour les estofes des parties. Voici pour la matiere generale, et puis je dirai un mot de la disposition" (*Aux lecteurs*, 6). The seven titles of the books are meant to pair "effet" and "cause" in a standard causality, where causes receive the primary emphasis, since man cannot always see beyond them. However, as d'Aubigné focuses his narration, "effets" are more immediately striking and of greater concern than "causes." In this way d'Aubigné likens himself to God, for by showing effects *before* their causes (past before present) he possesses divine insight: "[Dieu] qui préveu[t] les effects dés le naistre des choses. . . ." God, too, is a writer: "Dieu qui d'un style vif, comme il te plaist, escris / le secret plus obscur en l'obscur des esprits" (*Misères*, 43). In addition, d'Aubigné allocates specific styles to different books.[26] What is perhaps most significant about d'Aubigné's choices is that they acknowledge an awareness of narrative style that figures a tension between "truth" and the "telling of it." That is, literature may necessarily exceed the approved bounds of factual relation. *Misères*, for example, is to be written "d'un style bas et tragique, *n'excedant que fort peu les loix de la narration*" (*Avis*, 6; my emphasis). *Misères* is the book that provides the most straightforward historical framework. Its style conforms to the generic imperatives of history and minimizes personal reconstruction of events. *Feux*, however, contains avowedly personal interventions as it is "tout entier au *sentiment de la religion de l'autheur*" (*Aux lecteurs*, 6; my emphasis). Thus, in miniature, d'Aubigné's stylistic labelling of the books that compose *Les Tragiques* epitomizes the tension between fact and fledgling fiction (or personal interpretation). Writing may not always conform to prescribed style, because its content surpasses the norm. The confines of truth may need to be stretched. These distinctions also convey d'Aubigné's unique theo-literary approach to his subject, for they mingle the "style . . . poétique" in *Fers* (*Aux lecteurs*, 6) with the "style . . . théologien" (*Aux lecteurs*, 7) in *Vengeances*.

The "tableaux celestes" in *Fers* are, as Mitchell Greenberg discovers[27] and as d'Aubigné himself alerts us, written in a "style . . . plus hardi que les autres" (*Aux lecteurs*, 6). They are probably one of the more daring examples of permission for writing in the *Tragiques*, for they are "blasmées [parce que] nul n'avoit jamais entrepris de peindre les affaires de la terre au Ciel, bien que les celestes en terre" (*Aux lecteurs*, 6). Calvin stresses that the representation of the divine, the "uncreated," is to be avoided at all costs in artistic endeavor. "Toute représentation du Christ fausse, en effet, sa nature. . . . On ne doit que représenter le créé."[28] Calvin mandates in

---

[26]Sauerwein, *Agrippa d'Aubigné*. Cf. Chapter One, where he comments on these stylistic classifications.

[27]Mitchell Greenberg, "The Poetics of Trompe-l'oeil: D'Aubigné's 'Tableaux célestes,'" *Neophilologus* 52 (1979): 1-22.

[28]Wencelius, 163, 183.

the *Institution de la religion chrestienne*: "Or Dieu defend en general toutes remembrances que les hommes luy cuydent faire, soit de marteaux ou de pinceaux, parce que tout cela dérogue à sa Maiesté."[29] D'Aubigné here flouts Calvin's strictures. He does so mimetically, rather than through verbal description, using the painterly technique that, in the Renaissance, is commonly deemed more precise (*ut pictura poesis*) than writing. We find an example in the anthropomorphic God of the *Chambre Doree* (1-30) for, although d'Aubigné is writing and using words to describe, he should, as a Calvinist, choose a more stylized or abstract manner of description. Instead, he applies words with painterly impasto, shaping representation that will approximate as closely as possible their model as he perceives it. An illustration of his more concrete imagery may be obtained by contrasting his depiction of Satan with de Bèze's description of Satan in the *Abraham sacrifiant*. D'Aubigné shows an active dialogic drama between Satan and God:

> [Dieu lui demande] 'D'où viens-tu, faux Satan? . . .
> Lors le trompeur trompé d'asseuré devint blesme,
> L'enchanteur se trouva desenchanté luy-mesme . . .
> Le crespe blanchissant qui les cheveux luy coeuvre
> Se change en mesme peau que porte la couleuvre . . .
> . . . un changement estrange
> Luy donna front de diable et osta celuy d'ange . . .
> Tout ce blanc se ternit: ces ailes, peu à peu
> Noires, se vont tachans de cent marques de feu . . .
> (*Fers*, 51-75)

This is de Bèze's terse, carefully anti-imagic description:

> Satan en habit de moyne [dit] . . . je vay, je vien, jour et nuit je travaille . . . Regne le Dieu en son haut firmament: mais pour le moins la terre est à moy.[30]

Satan is portrayed by de Bèze through his iniquitous *speech,* but for fear of contaminating the reader, no precise *vision* of him is provided, for this would increase his plausibility. D'Aubigné, however, does not fear to depict Satan, and does so elaborately. By showing God's triumph over Satan, d'Aubigné describes the victory of the Word over image. Image's traditional status as most potent medium for presence and immediacy is now debunked. Through the association of his writing with God's Word, d'Aubigné valorizes his own endeavor.

D'Aubigné, like Calvin, wants to disentangle religion from the secular grasp through privileging his word over image. Word and image are

---

[29]Calvin, *L'Institution,* I.xi.125-26.
[30]De Bèze, *Abraham sacrifiant,* 37.

explicitly contrasted: images and ideas are found at court, while God's
Word roams deserted expanses:

> Dans ces cabinets lambrissez,
> D'idoles de cour tapissez,
> N'est pas la verité connue:
> La voix du Seigneur des Seigneurs
> S'écrie sur la roche cornue.
>
> (Préface, 337-41)

Thus, containment and limitation characterize images, while expansiveness
and freedom are attributes of the Word.

D'Aubigné seeks to make his writing an active instrument to remediate
the state of both interior and exterior contamination of which the image
of the famished mother who becomes a wolf and devours her child is a
powerful example: "tout est troublé, confus, en l'âme qui se trouve /
N'avoir plus rien de mere, et avoir tout de louve" (Misères, 533). But, unlike
Calvin and de Bèze, he does not intend to subordinate his personal reactions
and prejudices to God's will. Certain of his election, he is confident that
his own will does not diverge from that of God. He appropriates the Bible
to his personal circumstance: "j'ai de jour le pilier, de nuict les feux pour
guides" (Misères, 22). Upon occasion, he is forthright in his assertion of
distinction; however, more frequently in Les Tragiques he feels compelled
to dissimulate his authorship. He claims to be a witness ("mes yeux sont
tesmoins du subjet de mes vers [Misères, 371]) rather than judge ("fidelle
tesmoin et jamais juge" [Aux lecteurs, 8]), for instance, since to set himself
up as judge would be to threaten God's sole prerogative of judgment. The
images of violence which proliferate in the text may also be read as indirect
testimony to the tension d'Aubigné feels concerning his as-yet-unlegitimized
status as a writer.[31] Similarly, d'Aubigné's work is torn from him ("arraché")
to go forth into the world. He cannot yet permit himself an absolute
identity with his literary work. It, not he, is agent of his self-expression.
He does not even dare to publish his name with his work, alternatively
excusing himself coyly under the guise of convention ("quant à son nom,
on n'exprime point les noms dans les tableaux" [Aux lecteurs, 9]) or proferring
the pseudonymous LBDD ("le bouc du désert") which attests to his feeling
of alienation from his fellow Calvinists and the court.

However, if d'Aubigné is unable to permit himself totally free expression,
the symbiotic relationship he maintains with his book provides a strong
substitute. His preface is actually a dialogue between the two ("l'auteur à
son livre") in which Christ's resurrection and redemption of sinners is

---

[31]René Girard, Violence and the Sacred (Baltimore: Johns Hopkins University Press, 1971),
102. Images of twins, Girard notes, are cosmic figures of violence. Pairs such as the "bessons"
battling on their "mère affligee" (Misères, v. 97) or Abel and Cain can bear out this conflict.

recalled when d'Aubigné tells his book that "*mon* exil *te* delivre" (*Préface*, 3; my emphasis), and the book is paradoxically, like Christ, "né dans le tombeau" (*Préface*, 2). D'Aubigné also immediately implicates the reader in the book's production and in its interpretation. Finding the book likeable, despite its forbidding appearance, ("ta trenche n'a or ne couleur, / Ta couverture sans valeur / Permet, s'il y a quelque joye, / Aux bons la trouver au dedans; / Aux autres fascheux je t'envoye / Pour leur faire grincer les dents") is constituted as proof of election and, consequently, of salvation. The book's mission is to "plaire aux bons et plaire à peu" (*Préface*, 48), while most readers "en ta lecture / Fronçans le sourcil de travers / Trouveront bien ta couverture [desagreable] / Plus agreable que tes vers" (*Préface*, 39-41). As at the Last Judgment, d'Aubigné's book separates good from evil: "heureux livre qui en deux rangs / Distingue la trouppe ennemie" (*Préface*, 52). In order to approve of the book, it is necessary to *read* it correctly, as opposed to "ceux que la peur a revoltez / [qui] diffameront tes veritez, / Comme faict l'ignorante lie" (*Préface*, 49-51). Thus, reading leads to recognition of salvation. Words and their written transcription will lead to redemption if he who utters them, or reads them, is right-intentioned. Otherwise, d'Aubigné warns, this "apophétie" will be realized to those of unfaithful hearts and mouths, to those who deliberately *misread*:

> Quand ta bouche renoncera
> Ton Dieu, ton Dieu la percera
> Punissant le membre coupable;
> Quand ton coeur, desloyal moqueur,
> Comme elle sera punissable,
> Alors Dieu percera ton coeur.
>   (*Préface*, 325-29)

For d'Aubigné, writing may be either medicine or poison. Those who read it correctly will find it a cure against secular evil and damnation:

> Je n'excuse pas mes escrits
> Pour ceux-la qui y sont repris:
> Mon plaisir est de leur desplaire.
> Amis, je trouve en la raison
> Pour vous et pour eux fruict contraire,
> La medecine et le poison.
>   (*Préface*, 367-72)

D'Aubigné writes to renounce the world, embrace his death and hasten his union with God:

> Aujourd'hui abordé au port
> D'une douce et civile mort, . . .
> D'autre humeur je fai d'autres vers,

Marri d'avoir laissé au monde
Ce qui plaist au monde pervers . . .
[Je m'exile] où mon ame veut que je meure,
Furieuse de sainct amour.

(*Préface*, 91-132)

However, this contention is ironic, for in claiming to die to the world and even to himself, he is only at the beginning of the vast textual project of *Les Tragiques,* a work which perpetrates d'Aubigné's identity.

Concurrent with this theme is the emphasis which runs through *Les Tragiques* on the relationship between the author and his book, speech and writing, personal experience and revealed history. In many cases d'Aubigné singularizes himself, pointing out the extraordinary import of his writing act by comparing himself with historical figures such as "Cesar" and "Hannibal" (". . . par un chemin tout neuf, car je ne treuve pas / Qu'autre homme l'ait jamais escorché de ses pas" [*Misères,* 20]) or likening himself to biblical models such as David. This latter comparison is even more significant, as Calvinists endorse the Psalmist as the only permissible model for "literary" inspiration. Calvin states,

de ma part, en me conformant à la façon que Dieu a ici tenue, je m'efforcerai de suivre en bref le vrai fil du texte, et . . . je mettrai peine seulement de mâcher les mots de David, afin qu'on puisse les digérer. Pour ce faire j'ai délibéré . . . me restreindre tellement . . . que je n'ai voulu sinon esclairer la simple substance du texte.[32]

David's songs in every way subordinate themselves to God's Word:

Ainsi on peut voir que la raison de nostre entendement, de quelque costé qu'elle se tourne, est purement suiette à vanité. Ce que recognoissoit David en soy-mesme, quand il demandoit qu'entendement luy fust donné de Dieu, pour apprendre droitement ses préceptes. Car celuy qui désire nouvel entendement signifie que le sien n'est pas suffisant. Car en désirant que Dieu luy crée un coeur nouveau, il ne s'attribue pas le commencement de telle création.[33]

D'Aubigné sees in himself similarities with David,[34] but these display a more active character in his being. For example, he does not refer in detail to the *personage* David, but rather mentions the *weapon* with which David slew Goliath, thereby emphasizing process over person, word over image.

[32]Calvin, "Premier Sermon sur le Pseaume 119," cited in Stauffer, *Dieu,* 209.

[33]Calvin, *L'Institution,* II.ii.54.

[34]Cf. d'Aubigné, *Méditations,* 550. "David se plaignoit d'estre mis en oubli du coeur des hommes comme un mort est d'estre estimé autant qu'un vaisseau de nul usage: mais c'est bien pis d'estre comme mis en oubli de son Dieu et retranché d'entre les vaisseaux de la cité. 'Tu m'as mis en une fosse des plus basses es lieux ténébreux et profonds.'"

He states that his verses will function as does David's slingshot: "Dieu ne veut qu'une fonde pour instrument de son courroux" (*Préface*, 239-40). D'Aubigné thus confers a vitality and an autonomy upon his verses that exceeds that of the Psalmist.[35] Also, in so doing, he employs a strategy that he will use throughout his literary career, and one that is integral to his ultimate articulation of a conception of self via a literary medium: he *textualizes himself*, writing himself into a mini-drama that is embedded in, yet propels, the text that contains it. He shows himself with Vérité, a dramatic personification, as they jointly ready their arms to do battle against injustice:

> Je commençois à arracher
> Des cailloux polis d'un rocher,
> Et elle tordoit une fonde;
> Puis nous jettions par l'univers, . . .
> Ses belles plaintes et mes vers.
>
> (*Préface*, 157-62)

Thus inscribed within his text as a "je" *persona* permitted and even required by the account, d'Aubigné contends for a more active writing self.

In order to do so, he must raise the question of what type of writing is legitimate. Here, he is not as advanced as he will be by the time of the publication of the *Avantures*. He refers negatively to the poetic compilation of his youth, *Le Printemps* ("un pire et plus heureux aisné / . . . moins plein de sagesse" [*Préface*, 56-57]). He shows, however, that he is beginning to trust the power of his word sufficiently to forsake traditional representationality ("Alors je n'adorois sinon / L'image" [*Préface*, 97]) in favor of the word. In this respect, he is a good Calvinist, rejecting idolatrous image in favor of the unadorned word. But he is different in that he *will* incorporate highly imaged descriptions in his writing, with the express purpose of subverting them through word as discourse. The allegorical images in the *Chambre Doree* are good examples of this.

D'Aubigné knows that, in order to infuse his words with strength, he must somehow surmount the schism between words and things that the sixteenth century perceives. His words must become action, his phrases *praxis* rather than painterly description. He is beginning to perceive the problem of the

---

[35]The Psalmist is, in fact, the accepted model for lyrical inspiration for Calvinists. However, d'Aubigné develops the individual side of David's personality, emphasizing his free choice of idiom and expression over the stress other Calvinists place on the fact that David is inspired by God. This is similar to the manner in the *Méditations* in which he deviates not only from the phrasing of the Psalm, but even from its intent. D'Aubigné never allows the Davidic model to diminish his own role. The lyrical outbursts strewn throughout the *Tragiques* are always circumscribed by d'Aubigné's firm grasp of history, his polemic aims, and his consciousness of himself as the source from which his text derives.

mythe de l'homme qui a perdu le verbe. . . . C'est sur cette toile
de fond du verbe perdu que s'éclaire la réponse de Hamlet: "Que
lisez-vous, Monseigneur?–Des mots, des mots, des mots." La séparation
de l'univers réel et l'univers verbal prend ici son sens le plus dramatique,
réduisant l'homme à n'avoir par le langage aucune prise sur le réel.
Paradoxalement, cette vacuité sémantique du mot semble liée à
l'origine à un excès de richesse.[36]

Painterly representation, now stages removed from its model and, hence,
itself a form of feigning, constitutes the "vacuité sémantique." Calvinism's
literary application of the theological "plain style" evinces an effort to
counter "un excès de langage." D'Aubigné must find a verbal form that is
based on action rather than on a duplication of something seen. Image-words,
words that merely describe or attempt to reproduce an object, are derivative
and deceitful. In this regard, d'Aubigné is in accord with Montaigne who,
attacking flattering and deceptive rhetoric, notes, as Claude-Gilbert DuBois
analyzes it, that

l'éloquence . . . est l'art de l'illusion par excellence dont toute la
force réside dans le paraître. Le mot n'est pas l'object mais l'habit
dont on le vêt . . . l'efficacité de la parole réside dans une duperie:
c'est l'art d'escamoter la différence entre les mots et les choses.[37]

D'Aubigné further revises Calvinism in the course of Les Tragiques, for his
word grows from the Word of God in a way that Calvin acknowledges

(. . . toutes inventions humaines qui ne sont établies en la parole
de Dieu ne peuvent porter l'examen de l'Esprit, qu'elles ne soyent
destruites et anéanties. . . . Telle manière de gens facent la perte
de leur ouvrage, c'est à dire que ce qu'ils ont adiousté du leur parmy
la parolle de Dieu, périsse et soit mis sous le pied.)[38]

yet also begins to stand separate from it.
    The progression of the subject matter of the seven books attests to
d'Aubigné's gradual liberation from Calvinist constraints. He begins with
Misères, which provides the historical context and contains, in germ, the
major themes of Les Tragiques. He ends, however, with Jugement, by which
time the writer figures God at the Last Judgment, and writing is valorized
as an implement of sacred intervention into human history. Indeed,
d'Aubigné's writing figures its own completion and fullness for, through
the elaboration of the network of themes first sketched out in Misères and

---

[36]Claude-Gilbert Du Bois, Mythe et langage au seizième siècle (Bordeaux: Ducros, 1970),
41.

[37]Du Bois, Mythe et langage, 45.

[38]Calvin, L'Institution, III.v.154.

their resolution in *Jugement,* the book actually returns in a chiasmus to the beginning where the final themes are first announced.[39] Throughout *Les Tragiques,* images of writing can be found in abundance: references to hands, ink, books and paper inscribe a likeness to God and a permission for literary creation within the very work. Focus on writing is spotlighted for the reader by the use of terms such as "trace," "la plume," "peindre," "style," "escrits," "vers," and "discours."

The first example d'Aubigné employs in *Misères* is, significantly, historical rather than biblical, thus signalling his intent to write a work which is not purely biblically derivative. He refers to Hannibal and makes his first allusion to writing when he describes Hannibal etching, by "feux d'aigre humeur" (*Misères,* 3), his fame on the mountains he has scaled, just as d'Aubigné will engrave his literary personality on the works he presents. This image is similar to Calvin's vocabulary when he describes the divine superimposed on the human heart.[40] D'Aubigné proposes to graft his discourse onto the biblical Word in such a way that his does not negate the prior existence of the latter, yet becomes an independent creation rather than (as it would be with de Bèze) a re-saying of the precursor: "le recours presque exclusif à la Bible comme source [produit ce phénomène]: . . . le fait est donné, non produit."[41] D'Aubigné's works will produce *new* "faits." The problem he must confront is how to legitimize his own voice while writing within such a context, since Calvin feels that "laying claim to any kind of merit or desert for any of one's works is a dangerous sign of reprobation."[42] Indeed, while such images of palimpsests and layered writing may be found in other sixteenth-century writers, they are even more significant for d'Aubigné, who is writing in, through and against not another *human* model–be it classical, mythological or contemporary–but rather against a transcendent entity, the revealed Word of God. In order

---

[39]Du Bartas attempts to achieve a similar aim in the stylized manner in which he portrays the title of *La Sepmaine* in the form of a globe. Although such circles are fairly common typographical devices in the sixteenth century, there are other forms from which Du Bartas may choose, so the selection must be given the value its choice compels. In general, the Renaissance construes circularity as emblematic of perfection. Du Bartas' explicit creation account deals with the construction of the globe, just as d'Aubigné's deals with the process of salvation history.

LA
SEPMAINE
OU CREATION
DU   MONDE   DE
G. DE SALVSTE
SEIGNEVR DV
BARTAS.

[40]Calvin, *L'Institution,* I.i.44.

[41]De Bèze, *Chrestiennes,* 27.

[42]Lewalski, *Protestant,* 16.

even to conceive of writing, he must, at least initially, adopt the role of challenger to his own theological belief system.

One strategy d'Aubigné uses to circumvent this interdiction is that of the manipulation of source material in a reversed fashion. For instance, his presentation of the starving mother who becomes "louve" may be a reversed figuring of the Abraham and Isaac story. As in his treatment of David, here again d'Aubigné focuses on the *instruments* of human action rather than on personalities. The knife the mother holds readily recalls the knife with which Abraham is to sacrifice his son: ". . . le funeste couteau / Quand, pour sacrifier de son ventre l'agneau. . ." (*Misères*, 527-28). Through such revisionist episodes, the reader is not merely, as Soulié suggests, "invité à participer à ce renouvellement du regard qui permet de contempler les faits et les signes de Dieu à travers . . . la réalité,"[43] but also is compelled to perceive the *differences* between the biblical story and d'Aubigné's narrative. It is in these subversive interstices that d'Aubigné begins to insert a unique conception of the writing self. The Bible needs human voice to "re-speak" it. Similarly, d'Aubigné calls for the active involvement of his reader to rehearse his text: the potential is inherent in his words, but the reader must release it and therefore participate in its dynamism. D'Aubigné seeks what Geoffrey Hartmann terms a "hermeneutics of response," hoping that

> Scripture is not wholly other, or that the strain of its higher or enigmatic style will not prove discontinuous with secular literature. [He] insists on the history of reception as more than passive: it has an authority of its own that supplants or invests the sacred text.[44]

Thus, as with the *Aux lecteurs, Misères* opens on a dialogic note, as though in mid-stream of an interrupted conversation: "Puis qu'il faut s'attaquer aux legions de Rome. . ." (*Misères*, 1). The reader is continually called to order through the use of apostrophe and direct address which compel the reader's engagement: "Vous n'estes spectateurs, vous estes personnages" (*Misères*, 170). The "je" interventions are abrupt and pre-emptive, creating a tension within the act of reading, for the "je" statement pulls the reader away from the narrative flow. Such disruptions mirror the ambivalence d'Aubigné feels as he writes, dialoguing with a pre-existing model, and trying to impose his own voice. This tension determines style. The reader's unease with his role and reluctance to be drawn into the grim drama are quite apparent in the preface. D'Aubigné acts more like a coercer instead of a persuader. He and the reader must work through an essentially adversarial relationship before authorial intent can be realized. With no transitional phrase, for instance, d'Aubigné asserts, "je veux peindre la France" (*Misères*, 97), shattering the former narrative continuity of the book. In the midst

---

[43]Soulié, *L'Inspiration biblique*, 32.
[44]Hartmann, *Criticism*, 156.

of following one line of thought, d'Aubigné darts off to pursue another, interrupting "ici je veux sortir du general discours" (*Misères,* 367).

Another tension he must resolve is that between his Calvinist distrust of images, and his need to vivdly animate his written word. Later, in the *Avantures,* he will emblematically portray the primacy of word over image, while also demonstrating that the interpenetration of the two is necessary to full understanding. Here, he suggests an approach similar to that of the emblem: mere image, unaccompanied by word, is deceptive, yet image linked with word may be insightfully illuminated. The tension between the uncompromising presence he senses ("Voilà le front hideux de nos calamitez" [*Misères,* 679]) and the framed images of painting he attempts to use to portray it ("de la France qui meurt . . . autre pourtraict" [*Misères,* 424]) testify to the conflict between *verbum* (immediacy) and *res* (representation). This tension is resolved through an iconic form of reading, in which words function as directional arrows moving the reader through and beyond image to an apprehension of meaning. Image for d'Aubigné does not epitomize truth and, in fact, may seem to deny it, but rather is a stepping-stone to signification in a dialectic that parallels the apparent discrepancy, but actual relationship, between sin and salvation. Unmotivated or unexplained images are misleading: "meslé de cent couleurs, et les chaos estranges, / Bazes de ces tableaux. . ." (*Princes,* 735-36). "Couleurs" recalls the colors of rhetoric, or words manipulated and misused to abuse the credulous "qui sur un vrai subject [s'esgarent] en ces couleurs" (*Princes,* 1106); or again, it is "les poètes volages [qui] arborent ces couleurs. . ." (*Princes,* 943-44). D'Aubigné envisions a schism of self unless language coherence is restored:

> Au fil de ces fureurs ma fureur se consume,
> Je laisse ce sujet, ma main quitte ma plume,
> Mon coeur s'estonne en soy; mon sourcil refrongné,
> L'esprit de son sujet se retire esloigné.
> (*Princes,* 1099-1112)

The multiple selves–the Calvinist self, the writing self, the prophetic self, the self as it evolves textually in time–inscribed throughout his work can only attain a unified conception if his word is true to his intention and if action follows faithful to his utterance.

In *Les Tragiques,* the narrative becomes active, rather than descriptive or prescriptive. D'Aubigné changes his conception of the purpose of the conventional analogy between painting and poetry (*ut pictura poesis*) so that painting is endowed with a voice in *Les Tragiques* ("un pourtraict reprochant" [*Misères,* 556]); it is woven into a complex inter-referential system of response situated *en abyme* ("miroir de son miroir," [*Misères,* 556]), just as d'Aubigné is written into his own work, and participates in the signifying attributes customarily accorded to writing. He speaks, for instance, of the "traiteresse Pandore" who, through representational writing, "apporta nos malheurs." Pandore intends to depict human suffering. But what she portrays is an "enigme," and what she writes is ultimately ineffectual, since "aprés la flamme [de la souffrance] esteinte encore vit l'ardeur" (*Misères,* 992) of hope. Pandore is, for d'Aubigné, an epitome of deceptive (because incomplete and reductive) writing. The fact that "marquant pour se moquer" is truncated and has no specified object (usually, "se moquer *de* quelque chose") reverses her intention, so that she mocks *herself* through her attempt at artistic creation. She is shown "peignant sur son champ noir l'enigme de nos pleurs . . . / Marquant pour se moquer sur ses tapisseries / . . . Mesme escrivant" (*Misères,* 989-90). This is an emblematic mingling of word and image. Pandore and her actions are the image framed by, and demythified by, d'Aubigné's discourse. He implicitly requires Pandore, in order to be able to comment upon her, but explicitly moves beyond her presence to both incorporate and subvert her intention. D'Aubigné's discourse possesses extraordinary incorporative powers; it subsumes other art forms, such as the "peinture," the "tapisserie," the "emblesme" and the "devise" which, as d'Aubigné portrays it, is no longer a static representation but rather (employing as it does graphic, active verbs) is activated by a dramatic impulsion of its own: ". . . sur nos lis tant *foulez* le joug des Medicis. . ." (*Misères,* 800; my emphasis). Based on an *impresa,* this image is intended to convey the "essence" of the Médicis family. The evocative verb "foulez" is d'Aubigné's opinion of the Médicis' abusive treatment of France. Another example is found in the suggestive verb "crotter" in the following *devise* that succinctly summarizes the Pope's attitude toward France during the Wars of Religion: "la pantoufle crott[e] le lys de la couronne" (*Misères,* 1218). D'Aubigné's is a commentary on the image of the Pope's *devise.* It it uses the image, but describes it in a way inherent to, yet contrary to, the reason why the *devise* is originally chosen. The extended and personalized narratives expressed in such *devises* exemplify another strategy by which d'Aubigné inserts his own narrative into the genre of the epic, and constitute instances of his individualized utterance. Elsewhere, his expression is explicitly personal: "Ne pense pas . . . mon lecteur, que je conte / A ma gloire ce poinct, je l'escris à ma honte" (*Misères,* 1073-74). It appears that painting and seeing are used to convey more generalized experience, while hearing, associated with written transcription of the spoken word, expresses more personal events. Also, seeing may produce an impression, but only an apprehension of the word leads to action. Therefore, d'Aubigné links seeing with pagan habits: they rely on images (form) rather than accounting for content (which calls for action)

> Payens, qui adorez l'image de Nature,
> En qui la vive voix, l'exemple et l'Escriture
> N'authorise le vrai, qui dites: "Je ne croi
> Si du doigt et de l'oeil je ne touche et ne voi,"

> Croyez comme Thomas, au moins aprés la veue. . . .
>
> *(Jugement, 543-47)*

Apprehension through image is surpassed through reliance on the word that God dictates:

> Cet oeil vid les dangers, sa main porta le faix, . . .
> La Paraclet t'aprit à respondre aux harangues
> De tous ambassadeurs, mesme en leurs propres langues.
>
> *(La Chambre Doree, 965-68)*

Thus, images of painting and other art forms are englobed and surpassed by writing. D'Aubigné opposes his representations to idolatrous images.[45]

The insistence *Misères* places on considerations of language is maintained throughout the *Tragiques* and attests to d'Aubigné's concern over his role as a Calvinist and as a writer. *Misères* concludes with a biblically saturated invocation to God, calling for the restitution of the prelapsarian truthful utterance which is articulated within the confines of his writing:

> Leve ton bras de fer, haste tes pieds de laine,
> . . . Frappe du ciel Babel . . .
> Voila vostre evangile, engeance de Loyole, . . .
> C'est vostre instruction d'establir la puissance
> De Rome, sous couleur de points de conscience,
> Et, sous, le nom menti de Jesus, esgorger . . .
>
> *(Misères, 1245-1380)*

Such an emphasis on communication brings into the foreground the writing subject:

> c'est à la fin du xvie siècle . . . que l'on commence à supposer qu'un texte est exclusivement constitué par un sujet dont les intentions se manifestent dans le texte, que ces intentions sont réparables par le lecteur et que, d'autre part, le texte peut arranger les intentions du lecteur afin de les faire coincider avec celle de l'auteur.[46]

Despite the Calvinist prohibition of literature, d'Aubigné renders his historical epic poem a vehicle for personal expression that enables the writing self. Unlike Calvin, who insists that when one reads the Bible, one may only do so with the aim of finding Christ alone in it,[47] d'Aubigné presents us

---

[45]Du Bartas evidences a similar concern in *La Judit* where Judit's discourse, animated by the Word, textually enacts the progressive silencing and impotence of the pagan Holoferne. Holoferne's fatal error is his reliance on images unsubstantiated by narrative. For instance, Judit bedecks herself as an idolatrous object of worship in order to lure Holoferne. This problem of the relationship of word and images will be discussed further in Chapter Five, concerning the *Avantures*.

[46]Langer, "Les Tragiques," 71.

[47]Forstmann, *Word and Spirit*, 64.

with a text in which we may perceive both God and d'Aubigné's textualized self. By the time the *Avantures* are written, we find a fully developed d'Aubigné.

Language, Authorship and Authority[48]

In *Princes,* the second book of the *Tragiques,* the authority of princes is shown to be rooted in, and recognized through, language. Their abuses of power are mirrored in language: "par les escrits le mal resuscité / . . . Tranche et detruit l'erreur, et l'histoire par elles. / Mieux vaut à descouvert monstrer l'infection" (*Princes,* 1085-94). D'Aubigné purports to stand against them and fallen language, establishing his book as a sort of purified dictionary. He opposes the fertile abundance of his "vers bien aimez" to the "steriles discours" of the other (*Princes,* 55-57). Since the dialogue with which *Misères* begins is no longer possible because language is fallen, *Princes* is articulated on a confrontational axis, where "je" and "vous" spar with each other, and where "je" is always privileged:

Je veux, à coups de traits de la vive lumiere. . . . Vous qui avez donné ce subject à ma plume. . . (*Princes,* 1-9).

All the active verbs ("crever," "ouvrir," "percer" in the rest of the passage) are associated with "je" while "vous" is placed in the role of passive recipient; imperatives instruct him what to do. D'Aubigné's conception of self originates from the tension inherent in its antagonism toward another; this will be important for our discussion of *La Confession du Sieur de Sancy,* where d'Aubigné actually *adopts,* for polemic purposes, an antipathetic *persona.* He thus extends the habitual Calvinist stylistic reliance on antithesis to develop an entire drama of opposition. However, great care is needed in this procedure for, as can be seen in "vous qui avez donné ce subject à ma plume," the "vous" who is being excoriated is actually, paradoxically, perpetuated by being mentioned.

Another manner in which d'Aubigné writes images of himself into the text is through the continuing resort to historical *exempla,* as is the case with Hannibal.[49] Through the selection and accumulation of such models, by the end of *Les Tragiques* d'Aubigné moves outside of such molds to

---

[48]A conflict similar to that which d'Aubigné must resolve between authorship and authority is discussed by Jonathan Goldberg in *Voice Terminal Echo* (Chicago: University of Chicago Press, 1986), 49. He notes that "to live the poet's life means to surrender to another, authoring swallowed in authority. . . . Authority usurps the poet's role. . . . Power encompasses and straightens poetic production, producing the poet and 'his' text." D'Aubigné devises strategies to overcome this obstacle.

[49]He chooses models of exceptional historical prominence and acknowledged almost mythic charisma, such as Hannibal and Caesar. It is noteworthy that he chooses such non-religious models in his apparently religious drama. Acting decisively in history is very important to him, as we can see from these prototypes. Writing is the form his action takes. His writing is equally as forceful as the memorable deeds of these men.

create his own writing *persona* within the text. Here, however, his self is still subordinate to his undertaking: "je voi ce que je veux, et non ce que je puis; / Je voi mon entreprise et non ce que je suis" (*Princes*, 43). Before he can reap the harvest of his literary endeavor, he must first acknowledge the historical reality from which it springs and resign himself to gathering its "fruicts amers" (*Princes*, 78). Writing, therefore, retains some vestiges of its Calvinist association with sin: one is the *author* of one's misdoing, just as in *Princes* liars "blasment les pechez desquels ils sont autheurs" (128). Writing may, however, be condoned if it is divinely inspired: "ces escoliers d'erreur n'ont pas le style apris / Que l'Esprit de lumiere aprend à noz esprits" (*Princes*, 435-36). This poses a dilemma for the reader. As a Calvinist, d'Aubigné may not invoke the classical humanist muse or the divine furor of the Pléiade: "vos rhymeurs hypocrites, / Desguisez, ont changé tant de phrases escrites / Aux prophanes amours. . . . / Ils colorent encor leurs pompeuses prieres / De fleurs des vieux payens et fables mensongeres" (*Princes*, 429-34). In addition, he may not, as a flawed human vessel, in any way claim to deserve divine inspiration. How, then, is d'Aubigné to valorize his writing?

In order to be elect, sin is paradoxically required as the historical point of reference that enables a reorientation of language so that one may "prononc[e] de Canaan la langue" (*Princes*, 442). Then, d'Aubigné reasons, one may be permitted to display the self. The most efficacious writers, he notes, are those "qui règnent sur eux mesmes" (*Princes*, 665). This constant vigilance also connotes a strong self that must be cultivated and perfected.

Another representation of d'Aubigné's dilemma as a writer surfaces at this juncture. It is presented allegorically, through the vehicle of a young boy, newly arrived at court, who is asked to choose between Fortune and Virtue. He notices the lack of congruity between words and things at court. More importantly, he signals the signification of careful reading as a guarantor of salvation. The misguided nobles at court read, as will Faeneste later, incorrectly and incompletely, bastardizing meaning and appropriating words to their own inaccurate sense: "lisants ils ont pillé . . . / Les poinctes pour escrire . . . [ils] reni[ent] [leur] salut quand il y va du gain" (*Princes*, 1271). The youth's meditation on truth and writing's relationship to it acts as a signpost for messages of extreme importance to the reader, signalling authorial intervention.[50] In addition, the emphasis on writing, its implements, and reading which runs as a theme throughout *Les Tragiques* highlights the self-consciousness d'Aubigné experiences concerning his act of literary creation and testifies to a motive far beyond that of historical fact-gathering for a Protestant polemic. *Princes* ends, appropriately, on a literary note,

---

[50]Jean Crespin, *Histoire des martyrs*, ed. Bénoîst (Toulouse: Société des livres religieux, 2d éd., 1885-89). Crespin places typographical arrows in his text to alert readers to salient points. Cf. p. 251, for example.

imbricating an emblem within the narrative. That is, it combines words that are evocative of a picture, as well as words that function as the picture's caption, the gist the reader is meant to extract from the emblem. The haughty Catholics, imaged as unpliant oak trees, are warned that they shall fall before the mighty wind of the Protestant army:

> Vous y serez compris. Comme lors que l'esclat
> D'un foudre exterminant vient renverser à plat
> Les chesnes resistans et les cedres superbes, . . .
> [On vous verra] Avoir eu part à l'ombre, avoir part au danger.
> (*Princes*, 1517-26)

"Vous" reopens the confrontational situation of the book, acting, along with "avoir part . . . au danger," as a frame for the picture of the "chesne . . . renversé à plat." The emblem functions as a concluding warning, in potent miniature, to those who do not have ears to heed or eyes to *read* correctly. It is a warning, integrally attached to the text, to read attentively. Authority is negatively compared to authorship: the latter insists on fidelity to meaning, while the former, as with *Princes,* fosters duplicity and confusion in language.

Signs and Substance

The question of faithful signifying is further elaborated in *La Chambre Doree,* the most framed and allegorical of all the books. Significantly, d'Aubigné chooses to portray injustice and abuse of power in a mode that Calvin explicitly condemns. Allegories set up stylized types which, like painting, seem two-dimensional. Each allegorical figure is endowed with a set of qualities, rather like the sixteenth-century grammar books (such as that of M. de La Porte, *Les Epithètes*)[51] which list *attributs* or adjectives that can only properly be paired with certain nouns. A limitation of meaning is thus effected, which also produces limits as to the penetrability of each allegorical type. Allegories *seem* to invite reading so as to decipher their content, but in reality they block discerning reading and only permit a reassemblage of gnomic elements. Impassive and inscrutable, allegory conceals more than it conveys.[52] Out of such eventual hermeticism arises the possibility of errant interpretation which Calvin denounces: "Je n'introduy icy nulle figures ne paraboles, afin qu'on ne me reproche point que je cherche des subterfuges, en m'esloignant du texte."[53] In such a way, allegories

---

[51]De la Porte, *Les Epithètes.*

[52]Goldberg, *Voice,* 29. "In its etymology allegory (allosagoreuein) means a speaking beside the point, cryptic private utterance, voice 'present' to itself, not out in the open. . . . In allegory, the figures (characters) are parts for wholes. . . ." While simple personifications may not be misleading, the extensive allegorical development of the *Chambre Doree* is deliberately so, for it epitomizes the dangerous mixture of sacred aspirations with profane debasement.

[53] Calvin, *L'Institution,* IV.xvii.401.

epitomize enfleshment, or the enmiring of spiritual capabilities. Allegories are signs in themselves devoid of substance. It is possible that they may point to reality, but the disruptive way in which they are read opens the possibility that the signifier will not be linked to that which is signified. This is analogous to the way Calvinists perceive Catholic sacraments, for Calvin "would say that the *reality,* the thing or the *truth-of-the-thing* is, by definition, the *non-sign.*"[54] For d'Aubigné to write the *Chambre Doree* in the spirit of Calvinist polemic and aim at denouncing Catholic and princely abuses, he must liberate himself from the Calvinist interdiction of allegory in order to use it as a tool. He signals his intent to move beyond Calvinist confines by beginning the *Chambre Doree* with a representation of God, something which Calvin expressly forbids:

> Bref, s'il n'estoit ainsi que la cognoissance qu'on cuide avoir de Dieu par les images fust menteuse et bastarde, les Prophètes ne les con-damneroyent pas ainsi sans exception. Pour le moins, j'ay ceci gagné qu'en disant que ce n'est que mensonge et vanité de vouloir figurer Dieu par images visibles. . . .[55]

Nevertheless, d'Aubigné portrays God enthroned in majesty, providing a celestial frame for the *Chambre Doree,* and a viewpoint from the heavens which the author dares to share:

> Au Palais flamboyant du haut ciel empyree
> Reluit l'Eternel en presence adoree
> Par les Anges heureux . . .
> Au moindre clin d'oeil du Siegneur des Seigneurs
> Ils partent de la main. . . .
> (*La Chambre Doree,* 1-9)

This stylized, yet anthropomorphic and even familiar representation of God poses questions as to d'Aubigné's perception of himself at this stage in *Les Tragiques.* God, who "winks" at the angels, is a God rather reduced in awesomeness: d'Aubigné feels on comfortable terms with Him. The very fact of inscribing an image of God into his manuscript confers a great deal of power on the author. D'Aubigné's authorial presence is transported to the heavens; like God, he "plana sur le haut de la nue" (*Chambre Doree,* 161). The author is also like God, *primum mobile* of the universe, in that his actions propel the text; when God hears out Justice's tearful complaint, he "met l'espee au costé et marche à la *vengeance,*" (*Chambre Doree,* 138; my emphasis) thus prefiguring the title of the sixth book of *Les Tragiques.* The factor motivating God's action is the suffering of the martyrs, which

---

[54]Joseph Fitzer, "The Augustinian Roots of Calvin's Eucharistic Thought," *Augustinian Studies* 7 (1976): 95.

[55]Calvin, *L'Institution,* I.xi.126.

will be described in *Feux*. As d'Aubigné is ultimately, as author, the true motivating force behind God's action in the text in that he is the director behind the script, we may infer that d'Aubigné views himself as a living, literary martyr who animates salvation history.

D'Aubigné introduces considerations of language in order to explain why history needs to be saved. God condemns the tower of Babel, built of martyrs' ashes and skulls, symbolizing that human language, with its unholy mixture of sacred and profane, brings death. By incorporating into his work the secular images and abuses he denounces, d'Aubigné opens himself up to a similar charge.[56] He seems to succumb to a similar temptation when he begins to describe the allegorical figures of the *Chambre Doree*, for they are elaborately detailed and seem to impede the progression of the narrative. However, the ponderous pace of the *Chambre Doree* is expressly designed by d'Aubigné to stress the dead weight of images, like Catholic objects of worship, which are unanimated by the Word. The narrative is *not intended* to function; but he is permitting it to be temporarily blocked to prove his point (which is only more plausible when one contrasts the pace of the *Chambre Doree* with the quick movement of *Feux*).

It is for this reason that d'Aubigné insists on "pourtraicts" rather than on drama. D'Aubigné animates his allegorical presentation at only one juncture, in heaven, where the allegorical figures are permitted to speak. On earth, however, they are mute and static, and are allowed no determining voice which might influence the reader's interpretation of them. Also, the present tense is, appropriately, used in heaven, while the more passive imperfect is used for allegories on earth. Deictics are continually used, both to alert the reader to a particular point of interest, as well as to further slow the narrative by providing precise spatial and temporal loci: (là . . . à droite . . . au dernier coin . . . [*Chambre Doree*, 470-510]). Accompanying this image-saturated presentation is the parallel theme of incorrect writing. Words misused or scantily founded are "ridicules fables," made of "vent," and the decrees of such allegorical shams of justice "devien[nent] un arrest sans arrest" (*Chambre Doree*, 424). Paradoxically, unlike tableaux, which are static and framed and which the allegory here recalls, the effect of the allegory is to produce ceaseless change, greatly reminiscent of Satan's metamorphoses in *Fers*. This is because no equivalence between word and thing can be achieved through painterly representation. The allegorical figure "Formalité," for example, cooperates in causing the schism between speech and meaning: ". . . pour jetter dans les yeux des juges / La poussiere / . . . Erreur d'authorité . . . / [Elle] oste l'estre à la chose . . ." (*Chambre*

---

[56]He hereby creates a dilemma which he will not fully resolve until the composition of the *Avantures*. He still, at this point, half believes that the Calvinist distrust of poets as "feigners" is correct: "Les poètes ont feint que leur Dieu Juppiter / Estan venu du Ciel les hommes visiter / Punit. . . ." *Chambre Doree*, v. 187-89.

Doree, 481-90) and, hence, no salubrious stasis can be maintained. Writing that is improperly motivated produces death ("qui font de la plume / un outil de bourreau. . . . / Ces plumes sont stilets des assassins gagés" [*Chambre Doree,* 499-500]). Under such circumstances there can be no authorship, but only arbitrary authority: the would-be writer becomes the written-upon, adding another layer of meaning to the palimpsest of d'Aubigné's text ("ces plumes / . . . dont on escrit au dos des captifs affligés" [*Chambre Doree,* 499]).

The writer is figured as he who portrays the Catholics inscribing the death sentence upon their victims, and as the victim who endures this. D'Aubigné's images of writing lead him to contrast the human with the divine book. Misleading painting is associated with the former's fallen word: because language is shattered, no true reading is possible:

> Les rangs des condamnez . . .
> Portent les diables *peints*: les Anges en effect
> Leur vont tenant la main autrement qu'en portraict;
> Les hommes sur le corps desployent leurs injures,
> Mais ne donnent le ciel ne l'enfer qu'en *peinctures* . . .
> L'idolatre qui fait son salut en image
> Par images anime et retient son courage.
> (*Chambre Doree,* 548-58; my emphasis)

Reliance on images is misleading. Human writing is a perversion of language when it relies on pictorial, mimetic description. Authority, a form of social *inscription,* thus takes on a pejorative connotation: ". . . estendart . . . où est peint Ferdinand, sa compagne Isabelle / Et Sixte Pape, *autheurs* de la secte bourrelle" (*Chambre Doree,* 564-66; my emphasis).

In these circumstances, only one certain of his election may proffer his writing to be endorsed. Like the martyrs, his voice expresses a perfect equivalence of word with thing. As opposed to "ces bouches d'erreur," his praise of the martyrs is "muette, au Pere seul s'envolle / . . . Dieu à ses tesmoins a donné . . . / La langue estant couppee, une celeste voix" (*Chambre Doree,* 645-52). Through God's grace, the restoration of prelapsarian communication is achieved. The allegories d'Aubigné describes are revealed, before the fact, as "spectacles plaisans et feintes tragedies" (*Chambre Doree,* 619), for the martyr's suffering on earth will be abundantly redeemed in heaven. God is now the author, and legitimizes writing: "il . . . escrit . . . en son registre eternel tous nos maux" (*Chambre Doree,* 668).

With this resolution, the allegorical presentation is carried into historical process. The Inquisition is denounced through allegory. Human history is seen to be as flimsy and deceitful as allegory, unless it is directed by God. An early d'Aubigné appears to speak out against the very strategies he will employ in the composition of the *Avantures,* averring that "le vrai fruict de toute l'Histoire . . . est de connoistre en la folie et foiblesse des hommes, le jugement et la force de Dieu."[57] However, d'Aubigné proceeds to subvert this affirmation by implicitly comparing God as craftsman with himself as writer. The similarities are too great for the reader not to realize d'Aubigné's valorization of his art. God's act of selecting materials, for instance, parallels d'Aubigné's act of literary creation: "l'ouvrier parfaict de tous, cet artisan supreme / Tire de mort la vie, et du mal le bien mesme" (Chambre Doree, 665). Similarly, in Feux, d'Aubigné "os[e] bien eslire / Quelques martyrs choisis" (Feux, 29-30). God brings life out of death, as d'Aubigné the writer does elsewhere in Les Tragiques: "Vous, Gastine et Croquet, sortez de vos tombeaux" (Feux, 719); "du berceau, du tombeau je releve une fille" (Feux, 997). God writes our salvation. D'Aubigné, through another reference to superimposed discourse, grafts his text onto that of the Bible so that his narrative, too, plays a role in salvation history. He obliterates profane speech through the assertion of his writing, wielded as a weapon to militate for the Word. He warns his adversaries,

> Vous en avez chez vous une marque certaine
> Dans vostre grand Palais, où vous n'avez point leu, . . .
> Par un prophete ancien une histoire tracee
> Dont les traits par dessus d'autres traits desguisez
> Ne se descouvrent plus qu'aux esprits advisez.
>
> (Chambre Doree, 682-87)

His writing, which is only perceptible to the enlightened elect, calls for a new kind of writing, an ability to discern d'Aubigné's writing interwoven with the words of former prophets. Salvation is effected through directed reading, the discernment of the aspects of truth and transcendence among the multiple layers of confused human discourse.

D'Aubigné proceeds to reject allegory, the very method he uses to write the Chambre Doree: "fi des puants vocables / Qui m'ont changé mon style et mon sens à l'envers!" (Chambre Doree, 927). D'Aubigné as writing subject is oddly acted upon here; he claims that he is the object of external manipulation, and calls for God to be the subject who writes upon him, in terms reminiscent of Calvin's theory of biblical dictation[58] by the Holy Spirit: "Je diray en ce lieu / Ce que sur mon papier dicte l'Esprit de Dieu" (Chambre Doree, 958). The tension d'Aubigné feels concerning literary

---

[57]D'Aubigné, Histoire universelle, vol. 1, 10.

[58]Stauffer, Dieu, 63-64. Stauffer notes that Calvin considers that the writers of the Bible are not independent entities, but are rather accessories. They transcribe the Word as it is dictated to them. Calvin therefore refers to himself as an "instrument," evoking "une certaine passivité humaine": "Les exégètes de la Bible . . . pour qu'ils renoncent à leurs fantaisies exégétiques, pour que leur interprétation ne soit pas le fruict de leur invention personnelle, il faut . . . que l'Esprit qui a parlé par les Prophètes intervienne à nouveau pour communiquer l'intelligence de sa Parole."

creation is very evident here; he resorts to the subterfuge of appearing to renounce the entire literary construction of the *Chambre Doree*. However, were this truly the intent, the *Chambre Doree* would never have been published as part of *Les Tragiques*. Rather than cower behind the Davidic model with which he concludes the *Chambre Doree*, d'Aubigné actually assimilates that model to himself; he is not overwhelmed by it but rather appropriates it, in a supreme act of literary self-assertion, ordering his readers to attend to him: "Lisez, Persécuteurs, le reste de mes chants. . . ." While he *claims* that "ma voix se taist: oyez sonner pour elle / La harpe qu'animoit une force eternelle / Oyez David," in reality it is *his* voice, and not David's, that remains, narrating "en prophetique vers" (*Chambre Doree*, 1001-1009). For it is he, as author, who allows David's presence in the poem; "la main qui fit sonner ceste harpe divine" is certainly David's but, also, through his appropriation and re-activation of the example, d'Aubigné's.

Election and Expression

The summons is rearticulated in the deictic with which *Feux* opens, and situates the reader with the author in a privileged place from which they watch salvation history unroll: "Voicy marcher de rang par la porte sacree . . . L'enseigne d'Israel . . . / Au roolle des esleus" (*Feux*, 1-11). The ambiguity of the term "roolle" extends its significance to include the scroll upon which salvation is inscribed; that is, d'Aubigné's text. He explicitly links his text with the register of the elect by pointing out their mutual purpose: "Valeureux chevaliers, / . . . qui estes, devant les fondemens du monde, / Au roolle des esleus . . . / Condui mon oeuvre, ô Dieu! à ton nom, donne moy / Qu'entre tant de martyrs, champions de la foy / . . . Je puisse consacrer un tableau pour exemple" (*Feux*, 1-22). Read in proximity with the neighboring nefarious allegorical images of the *Chambre Doree*, the images of the martyrs in *Feux* are, on the other hand, sanctioned. Painting has both a positive and a negative sense for d'Aubigné, but even in its positive sense it requires completion by writing. D'Aubigné figures the martyrs' agonies as tableaux that he completes through his commentary. His book thus becomes the instrument for his *rapprochement* with God: God enrolls his martyrs, and d'Aubigné participates in this act of memorializing. As God views in perspective and knows all human history, the prophetic stance that d'Aubigné begins to articulate in *Chambre Doree* englobes past, present and future.

D'Aubigné's sentiment of election leads him to articulate a richer yet more fragmented conception of self, a sort of dualistic vision that establishes the diptych of sinful and redeemed self. Both selves are integral to the writing act. The sinful self provides the experience, while the redeemed self gives the commentary upon it:

Dormant sur tel dessein, en mon esprit ravi
J'eus un songe au matin, parmi lequel je vi
Ma conscience en face, ou au moins son image,
Qui avoit au visage les traicts de mon visage.
Elle me prend la main en disant: "Mais comment
De tant de dons de Dieu ton foible entendement
Veut-il faire le choix? Oses-tu bien eslire
Quelques martyrs choisis, leur triomphe descrire,
Et laisser à l'oubli comme moins valeureux
Les vainqueurs de la mort, comme eux victorieux?
J'ai peur que cette bande ainsi par toy choisie
Serv' au style du siecle et à la poesie,
Et que les rudes noms, d'un tel style ennemis,
Ayent entre les pareils la difference mis."
Je responds: "Tu sçais bien que mentir je ne t'ose,
Mirouer de mon esprit; tu as touché la cause
La premiere du choix, joint que ma jeun' ardeur
A ce haut dessein espoinçonné mon coeur,
Pour au siecle donner les boutons de ces choses
Et l'envoyer ailleurs en amasser les roses.
Que si Dieu prend à gré ces premices, je veux
Quand mes fruicts seront meurs lui payer d'autres voeux,
Me livrer aux travaux de la pesante histoire,
Et en prose coucher les hauts faits de sa gloire:
Alors ces heureux noms sans eslite et sans choix
Luiront en mes escrits plus que les noms des Rois."
Ayant fait cette paix avec ma conscience,
Je m'advance au labeur avec cette asseurance
Que, plus riche et moins beau, j'escris fidellement
D'un style qui ne peut enrichir l'argument.

                              (*Feux,* 23-52)

D'Aubigné the writer extracts experience from d'Aubigné the historical *personnage*; the writer then refers to himself in his text as "je," and perceives his mirror image, "ma conscience en face." This sort of *dédoublement* figures the self-images that proliferate *en abyme* elsewhere in d'Aubigné's work, and attests to an extreme degree of self-reflection. Here, too, d'Aubigné differs from other Reformist writers, for "in the Reformers, conscience is largely depersonalized, . . . at least they speak of God rather than conscience." Like Calvinists, d'Aubigné wishes to avoid depiction that relies on images:

les Imprimeurs sont curieux de representer en taille-douce les Autheurs aux premieres pages de leurs livres: tel soin est inutile, car il ne profite point au Lecteur de voir le visage et les lineamens de celui qui l'enseigne, mais bien ceux de l'ame.[59]

Yet he does wish to describe himself as author of his book. That is why he incorporates dynamic descriptions of himself into the text: they are meant not to be representational in a mimetic sense, but rather to convey his personal essence, "l'âme" (rather like a *devise* without images).

D'Aubigné resembles another historical entity: he is like John, the author of *Revelation* who, "ravy," exists both physically and "in the Spirit." Like John, d'Aubigné's historico-religious evolving sense of self finds its outlet in a theo-literary vehicle.

D'Aubigné meditates, through this internal dialogue, on the nature of his writing. This is a self-conscious portrayal by the author *of himself in the act of writing.* "J'ay peur," the redeemed self says to d'Aubigné, "que cette bande ainsi par toy choisie / Serve au siecle, et à sa poésie." D'Aubigné, himself the sinner whose writing is dialectically redeemed, responds, "mentir je ne t'ose." He then proceeds to detail an elaborate program of writing, boldly unveiling his authorial intention: "je veux . . . me livrer aux travaux de la presante histoire," he says, announcing the future project of the *Histoire universelle.* He also reflects on what sort of writing may be sanctioned, rejecting the frivolous *Printemps* of his youth ("pour au siecle donner les boutons de ces choses") and limiting his stylistic adornment to that which will best convey truth. However, it is important that it is *he* who makes the choice: no muse comes to counsel him, and God does not force him to any recognition of the need for such a program of writing. D'Aubigné asserts his independence by making his own judgments. If he limits himself, it is nevertheless within the framework of self-assertion and self-determination. He is active and resourceful: "je veux . . . me livrer . . . je m'advance . . . j'écris."

D'Aubigné's writing is expressed in organic metaphors: he is the bearer of fruit which must ripen: "quand mes fruicts . . . seront . . . meurs." The literary fruits also have a theological role: they are the "prémices," first-fruits or offerings to God. Writing is not alien to d'Aubigné's selfhood, but rather an extension and expression of it. Finally, the dialogue serves to confirm his conception of self, of election and of the legitimacy of writing: "Ainsi fait ceste paix avec ma conscience / Je m'advance en labeur avec ceste asseurance / Que, plus riche et moins beau, *j'escris fidellement*" (my emphasis). He opts for the "plain style," but the object of the fidelity he guarantees is not specified: is it to the Bible, to Calvinism or, more likely, to d'Aubigné's own conception of truth? The dialogue, by inscribing

---

[59]Here, too, d'Aubigné differs from other Reformed writers for, as Quirinus Breen notes in *John Calvin: A Study in French Humanism* (Grand Rapids: Eerdmans, 1931), 72, "in the Reformers conscience is largely personalized. . . . They speak of God rather than conscience." Second quote, d'Aubigné, *Histoire,* I.9.

the self within the text, sets up an intimate equation between selfhood and writing. D'Aubigné must find a way to reconcile with his "conscience," so that he may be theologically faithful as well as creative literarily. He has an activist manner of expressing himself that furthers the comparison the reader is brought to draw between God as creator and d'Aubigné as literary creator ("je veux . . . / En prose coucher les hauts faicts . . . / Alors ces heureux noms sans eslite et sans choix / Luiront en mes escrits."). Through the dreaming and doubling of self, d'Aubigné expands his writing self to incorporate and surpass the prophetic model: he is no longer the mere transmitter of God's Word, but rather is also the agent of the efficacy of his *own* voice in the world.

The prophetic voice undergoes several stages in its path toward expression. A period of *kenosis,* in which the self is emptied-out in order to be divinely inflated, is analogous to the initial disclaimers we note in *Les Tragiques* in which d'Aubigné states that he is unfit to be God's messenger. The prophet is then filled with the divine Word, which he releases in a stance of saying-forth, explicitly confining himself to the role of mere vehicle. Finally, the prophet as a tool is abandoned after his mission is fulfilled.[60] D'Aubigné intentionally deviates from this model in one crucial respect: he never undergoes the period of abandonment. Replacing the void left by the evacuation of God's utterance by his *own* word, d'Aubigné reconstitutes his "self." As one of the elect, he asserts his own right of choice. He chooses to be God's instrument. By this act of renunciation, consciously and willingly, he sets the conditions necessary for a selfpossession. He passes from the self as vehicle to the self as agent. They are similar in intentionality, but d'Aubigné's revised formulation contains an independent assertion: the power of the writer's word ("ames dessous l'autel victimes des idolles / . . . Je preste à vos courroux le *fiel de mes paroles*" [*Feux,* 52; my emphasis]). We may liken d'Aubigné's innovation to the model a similarly self-conscious Protestant literary creator, Milton, devises. To redeem speech, he proposes four steps in which, first, the poet prepares himself to be God's agent, then is infused with the Word. Then, however, Milton revises the traditional prophetic stance: the writer is free to exercise his own creativity, finally offering his epic as evidence that he is the direct recipient of divine inspiration.[61] In like fashion, in the foregoing quotation, d'Aubigné "preste [sa] parole," but never relinquishes authority over it. He thereby asserts his right to ownership.

Like God, d'Aubigné may elect the materials with which he will work. He uses "mots" to write of the "maux" the martyrs experience (*Chambre Doree,* 668). The word-play between "maux" and "mots" (God is a writer

---

[60]Harold Bloom, *A Map of Misreading* (Oxford: Oxford University Press, 1975), 96-100.

[61]R.L. Entzminger, *Divine Word: Milton and the Redemption of Language* (Pittsburgh: Duquesne University Press, 1985), 22.

who "escrit en son registre éternel tous nos maux") establishes the equation between Protestant suffering which gives rise to writing, and God's approval of writing. The "roolle des esleus" in *Feux* can be read as a guarantor of the written word: the é-*lus*, the elect, are those martyrs who in *Les Tragiques* are "read out of" Inquisitorial records to be inscribed *in* the texts of both God and d'Aubigné. Certainly one of d'Aubigné's purposes in writing is to "enroller" just as God does. Ulrich Langer notes that "le texte [de d'Aubigné] est un deuxième Saint-Esprit [pratique une deuxième élection]. En cela, d'Aubigné transcende le schéma de l'artiste calviniste."[62]

In *Feux*, d'Aubigné borrows from a contemporary prose source, Jean Crespin's *Histoire des martyrs*. It is instructive to contrast the manner in which d'Aubigné manipulates these materials with that of Crespin. D'Aubigné reveals far greater freedom of invention, while Crespin illustrates the typical Calvinist effacement of the authorial self. The Genevan printer is more a compiler than an author. His purpose in writing is purely polemic and didactic, a witness to the martyrs of the Calvinist faith:

> or nostre devoir sera de remercier le Seigneur et de l'invoquer d'affection ardente, lui recommandant sa cause et sa querelle, et que de plus en plus la celeste doctrine de son Evangile soit manifeste au milieu des horribles confusions de ce dernier aage du monde.[63]

All authorship is God's alone: "ce grand Dieu, et sa voix effroyable / Armé d'autorité, qui demeure immuable."[64] Reminiscent of Calvin's injunction against allegory, Crespin proclaims the only possible purpose for writing: "la parole du Seigneur doit servir aux fideles d'instruction, pour repousser tous tentations et allechemens qui les pourroyent distraire ou divertir du droit chemin."[65] D'Aubigné, too, wishes to remember the martyrs' confessions, but he simultaneously glorifies his own writing act, since it is only through his words that they will be immortalized. His "je" is omnipresent in the text, recording its reactions, making its selections: "De qui puis-je choisir l'exemple et le courage? . . . J'honorerai. . . . Passeray-je la mer de tant de longs propos / Pour enroller . . . Je veux tirer à part. . . ." Crespin's "je," however, is rarely heard even in his preface, and is nonexistent after that. Thus, d'Aubigné differs significantly from Crespin in intention and method. Unlike Crespin, who often quotes entire speeches or letters of the martyrs verbatim, d'Aubigné does not aim at an encyclopedic cataloguing of material, but rather effects a selection of those instances most likely to fulfill his requirement: "esmouvoir." He frees himself from concerns such as those Crespin demonstrates by promising to record all such material in

---

[62]Langer, *"Les Tragiques,"* 71.

[63]Crespin, *Histoire,* III.v.

[64]Ibid., II.vii.

[65]Ibid., I.a.1., roto.

the *Histoire universelle*. History is thereby relegated to a supplemental, secondary status. It is a mere repository, and puts forward no analysis of the material it contains. Usually privileged over subjective interpretation, history is now subordinated to it. D'Aubigné thus significantly evolves toward permissions for fiction implicit in the legitimation of literary creation. In *Sa Vie* he will make more explicit the new, unprecedented role reversal of history and fiction that he effects through his writing.

In the only instance in *Feux* in which d'Aubigné reproduces a large segment of a martyr's harangue, the martyr's "je" is blurred into d'Aubigné's "je," so that d'Aubigné ultimately appropriates the words to himself.[66] D'Aubigné's narrative surrounds and frames the martyr's speech, resuming immediately after he falls silent, so that the reader is deceived into relying more on the authorial voice for direction, and attribution of the speech to the martyr becomes merely a secondary concern.

Just as God should provide the ultimate reference for all our speech, so d'Aubigné sees his writing act as divinely motivated. He differs from Crespin, who means merely to glorify God, a natural, human impulsion. Because writing can, for d'Aubigné, become a testament of the individual author's salvation, he perceives narrative as the portrayal of divine discourse acting through humanity. His word constitutes a new, intermediate stage before the ultimate realization of salvation: ". . . de mes paroles / En attendant le jour que . . . Les pourtaux du Paradis ouvr[iront]" (*Feux*, 54-56). Consequently, d'Aubigné develops the isolated episodes he borrows from Crespin into full-fledged mini-drama, inventing dramatic detail and judiciously emphasizing traits likely to make the martyr's experience more vivid: the martyr is not just an image; his witness speaks to us through d'Aubigné's rephrasing. Similarly, God's Word surpasses two-dimensional attempts at representationality. The technique with which the martyrs are drawn is similar to that used for the allegories in *La Chambre Doree:* these are quick, simple sketches with salient points highlighted. There is, however, one major difference: the allegories are portrayed as static images, while the martyrs are perceived in terms of the significance of their *discourse* and the instructions to the faithful they utter in their agony. Writing is also privileged in the latter case, further strengthening the perception of the legitimacy of d'Aubigné's writing act. For instance, the martyr Norris *writes* his own salvation in blood: "Sur ces tapis aigus [d'espines] ainsi jusqu'à sa place / A ceux qui la suivront il a rougi *la trace* / Vray *trace* du ciel. . ." (*Feux*, 140-43; my emphasis). Proper reading is also called for; Norris' writing is meant for others to read and follow. Similarly, Marie Stuart is a writer who literally inscribes on her "livret," a book of prayers she holds at her execution, a prescription for salvation: she writes, "C'est ma main qui t'escrit ces dernieres paroles: / Si tu veux suyvre Dieu, fuy de loin les

---

[66]Cf. Montalchine's "seul, seule, et seullement" speech in *Feux*, v. 655-700.

idoles; . . . Ces doigts victorieux ne graverent cecy / En cire seulement, mais en l'esprit aussi" (*Feux*, 241-52). When the martyrs are forbidden to speak, the written word speaks for them, reversing, as d'Aubigné intends, the customary privileging of orality over textuality, of Word over d'Aubigné's word. Both Word and word ("vers") are associated with truth ("veritez"), however; when the martyr caged above the street sees the Catholic monstrance passing by, he abominates it in "vers" of "pures veritez" (*Feux*, 410). The sonorous anaphora links verses with truth, showing how words prevail over image, the "idolle": "langues fausses et foles / . . . ce mal vient de servir aux idoles / Parfaicts imitateurs des abusés payens" (*Feux*, 1327-29).

The written word subordinates orality in *Feux* by its power of inspiration; the martyrs themselves stand firm due to their *reading* of their predecessors' examples of courage: "Cette-ci, en *lisant* avec frequents souspirs, / L'incroyable constance et l'effort des martyrs, / . . . la crainte fut esteinte" (*Feux*, 479-81). This image *en abyme* of martyrs inspiring future martyrs and of martyrs reading d'Aubigné's text is reminiscent of d'Aubigné's textualized images of self inscribed elsewhere in *Les Tragiques*. The writer writes of readers reading both his works and those of others (permitted by his textual mention). Reader and writer thus merge through the medium of the text.

Such a relationship is not apparent in Crespin. Crespin's technique is that of a mosaic, in which peripherally-related incidents are strung together by the thread of religious persecution. D'Aubigné, however, does not describe distinct, contiguous models of martyrdom, but rather makes each martyr an entity who articulates a conception of himself as one who embodies God's inscription on history. Each martyr is a coherent whole, self-contained yet dialectically participating in a continuous discourse between the human and the divine. D'Aubigné "individualizes" his martyrs. Unlike Crespin who, more typically Calvinist, empties out the self so that Everyman may conform to the general lineaments which remain, d'Aubigné writes a *narrative of the self*. In so doing, he implicitly strengthens his case for the existence of his own writing self.

Tension about his self-assertion as a writer nevertheless persists in *Feux*. It can be discerned in the reversal of the writing subject into an object, the written-upon discussed earlier. Such an effect is produced through the strength of the *exempla* themselves: it is as though d'Aubigné is not empowered to select them, but rather must yield to their assertion: *They* compel his selection: "le vaillant Gardiner *me contraint* cette fois / D'animer mon discours de ce courage anglois" (*Feux*, 291-92; my emphasis). Elsewhere, the pre-emptive nature of the materials is equally strong: passive grammatical constructions show that d'Aubigné sometimes feels overwhelmed by the power of the *exempla*. He claims, "maint exemple *me* cerche, et *je ne cerche pas* / . . . ces exemples m'ennuient, / Ils poursuyvent mes vers et mes yeux qui les fuyent" (*Vengeances*, 923-26; my emphasis). Another indication that d'Aubigné has misgivings about the Calvinist perception of his writing act is the reappearance of disclaimers such as we remark in the preface. He demurs, uncharacteristically, "je ne fay qu'un indice à un plus gros ouvrage" (*Feux*, 609). Yet, with the plethora of allusions to the *Histoire universelle*, it is possible that d'Aubigné is not modestly devaluing his work in order to compare it with a transcendent model (the Bible? the "roolle des esleus"?) but rather, referring to a complete, coherent *literary corpus* of his own, of which the *Histoire universelle* is part. In *Les Tragiques*, then, he selectively details certain striking instances that he will later more thoroughly document, but less creatively interpret, in the *Histoire*. This ability to perceive his written work and, hence, himself as a writer (for he finds the two inseparable: "mon dessein s'estend autant que ma vie et mon pouvoir"[67]) as existing on multiple planes and for diverse purposes, attests to d'Aubigné's self-conscious, thoughtful authorial perspective, and counteracts the Calvinist prohibition of writing. The script may still be, in some respects, that of the other: God. Or, it may be that of the other: d'Aubigné, writing in a different style and for a different purpose. Such questions do not alter the essential assertive course d'Aubigné chooses; he proceeds soon after to equate the effect of his rhetoric with divine onomastic powers, altering the connotative power of words: "Que le *nom* de la *mort* autrement effroyable / Bien cognu, bien pesé, nous deviene *agreable*," (*Feux*, 893; my emphasis) and of names: "le Pape [Clement] *non* Clement" (*Feux*, 1207; my emphasis).

Similar considerations prevail in *Fers*. Again in un-Calvinist fashion, d'Aubigné, as in the *Chambre Doree*, represents God pictorially. Acknowledging the tension inherent in such a depiction, d'Aubigné modifies his stance, describing God "sans définir de l'Eternel la place." That is, he permits a recounting of God's anthropomorphic *actions* as a type of *depiction*:

> Dieu retira les yeux de la terre ennemie: . . .
> [il] se rassit en son throsne et d'honneur couronné
> Fit aux peuples du ciel voir son chef rayonné . . .
> Un chacun en son lieu
> Exstatic reluisoit de la face de Dieu.

(Fers, 1-32)

By describing God, d'Aubigné makes himself part of the company of "les peuples du ciel," the only one permitted to look upon the divine visage. He thereby proclaims a unique status for his writing, a standing similar to that of the Bible: "mais comme il est permis aux tesmoignages saincts / Comprendre le celeste aux termes des humains" (*Fers*, 19-20). These remarks are enclosed in parentheses, a technique that may indicate a stylistic tension, the site of tension or hesitation.[68] We may interpret the parenthetical

---

[67]D'Aubigné, *Histoire*, 8.

[68]A similar phenomenon occurs with the use of the apostrophe. Cf. Jonathan Culler, *The Pursuit of Signs* (Ithaca: Cornell University Press, 1981), 142-48.

statements about d'Aubigné's inability to perceive and write about God as evidence that d'Aubigné is consciously liberating himself from Calvinist constraints. Further support is brought by an examination of the manner in which d'Aubigné likens himself to God; God's anger and subsequent action are shared by the poet. The very fact that it is d'Aubigné's page that records God's decisions points to d'Aubigné's essential role as God's agent:

> . . . Tes derniers jugemens, les arrets de ton ire,
> Il faut faire une pose et finir ces discours
> Par une vision qui couronne ces jours.
> L'esprit ayant encor congé par son extase
> De ne suivre, escrivant, du vulgaire la phrase.

(Fers, 1442-47)

Other evidence that d'Aubigné's poetics is shaped within zones of tension can be found in *Fers*. One example is that d'Aubigné seems to indicate that his book–to the extent that it reiterates human history–is written by Satan. Satan over-determines human actions, using them to his own purposes. Indeed, two of the book titles of *Les Tragiques* are included in Satan's statement to God: "je vien de redresser emprise sur emprise: / Les *fers* aprés les *feux* encontre ton Eglise" (*Fers*, 89-90; my emphasis). Thus Satan brags to God. This is, in fact, the exact spatial situation of d'Aubigné's two books, *Feux* following *Fers*. D'Aubigné is recounting, therefore, Satan's actions to the world. To this extent, content, if not form, is Satanically derived. *Les Tragiques* must, then, purify and neutralize history, reorienting it toward God. The poet is the agent of this change, as he relegates Satan, speechless ("la parole luy faut" [*Fers*, 75]) to the past tense, and confirms God's power through his actions in the present tense. The present has become the tense of revelation: God "sépare [Satan] de tous" and forces him to reveal his true, duplicitous nature. D'Aubigné's writing participates in a similar revelatory function.

Painting, however, with its deceptive illusions, is Satan's method of expression:[69] "Ces sont les Esprits noirs qui de subtils pinceaux / Ont mis au Vatican les excellens tableaux / Où l'Antechrist saoulé de vengeance et de playe. . ." (*Fers*, 256-57). Described only in the past tense, painting may depict only human history ("l'hideux portraict de la guerre civile / Une autre grande peinture est plus loing arrangee / Où pour le second coup babel est assiegee" [*Fers*, 391-92]); it may not represent divine subjects. Painting is only permissible as a conveyor of truth when it is accompanied by a commentary, as d'Aubigné pairs his painterly images in *Les Tragiques*

---

[69]Satan also embodies imagination ("comme l'idée il gaigna l'imagination" [*Feux*, v. 198]). D'Aubigné must work through this in order to draw fully on his powers of invention in the *Avantures*.

with appropriate glosses.[70] For instance, the angels contemplate, and comment in the present tense upon, images of the martyrs: "Tels serviteurs de Dieu, peintres ingenieux, / Par ouvrage divin representoyent aux yeux / Des martyrs bien heureux. . ." (Fers, 277). The martyrs are reified into images by their Catholic persecutors but are ultimately reanimated by the Word. Contrarily, a spectator is portrayed, en abyme, within the painting of the spectacle he contemplates. He is the infamous historical figure, Roi Sardanapale (Fers, 945); and d'Aubigné wields his written words to turn the tables and reify him as a framed, impotent image, just as the king tries to reify the martyrs.

Sacred history is written, not painted: "Dieu met en cette main la plume pour escrire / . . . doctement sacré une autre histoire, / . . . [par] les peintures advisent / Plus qu'un pinceau ne peut, et en l'histoire lisent. . ." (Fers, 307-20). Significantly, the angels and the elect are portrayed reading the very books of the Tragiques: "feux" are mentioned (318), and we see them "en l'histoire lisant / les premiers fers tirés"[71] (Fers, 320-21; my emphasis).

Those who, in the course of history, are inscribed in Les Tragiques, will resist Satan's wiles, will be the elect. God tells Satan, "fay selon ton dessein, les ames reservees / Qui sont en mon conseil avant le temps sauvees / Ton filet n'enclorra que les abandonnés" (Fers, 177-79). Predestination, therefore, is crucial for d'Aubigné's conception of the writing self. As reading Les Tragiques is the sole means of instructing us as to the outcome of the battle between God and Satan, d'Aubigné thus constitutes his work as the instrument of revelation. Salvation, after history, can be read in the heavens: "les yeux des bien-heureux / . . . lisent . . . dans le Ciel desguisé historien des terres, / ils lisent en leur paix les efforts de nos guerres" (Fers, 323).

---

[70]Painting and "tableaux" are invariably associated with evil or misrepresentation. When d'Aubigné describes the nefarious actions of those who oppose the Huguenots, he does so as though both he and the reader were viewing a painting; he gives directional indications, and refers to the organ of sight: "Voici Paris armé sous les loix du Guisard . . ." (Fers, 1351); "Tu verrois bien encor, . . . / Un double dueil forcé, le fils de l'adultère" (Fers, 1393); "Je voy l'amas des Rois et conseillers de terre / Qui changent une paix au progrez d'un guerre" (Fers, 1317). Writing, on the other hand, epitomizes and conveys truth: it is "l'escrit des véritez" (Fers, 1256). Sin is, indeed, ever-present as in a painting before the eyes of the world: "Les fidelles voyent bien aussi leurs péchez, qui se présentent incessamment noirs et hideux devant leur face; et de tant plus laids que les bons les hayssent" (Méditations, 560). On the other hand, God himself, the Word, cannot be seen: representation is a fallen thing, to be surpassed by reliance on the Word and its transcription: "C'est là que nous parviendrons à ce que l'homme n'a peu supporter, à la lumière inaccessible qui esblouyt . . . C'est là ou nous attent cette béatitude, qui n'a peu estre dépeinte dignement, ni par la Majesté de Sina, ni par le splendide palais qu'Ezechiel nous a représenté, ni par le glorieux estat de la Transfiguration, non plus par le portraict de celui qui parut à Sainct Jean entre les chandeliers, ni par l'estat excellent de la triomphante Jérusalem: c'est ce que nul oeil n'a peu voir. . ." (Méditations, 572).

[71]That d'Aubigné is meticulously constructing an inter-referential system among the books of the Tragiques is clear: we note previous references in the text to the titles of the books "Feux" and "Fers"; d'Aubigné here also refers back to "Princes."

The angels view celestial portraits of human history. Painting must be animated by a commentator; it cannot stand alone. Suddenly the voice recounting what they see is no longer that of the impersonal speaker but rather of d'Aubigné himself: "Ainsi voy-je. . ." (*Fers*, 513). He translates himself to the celestial sphere, the realm of omniscience. Such a "figure of flight maintains the beyond *within* a textuality that re-marks its indeterminate limits. . . . The re-marking effects as well the voice that casts itself into the beyond."[72] Flight provides d'Aubigné with a transcendent perspective from which to manipulate history and to mold it textually. Omnipotent now as well, d'Aubigné draws the reader into the band of the elect among whom he marches, directly appropriating a biblical quotation for his own purposes: "le Pillier du nuage à midi nous conduit, / La colonne de feu nous guidera la nuict" (*Fers*, 527-28), he claims, taking the reader with him in a re-enactment of the flight from Egypt. To emphasize his power to do so, d'Aubigné leaves unexplained for several pages *how* he is drawn up into the heavens, allowing us to assume that it is his own doing; later, he confesses that he is "par l'Ange consolant . . . mené dans les regions pures" (*Fers*, 1196-97).[73]

Elsewhere, he continues to assert his authority, and authorship, over the reader. D'Aubigné denies information to the reader and instructs him precisely how to interpret the limited information he is accorded: "Ne t'enquiers, mon lecteur, comment il vid et fit, / Mais donne gloire à Dieu en faisant ton profit" (*Fers*, 1203-4). D'Aubigné's desire to compose an *exemplum* of the experiences he recalls in *Fers* is apparent: "L'Ange m'en fait leçon disant: 'Voilà les restes / Des hauts secrets du ciel. . . . / C'est de tout l'advenir le registre . . ." (*Fers*, 1245-46); but he is unable to avoid contamination of the *exemplum* by his own subjectivity: "cependant qu'en luy, extatic je me pasme, / Tourne à bien les chaleurs de mon enthousiasme" (*Fers*, 1205-6). His self-consciousness imposes itself on the reader, slanting the reading act. In a fashion similar to the doubling dream discussed in *Feux*, d'Aubigné dialogues with himself:

> Retourne à ta moitié. . . .
> Escrits fidellement. . . .
> Ne chante que de Dieu, n'oubliant que lui mesme
> T'a retiré [de la mort].

> (*Fers*, 1417-26)

---

[72]Goldberg, *Voice*, 56.

[73]D'Aubigné, in an unusual twist, informs us that it is his "corps" that is taken up. Ordinarily, it is "l'âme" of the believer that is assumed into heaven. This may be an attempt to redeem his own corporeal nature through writing.

He then switches from an injunction to himself, to a first-person prayer proffered to God: "ta main m'a delivré, je te sacre la mienne. . . . / Tu m'as donné la voix, je te louerai, mon Dieu" (*Fers*, 1417-35). The two selves recall the distinction between sinful and redeemed selves which d'Aubigné must dialectically reconcile in order to write: "te" in the first quotation is the sinful self being instructed in the paths of righteousness (and, additionally, correct reading). "Te" becomes the "je" of the second quotation, now redeemed and free to praise the Lord.[74] In this way, d'Aubigné's expanded prophetic stance is more pronounced in *Fers* than in any other book. Significantly, in his preface, he calls this book more "poëtique et hardy" than the others. He falls into trances, speaks of his "enthousiasmes," and makes predictions. ("Paris, tu es reduite à digerer l'humain: / Trois cens mille des tiens perissent par la faim" [*Fers*, 1371-72]) as well as the "apophéties" ("Toy, Prince prisonnier . . . / Tu as de tels discours enseigné nos oreilles. . . . / Si un jour, oublieux, tu en perds la memoire / Dieu s'en souviendra bien à ta honte, à sa gloire" [*Fers*, 1025-30]). As discussed earlier, the "apophéties" may be seen as instances of permission for fiction, as the alternation of the spatial and temporal stance of the speaker permits a narrative manipulation similar to that which writing permits.

Literary self-consciousness is apparent in *Fers*; d'Aubigné intervenes to alert his reader to upcoming events, calling upon himself for his next book: "Venez, justes vengeurs . . . / Venez sçavoir comment / L'Eternel fait à poinct *vengeance* et *jugement*" (*Fers*, 1549-60; my emphasis). He also interrupts to discuss stylistic points: "Il faut faire une pause et finir ces discours" (*Fers*, 1443).

D'Aubigné continues to issue directives as to how his book is to be read, thus affirming indirectly his authorial stance. He fears that the "vain lecteur desjà en l'air s'esgare: / L'esprit mal preparé. . ." (*Vengeances*, 73). In addition, he warns the reader that his work is Calvinist, not to be interpreted allegorically, as are Catholic works ("vous n'aurez point de signe" [*Vengeances*, 82]). Narrative is valued over a mosaic of images. In a fashion similar to the narratizing he operates on Crespin's loosely-strung martyrology, d'Aubigné shows that Catholic reliance on mere images negates the voice and the Word: there is no syntax mediating among separate images, and hence no real communication is possible. Similarly, Calvin calls for a mutual examination of signifier and signified; if there is to be a sign, let it be explicated (and, necessarily, surpassed) in light of

---

[74]We may contrast this with the "je" / "tu" dialogue in de Bèze's *Chrestiennes méditations*, 95. Although the sinful "tu" addressed by the speaker is eventually saved, he is never permitted to speak. The self is never sufficiently redeemed as to be worthy of self-expression, but rather must wait passively as his salvation is narrated to, and for, him: "Crains tu les hommes puisque Dieu est pour toy? La mort te fait-elle peur? Elle est vaincue, et tournée en entrée de vie. Voilà donc tous tes ennemis dissipez: voilà bas tous ceux qui t'affligeoyent dedans et dehors."

how it is oriented to something beyond itself. This is similar to the iconic theory of reading we have postulated. Calvin observes,

> les Papistes confondent la vérité et le signe. Il y a d'autres hommes profanes qui séparent les signes d'avec la vérité . . . Quant à nous, suyvons le moyen entre ces deux extremitez: c'est-à-dire, retenons la *conjunction* qui a esté mise par le Seigneur: mais *distincte* de peur que ce qui est propre à l'un nous ne le transférions point faussement à l'autre.[75]

D'Aubigné asks that *Vengeances,* and all the books of *Les Tragiques,* be read plainly as they are written clearly and truly: they "seront exemples vrais de nos histoires sainctes" (*Vengeances,* 90).

It is d'Aubigné, rather than God, who explicitly directs the reader as he peruses *Les Tragiques,* for d'Aubigné now *interiorizes* his source of inspiration;[76] it is he, and not God, who now summons the powers of revenge (*Vengeances,* 96). Similarly, like God, he is capable, through his writing, of sacralizing things, people and history ("je sacre à la memoire / L'effroyable discours, la veritable histoire" [*Vengeances,* 369-70]). Also, like God, his writing foresees and announces future events: "le doigt qui escrivit . . . / sceut l'advenir escrire" (*Vengeances,* 419). His verses even become the literal instruments of vengeance: the Pope is eaten away by a mass of "vers" (worms / verses [*Vengeances,* 517]).

Language considerations play an important role in *Feux.* The Sainte-Barthélemy, for instance, is read as the sign of a dangerous semantic surplus, an over-determination of meaning, or death: it is the "signe plus grand / d'un excez sans mesure" (*Fers,* 1031-32). So extreme is the resulting disorientation of language that d'Aubigné momentarily appears to doubt his ability to write: "Où voulez-vous, mes yeux, courir, ville après ville, / . . . Quels mots trouverez-vous, quel style pour nommer . . . ?" (*Fers,* 1117-18). "Sauvé par grâce" (*Fers,* 155), he must invent a new, purified style and vocabulary; the former are disgraced and inadequate. With a similar intention, d'Aubigné reverses the customary process of reading in *Fers.* Ordinarily, reading proceeds from left to right, and meaning accumulates progressively. In the heavens, however, d'Aubigné situates himself and his reader ("nous") so that they are placed at the *right,* and atypically read from *right to left* the future in the stars: "A la gauche du ciel, au lieu de ces tableaux, / [les étoiles] font ce que nous lisons aprés dans les effects" (*Fers,* 1239-45). By reversing the normal order of reading, d'Aubigné reverses the causality of history. He knows effects *before* their causes, thus demonstrat-

---

[75]Calvin, "Epistre sur les Corinthiens," cited by Saussure, "La Notion des sacrements" in *Colloque Calvin* (Paris: PUF, 1965), 246 (my emphasis).

[76]Also, in *Vengeances,* the "poet explicitly encourages the impression that one is reading Scripture." Regosin, *D'Aubigné/s "Les Tragiques,"* 78.

ing his omnipotence in the text.[77] The future read in the stars is both God's divine "registre" and the *Tragiques* themselves, which record God's decree: "la vraye eternité . . . / C'est le registre sainct . . . / l'escrit des verités. / Tout y est bien marqué" (*Fers*, 1252-57). D'Aubigné sees, already inscribed in the heavens, that which he is writing. This can be construed either as meaning that his writing is merely derivative of the already-written or, more positively, as indicating that his writing is so effective that it merits inclusion on the heavenly rolls. This latter interpretation is made more plausible by the emphasis on d'Aubigné's privileged role as interpreter of sacred history. "Tout y est bien marqué, nul humain ne l'explique" (*Fers*, 1257), with one notable exception: d'Aubigné himself, who writes the *Tragiques* for the very purpose of deciphering God's edicts and thereby associating himself with the divine. This ability is, again, proof of his election: "Ce livre n'est ouvert qu'à la troupe angelique, / Puis aux esleus de Dieu" (*Fers*, 1258-59). Consequently, if his readers read correctly, they will find confirmation of their election in *Les Tragiques*.

Vengeance and Invention

D'Aubigné moves into *Vengeances*–the book and the act–fully empowered to express his writing self. His sources of *inventio* are two-fold. D'Aubigné enjoins the Lord to open the treasure-houses of truth and knowledge so that he may incorporate them into his writing: "Ouvre tes grands thresors, ouvre ton sanctuaire, / Ame de tout . . . / Ouvre ton temple sainct à moy, Seigneur, qui veux / Ton sacré, ton secret" (*Vengeances*, 1-4). He also draws upon a sense of worth and election which is, paradoxically, derived from his sin: "le mal bourgeonne en moy, en moy fleurit le vice, / Un printemps de pechés. . . . / Change moy, refai moy" (*Vengeance*, 33-35). Through his writing d'Aubigné acknowledges his rebirth and purified state. It is significant that simultaneous with d'Aubigné's invocation to the Lord he launches into the most extensive subjective confession of his sinful nature. It seems he speaks despite himself ("Que dans moy contre moy chantoit ma conscience," [*Vengeance*, 110]). He is, however, ultimately *affirmed* by such apparent self-negation, for in claiming to be merely "l'organe à la celeste voix" (*Vegeance*, 58), he still renders *his* writing the *only* vehicle for God's voice, and thereby valorizes his own narrative act. Like the doubled selves, sinner and saved, in *Feux* and *Fers*, this juxtaposition of apparently contrary concerns spatially portrays on the printed page the dialectical

---

[77]This attempt to read backward may be an attempt to counteract the Catholic, and also Renaissance tendency to view Nature as God's book. Du Bartas takes this view. (*La Sepmaine*, ed. André Baiche, I.v.289: "Le monde est un grand livre, où du souverain maistre / L'admirable artifice on lit en grosse lettre.") D'Aubigné appears to find this a reductive containment of the divine in the human, and wishes to reverse this trend. For more on reversed reading, see Chapter Five, in which Faeneste is shown to read "being" incorrectly, reversing it into misleading "appearance."

movement of salvation through sin which legitimized d'Aubigné's writing. In fact, for d'Aubigné writing is the vehicle and guarantor of salvation; death ensues from *ignoring* its imperative: "Que le doigt qui esmeut . . . / Resveille en moy . . . / Le zele. . . . / J'ay fuy tant de fois, j'ay desrobé ma vie / tant de fois, j'ay suivi la mort que j'a y fuie" (*Vengeances*, 101-6).[78]

Because of the active purpose of d'Aubigné's verses and because of the dynamic material from which they are shaped, d'Aubigné's written word is like the biblical Word in that its written form is a revocalization and perpetuation of his original utterance: writing attains a status equal to the privileged standing of orality, and the written witness is at least as efficacious as the eye-witnesses' secondary recounting.[79] It is an *écriture-parole*. As in our earlier discussion of d'Aubigné's treatment of images, in which he incorporates and reanimates them by commenting upon them through his written word, d'Aubigné here joins seeing (image) and hearing (word) to produce a unique form of writing.[80]

In *Jugement*, d'Aubigné continues to animate otherwise static images through his word, commanding the Lord to fulfill his writing (*Jugement*, 7-8). D'Aubigné, in this last book, pays deceptive lip-service to the subordinate posture of author as instrument; his word joins with the divine Word: "Donne force à ma voix, efficace à mes vers" (*Jugement*, 8). Yet by explicitly comparing himself with the stance of Christ at the Last Judgement, separating good on his right from evil on his left ("je retourne à la gauche, ô esclaves tondus" [*Jugement*, 81]), d'Aubigné thereby undermines such apparent humility and again succeeds in equating his word with that of the Lord. D'Aubigné becomes a judge, contrary to his statement in *Misères* that he would never play such a part.[81] Judgement occurs through writing. As a result, the reliable word always surpasses painterly artifice. D'Aubigné describes the

---

[78]Here d'Aubigné compares himself with Cain. However, having experienced a "schism of self" similar to that of Cain after his murder of Abel, d'Aubigné now finds self-unity through and in writing.

[79]"Scribes, qui demandez aux tesmoignages saincts / Qu'ils fascinent vos yeux de vos miracles feints / Si vous pouvez user des yeux et des oreilles / Entendez ces merveilles." *Vengeances*, vv. 1069-70.

[80]In terms of "interpersonal communication" which accords well with the highly personal, interventionist stance of d'Aubigné's writing self and in conjunction with theological and literary considerations, Walter Ong notes that an "oral-aural theology of revelation through the Word of God would entail an oral theology of the Trinity which could explicate the 'intersubjectivity' of the three persons in terms of communication conceived of as focused (analogically) in a world of sound rather than a world of space and light." (Walter Ong, *The Presence of the Word* [New York: Simon and Schuster, 1970], 181.) D'Aubigné's tripartite dialogue with God, writer and book, or between sinful self, redeemed self and reader, may figure a phenomenon like that which Ong describes.

[81]This is similar in intent to his preface in the *Histoire universelle*, where he elects to decide for himself, or at least to choose his own judge to adjudicate, the merit of history: "n'estant possible de plaire à tous à la fois, j'ay estimé qu'il se falloit régler aux meilleurs, et n'attendre pour juges aequinimes de ma louange, que ceux qui l'ont méritée pour eux," 1:2.

eve of the St. Bartholomew, evoking as in a painting the evils hidden beneath:

> Le somptueux apprest, l'amas, l'appareil feint,
> La pompe, les festins des doubles mariages
> Qui desguisoyent les coeurs et masquoyent les visages.

(Fers, 745-58).

Image is never adequate, and must be surpassed and redeemed by the word. A refusal to hear or to read the word is tantamount to damnation: "Payens, qui adorez l'image de la Nature / En qui la vive voix, l'exemple et l'Escriture / N'authorise le vrai. . ." (*Jugement*, 543-45). Writing is a register of misdoing, containing its own deceptions of rhetoric, fable and lie:

> Vrai est que les tyrans avec inique soin [rejètent]
> . . . La veritable voix . . .
> Avec art vous privant de . . . seures nouvelles. . . .
> Ils vous ont . . .
> Imbu vostre berceau de fables pour histoire.

(Jugement, 165-72)

Writing must be read dialectically in order to ensure salvation: "les livres sont ouverts, là paroissent les roolles / De nos sales pechés, de nos vaines paroles" (*Jugement*, 799-800). Images are "unauthorized," "inadequate," "invented" in the negative sense. They are incapable of portraying celestial reality.[82] For instance, concerning d'Aubigné's "tableaux célestes," Mitchell Greenberg observes that

> Painting . . . implies an immediate and total presence that is assimilable to our own reality. Thus, the mediation of the "tableaux" [mediation being a principle d'Aubigné, as a Calvinist, rejects] indicates a rhetorical ploy that changes history from a distanced intellectual past to an immediate present experience. . . . The picture appealing to our imagination rather than to reason is a corrupting influence.[83]

---

[82]They may, however, portray human reality: misdoings, punishments and sins are conveyed through images ("ces juges contemployent avec craintive face / Du siècle un vray portraict, du malheur le miroir" [*Fers*, vv. 1142-44]). These images are saturated with human pollution, and must be explicated by the word in order to be useful.

[83]Mitchell Greenberg, "D'Aubigné's 'Tableaux celestes,'" 18.

Icons (our paradigm for reading)[84] are to be distinguished from images just as idols, which the Calvinists abominate, must be forbidden in worship. The Greek word *eidolon* means something that is contained, idolatrous, a similacrum of presence that purports to be a totality. *Ikonen,* on the other hand, are not representational; they are symbolic. While the former pretend to the status of sign and yet, for d'Aubigné, never achieve the role of signifier, the latter are signifiers that bring us closer to the sign.[85] For d'Aubigné icons function in a truly Platonic sense, while images root us further in our limited, earthly existence. The revelation, according to Calvin, functions this way: "the revelation really [takes] place as the flesh directed beyond itself to something higher behind or beyond."[86] Literary and theological theory work much like each other in this respect.

Images do not function iconically, but *Les Tragiques* does. Refusing representation, it leads *beyond*: "ce ne sont [que] des tourmens inventés des cagots / Et presentés aux yeux des infirmes bigots; / La terre ne produict nul crayon qui nous trace / Ni du haut Paradis, ni de l'enfer la face" (*Jugement,* 957-60). Debating the nature of the pure sign, or image of God, quibblers and scoffers, the "docteurs" of the Sorbonne, waste their time in *Les Tragiques* wondering if the elect will ever look upon the face of God (*Jugement,* 1085-88). D'Aubigné denies the need to do so, claiming rather that the elect will mystically become consubstantial with the Lord. We thus see that the pictorial representation of God in the *Chambre Doree* is merely another inadequate *image-based* representation which d'Aubigné's writing now transcends. The gap between subject and object which such a depiction causes is now resolved through d'Aubigné's writing.

D'Aubigné likens his style of writing to Scripture in this literary rumination which comes as the culmination of all the other author-to-reader or author-to-self mediations we have discerned in *Les Tragiques*: "Enfans de vanité, qui voulez tout poli / A qui le stile sainct ne semble assez joli . . . / Endurez mes vocables / Longs et rudes" (*Jugement,* 361-65). He asserts himself unequivocally as the product of redeemed written expression.

[84]We adopt the icon as our paradigm for reading a text that is both literary and theological because that text, like the intent and actual artistic composition of the icon, leads beyond itself to something else. We may never accept the simple literal meaning of the text, but must accord it its full weight both as a literary document *and* as a signifying factor pointing to a theological truth.

[85]Calvin's doctrine of the mass separates the signifier from the signified (the mass from Christ) so that the sign appears as fractured. For this reason, I occasionally refer to signifier and signified as separate entities, even from the sign itself. This is a theological reading of a literary application of sign theory.

[86]Edward Willis, *Calvin's Catholic Christology: the function of the so-called "extra calvinisticum" in Calvin's Theology* (Leiden: E. J. Brill, 1966), 186.

This is why, for d'Aubigné, the theo-literary element of choice or election is so crucial. He can choose correctly: to write.[87]

The Shaping of the Self

By paradoxically sacralizing the secular through sinful agency, d'Aubigné shapes *himself* in the space between the word "livre" contained in the first verse of *Misères* and "Dieu," the last word of *Jugement.* This book is specifically linked with God's Word. The process is highly self-conscious. While *Les Tragiques* remains in an intermediate phase in d'Aubigné's literary creation due to the zones of tension between Calvinist adherence and self-expression which persist, it implicitly creates the permission for fiction of which d'Aubigné will avail himself in his later composition of the *Avantures.* It creates a "fictitious space,"[88] one in which the author may watch himself as he writes. Similarly, the incorporation of "tableaux" in *Les Tragiques,* and their legitimation through textual commentary, results in a *mise en question* of the reader's self:

> the tableaux . . . are both a "reading" and a "viewing" and depend equally on both these acts for their validation in the reader. Having succumbed to the basic illusion of virtual immediacy, the reader evidences the first break with a "unified" conception of his own "persona. . . ." The reader is distanced from his own intellect upon which is based his conception of himself, i.e. whole and separate, and he becomes the plaything of the text.[89]

The episodes of dreaming and doubling strewn throughout *Les Tragiques* are representative of this process, as well as emblematic of the dialectical resolution the writer operates between simultaneous sinful and redeemed selves. We also note the unusual temporal flexibility d'Aubigné inaugurates in this manner. The redeemed self does not chronologically follow the sinful self, but rather time folds back upon itself to clasp the two selves dialectically. This perception of time allows greater permission for the author's point of view in the narrative. In addition, it accords with the increased emphasis on the reader's role: to confirm election through correct reading.

---

[87]Published too late (in 1616) to possess efficacity for the Wars of Religion, d'Aubigné's text affirms its value despite its non-coincidence with event. The immediate presence of the spoken word is now coincidental; the text can stand as a literary monument without the need for oral endorsement.

[88]Selinger, *Calvin Against Himself,* 140. She also observes that "self-consciousness in Mannerist art is close to Calvin's self-consciously rhetorical expression of self-abnegation." D'Aubigné's revision of Calvinism as we read it may actually not be so far off his mentor's mark.

[89]Greenberg, "Tableaux célestes," 9.

Reading and writing are d'Aubigné's constant concerns in *Les Tragiques,* and they both have literary and theological connotations. *Les Tragiques,* like the Bible, has become the "source book" from which radiate out themes that d'Aubigné will further develop in his other works, just as it continually refers to its own components in the course of its construction. It inaugurates the inter-referential system of writing upon which d'Aubigné's conception of himself as a writer depends.

The entire *Tragiques* can be seen as a highly pictorial narrative framed as in an emblem. *Misères,* as we have seen, opens dialogically and with a historical frame. The intervening books all portray images of abuses of power and irreligiosity. The final book, *Jugement,* adds the caption to complete the emblem as it confirms the retribution meted out to sinners. At the very end, however, the frame dissolves, as d'Aubigné is united with God and his voice seems to be silenced. A perfect equivalence between words and things is reached, and no more speech is necessary. This ultimate silencing can also be interpreted as the effective empowering of d'Aubigné's textualized self, the book, to move into the world and act autonomously, apart from the historical d'Aubigné. Writing thus reaches its own apotheosis.

The writer as a literary figure appears to die in the last scene of *Jugement:* he is "ravy," "sans parole," and he "meurt," unable to look upon the glory of God. However, Christ has rendered "la mort morte."[90] Therefore, death is now life, and d'Aubigné's literary self is redeemed and resuscitated. D'Aubigné continues his theo-literary existence *in* God, while his book lives on, returning us to the first words of *Les Tragiques* and the renewed process of reading and salvation. D'Aubigné continues to exist in his book, due to the strategy of self-inscription he has devised: images of himself are incorporated into *Les Tragiques,* where they are animated by his word.

[90]Jacques Ellul, *L'Apocalypse: architecture en mouvement* (Brussels: Desclee, 1975), 146. Ellul comments upon d'Aubigné's phrase "la mort morte," noting that the Bible, too, should be interpreted through such a reversal, reading *backward* from the Apocalypse. In *Les Tragiques,* 129, God also tells us this; his book is to be read "bien au rebours."

4

Self and Other:
Writing and Scripture in
La Confession du Sieur de Sancy

THE PERMISSIONS FOR THE WRITING SELF which d'Aubigné progressively implants in *Les Méditations* and *Les Tragiques* enable the production of *La Confession du Sieur de Sancy,* a polemical work which is also richly confessional and evocative of the self. While a polemic work is not an atypical genre for a Calvinist writer, given the intense partisan climate of the Wars of Religion, this particular polemic is unusual in that it surpasses normal persuasive, rhetorical goals, and sets up a problematic relationship between the author and the multiplicity of voices heard in the text. Although a common tool of scholastic education is to encourage the speaker to envision himself in his opponent's position,[1] the strategy d'Aubigné employs in *Sancy* far outstrips such rhetorical tactics. First, he does not announce his intention to "try on" Sancy's *persona* as a didactic exercise, but rather forces the *reader* to discern gradually that the narrator and Sancy are not always the same. Secondly, d'Aubigné here meditates on issues which are of greater magnitude than *tours de force* in intellectual ingenuity: he is attempting to discuss the nature of truth and how, daringly, under certain circumstances fiction may be revalued as an aspect of truth.

Persona and Presentation

Following the example of Henri IV, Sancy, a nobleman, abjures Calvinism and converts to Catholicism in the hopes of securing personal and political gain. He thereby mingles profane with sacred considerations. A complex ambiguity results when d'Aubigné adopts the *persona* of Sancy, a character who is clearly repugnant to him. In so doing, he intentionally creates confusion in the narrative, for at times he speaks as Sancy, while at others he speaks as a distinct narrator. This is unlike other Calvinist and Catholic polemic in which, for the purpose of clarity and effectiveness, the speaking voice expresses its polemical beliefs without any possibility for confusion in the text. In d'Aubigné's construction, however, in which the interchange of pronouns creates the possibility of error. D'Aubigné revises polemic, including "multiple versions" of truth. He is not afraid to admit the option

---

[1]Perry Miller, *The New England Mind: The Seventeenth Century* (Boston: Beacon, 1961), 361.

of fiction, a new form of reading. The necessity for a strict interpretation may be seen as similar to Calvin's reason for opposing allegory, wherein the types may be misconstrued and misapplied and whereby a movement is effected *away* from the text to be explicated: "toute invention estrange par laquelle les hommes prétendent de servir à Dieu n'est autre chose que pollution de la vraye sainceté."[2] As Michel Foucault notes, such multiplicity causes textual uncertainty:

> la théorie de la représentation disparaît comme fondement général de tous les ordres possibles; le langage comme tableau spontané et quadrillage premier des choses, comme relais indispensables entre la représentation et les êtres, s'efface à son tour.[3]

Thus, when *Sancy* is contrasted with other, more conformist Calvinist polemical works, its audacity becomes evident. Marnix de Sainte-Aldegonde's *La Ruche française* has one narrating voice, a trenchant and wittily sarcastic narrator who enumerates Catholic abuses and attempts to discredit them through a logic of absurdity. Catholic misconduct, for instance, is flagrantly ridiculous and unconscionable. He asserts that "priestes and monkes may use all women at the pleasure."[4] While he does, for the sake of parody, purport to speak as his actual opponent would, he makes his sympathies obvious from the outset:

> For these Heretikes can steadfastly say, that they themselves are the Church of God. And to prove that, they introduce and bring in many goodly Texts out of Scripture: but they allege them only according to the letter: even as through the Church were nothing else . . . whereby is declared that the Church, with her power and authoritie, cannot be inclosed within the pales of Holy Scripture but that the Church may adde to the Scripture, but take from it what she thinks good, and therefore are many examples, and profound reasons alleged.[5]

Marnix does not change *personas* in mid-stream as does d'Aubigné in *Sancy,* and the voice he creates is quickly so repulsive that the reader establishes a simultaneous process of revision, in which the words uttered by the Catholics are immediately translated into the Calvinists' defense: "wherein is plainly declared that the Lutherans and Huguenots are heretiques, and ought to be burnt, notwithstanding that as well by Scripture, as by many examples, they shew *themselves to be the very Church of God.*"[6] Like many

---

[2]Calvin, *L'Institution,* I.x.24.

[3]Michel Foucault, *Les Mots et les choses* (Paris: Gallimard, 1966), 14.

[4]Marnix de Sainte-Aldegonde, *The Bee Hive of the Romish Church,* trans. George Gilpin the elder (London, 1636). Cf. II 4.

[5]Ibid., I 2 10.

[6]Ibid., I 10 (my emphasis).

other Protestant polemics, *La Ruche* conforms to exegetical practice: each enunciation derives its motivation from biblical passages with which it is thematically connected and spatially associated through the inclusion of these passages in the margin.[7] *Sancy* makes no such concessions to exegesis, allowing its fiction to wander far and wide, thus setting up the case for the lack of motivation and substance behind the fiction of its main character. Marnix's perspective is that of a non-literary creator; polemic is argument, without personal additions: "men ought to repose themselves and build upon the sincere Word of God only."[8] This is unlike d'Aubigné, who elaborates the Catholic privileging of tradition concomitant with Scripture into a system that reflects back upon the nature of writing[9] (that is, how may writing express truth if Scripture may be altered at the whim of church authorities?) while simultaneously contributing to Sancy's character as a man who performs his own revisions out of his desire to recant. Marnix merely notes the problem but does not incorporate it into a literary universe:

> . . . that the Pope may franckly ordaine and command contrary to the written ordinance and doctrine of the Apostle Paul . . . Christ never did command his Apostles to write.[10]

And although Marnix does point out the Catholic abuse of allegory

> . . . and sometimes they fetch a witnesse or authority out of Scripture by his neck, sometimes out of ye Fathers . . . as an Allegory . . . skipping and leaping like Monkies, from one place to another, and to helpe themselves with hands and feet . . . to wit, that the holy Church cannot err.[11]

he does not incarnate such abuse in the person of a fictional character, as d'Aubigné does with Sancy.

Henri Estienne's *Apologie pour Hérodote* contains clearly anti-Catholic elements and is even more straightforward than Marnix's work in condemning them. No fictional world is constructed here. Although his vocabulary is freighted with the same terms that d'Aubigné will develop into systems of fictional meditation (icons, idols, images, peintures, portraits), his presentation is limited to the strictly didactic:

---

[7]Some Catholic polemic works also include passages from the Bible, but they do not cite these passages in their entirety, as do the Calvinists. Marguérite de Navarre's poems often contain fragments of biblical passages.

[8]Marnix, I 4.

[9]Cf. *Sancy*, 238. "Je l'entends selon . . . le beau livre que vous avez fait imprimer, portant pour titre: *De L'Insuffisance des Sainctes Escritures.*" All other quotations in the text are from d'Aubigné, *Oeuvres.*

[10]Marnix, I 20.

[11]Ibid., 12.

Il n'y a Dieu quelconque en la présente image / . . . Ouvrage des humains, ne peut comprendre Dieu . . . / Pour bien rencontrer Dieu, pour trouver Jesus Christ / Il te faut feuilleter ton coeur et ton esprit / Ou lire incessamment les livres des prophètes . . . / Mais les baiseurs de bois qui leschent la peinture . . . / Périront à bon droit, comme ceus qui à tort / Ont adoré vivans les pourtrais de la mort.[12]

His narrating voice is single and constant, and while employing acerbic wit,[13] as do both Marnix and d'Aubigné, Estienne like Marnix avoids d'Aubigné's development of a critically humorous episode or observation into a full-fledged anecdote over which greater authorial manipulation may be exerted. That is, both Estienne and Marnix may note problems by cataloguing them. But fictional development allows for more intervention by the author, increased potential for him to sway the reader and impose his own viewpoint, partly because fictional characters are meant to be convincing and life-like. They *speak,* and have an effect through their declarations that "dumbe images" may not. Estienne bows to the Calvinist distrust of fiction that d'Aubigné, on the other hand, chooses to disregard. Estienne demurs concerning "ces fictions poétiques . . . [qu'il] confesse bien que . . . les poetes ont desguisé voire falsifié plusieurs histoires de la Bible . . .";[14] he will stick to the facts alone.

Du Plessis-Mornay's *De La Vérité de la religion chrestienne* continues the model of the writer's self-disavowal. His polemic, too, is univocal and didactic: "j'entreprens . . . par . . . ce peu que Dieu a mis en moy, de la convaincre et par ses Maximes et Tesmoignages propres sinon pour la faire revenir à meilleur sens."[15] For him, writing is as de Bèze mandates: "le fait [la Bible] est donné, non produit [vs. human writing]."[16] In fact, Du Plessis-Mornay's powers of invention are so consciously restricted that he refers to God as a "censeur"[17] of his writing. Unlike d'Aubigné, Du Plessis-Mornay intends to *assert* truth, rather than enter into the tricky, involved

[12]Henri Estienne, *Apologie,* I xxvii.

[13]We may compare this passage with Marnix's treatment of a similar theme: "Here again it . . . hath pleased our dearly beloved mother, the holy Church of Rome, to use her full and inestimable authoritie and power, and so without having any respect at all to that which is above written, hath . . . set to a certaine kind of serving of God, [as] Images, processions, palmes and palme bough, Albes . . . Miters . . . fooles hoodes . . . licking of rotten bones . . . and mumbling of *Pater Nosters* . . . before a dumb Image. . . ." *BeeHive,* I 15-16.

[14]For example, "quand nous lisons qu'Amadis, d'un bassin d'or qui avoit tousiours servi à laver les pieds, fit faire *l'image d'un dieu*. Et qui empescheroit Amadis de faire un *bassin* ou un *pot de chambre, de ce dieu,* aussi bien que de bassin *il avoit esté faict dieu?* Estienne, *Apologie,* I xiv-xv (my emphasis).

[15]Mornay, I 11.

[16]De Bèze, *Chrestiennes méditations,* 23.

[17]Mornay, *De La Vérité,* li recto.

process of *demonstrating* it: "qui aura leu seulement le titre de ce livre . . . s'il se veut ramentevoir combien de blasphèmes il oit contre Dieu et de sa Parole à toute heure. . . ."[18] He makes a dogmatic declaration, while d'Aubigné invites the reader into the process by which the right shall be ascertained (580).

Pierre Viret's *Des Cauteles* avoids any fictional invention. His strategy is to write a gloss upon Catholic doctrine. Ordinarily, Calvinists distrust glosses, for this is the scholastic procedure Catholics employ to interpret Scripture, with the result that the divine Word is deformed by their writing. Viret proposes to turn the tables and apply the strictures of their own technique to the Catholics:

> I have set them forth after the self-same manner and form as they are set down in the popish Masse book. . . . However, I am to beseech the Readers not to be lightly offended at them, although they seem very grosse and strange. Because I am to make them agree with the text, which is to be declared: and is in verie truth worthy the glose which shall be given thereunto which shall be . . . neat and pure.[19]

D'Aubigné surpasses the strategies of the other Calvinist writers because he is unceasingly aware of his *own* role to play in shaping the text. This is unlike the other Calvinists, for whom all writing other than Scripture is supplemental and open to suspicion, and for whom the sole book is God's, against which incomplete human writing stands in opposition:

> Car si on regarde combien l'esprit humain est enclin et fragile pour tomber en oubliance de Dieu, combien aussi il est facile à decliner en toutes espèces d'erreurs, de quelle convoitise il est mené pour se forger des religions estranges à chaque minute, de là on pourra voir combien il a esté nécessaire que Dieu eust ses registres authentiques pour y coucher sa vérité, à fin qu'elle ne périsse point par oubly, ou ne s'esvanouit par erreur, ou ne fust corrompue par l'audace des hommes.[20]

D'Aubigné, however, plays with the possibilities afforded him by writing, and in so doing develops strategies which permit the fuller articulation and expression of the writing self. The ease with which he moves back and forth from the role of Sancy to his narrating voice attests to a stronger self-conception.

The case for d'Aubigné's great innovations as contrasted with other Calvinist writers becomes more clear upon a close examination of *La*

---

[18]Ibid.

[19]Pierre Viret, *The Cauteles Canon and ceremonies* (London: Vautrollier, 1584), 111.

[20]D'Aubigné, *Sancy,* 280.

Confession du Sieur de Sancy. The title "confession" immediately instills ambiguity into the reader's notion of the text for, while this is a sort of confession, it is one made under false pretenses (we think Sancy is speaking, but he is a mere puppet animated by d'Aubigné's unavowed voice) for an unacknowledged ulterior motive (to convince the reader of the validity of the Calvinist stance over that of the Catholics). In addition, the speaker in a confession is customarily an "I" whose being relates with his utterance; here, it is a subverted "I," a "je" who is meant, in reality, to be construed in the third-person singular so that another "I," that of d'Aubigné, may surface. As Michel de Certeau queries concerning mystic expression, "is the 'I' a fiction of the Other which offers itself in its place?"[21]

Like the dualism of the other character's formulation, *Sancy* is divided into two sections. The first discusses the doctrines of the Catholic church, while the second analyzes Sancy's "personal" considerations in converting. In this sense, too, the work differs from an ordinary confession, for the focus is not squarely on the speaker, but more on the interplay of contemporary events and personalities. D'Aubigné redefines and broadens the confessional genre to include all of Catholicism, and not just Sancy, in his complaint. He simultaneously reveals the language employed by Catholics to be deceptive and reductive; holy sacraments become mere "things" to be recounted and are diminished to the human level (. . . "le sacrement de ma conversion. Je vous dis Sacrement, pour ce que vous m'avez promis de la faire conter" [576]). At the outset, then, the truly untrustworthy character in the text is the author himself, for he insists on duping his audience.

The signifying powers of language are now scattered and misleading ("ces signes seront une charge de livres; la chose signifiee, c'est l'esperance de parvenir" [576]). Sancy produces in the text signs without content. He is incapable of endowing them with reality. The reader quickly becomes aware of the need to listen to d'Aubigné's authorial voice behind Sancy's useless utterance, for d'Aubigné constitutes the only signifying system in the narrative. Sancy, who claims to be the signifier, is revealed to be the signified that d'Aubigné, the true signifier, designates. In this exchange, Sancy loses all ability to signify, to *mean* anything. His text, purportedly a confession, is repudiated and denigrated by its author, who calls it "ce petit avorton" (575), while the confessional information he is to divulge is equated with the base human functions: "ma declaration . . . laquelle je suis prest de signer de mon sang, à mes premieres hemorroides" (577). In *Les Tragiques,* the martyr Norris writes the story–a dynamic narrative–of his own salvation with the "trace" of his blood. No such use for Sancy's "sang," symbolic of his essence, is found here: Sancy produces nothing more than a vulgar, ineffectual image of "hémorroides." He engenders no

---

[21]Michel de Certeau, *Heterologies: The Discourse of the Other,* Theory and Interpretation of Literature, vol. 17 (Minneapolis: University of Minnesota Press, 1985), 96.

narrative but, exhibiting the Catholic tendency for enclosure of essence in things, merely further limits and abases his own humanity.[22] Similarly, Catholics are denied the ability to read correctly.[23] The final meaning of the book–that Sancy is duplicitous–thus only strengthens the case for the options of authorship, since the reader has to back down from his initial adversarial distrust of the author to concede the author's correct interpretation. The text thereby enacts, within the ranks of of its readers, the divisiveness that characterizes language in the sixteenth century ("les esprits des auditeurs furent mipartis" [575]). Words and things are separated; words no longer transparently exhibit that which they pretend to name. D'Aubigné thus stands at the threshold of an important historical transition, where he must come to terms with language's complexity and find a means of condoning it through literature.[24] As Michel Foucault observes in *Les Mots et les choses,*

> Mais à mesure que les choses s'enroulent sur elles-mêmes, ne demand-
> ant qu'à leur devenir le principe de leur intelligibilité et abandonnant
> l'espace de la représentation, l'homme à son tour entre, et pour la
> première fois, dans le champ du savoir occidental.[25]

By compelling the reader to join with him in resolving such problems, d'Aubigné makes the point that writing may nevertheless play a salubrious role if not yet (as is the case with the *Avantures*) a soteric one.

Through the elaborate interplay of floating pronouns and abruptly shifting speakers and interlocutors (for instance, we find such addresses as "j'advertis le Lecteur" and "Monsieur le Convertisseur, ne vous estonnez pas" in close proximity to each other [579-80]), d'Aubigné chooses to inaugurate a fundamental state of tension – predicated upon a free choice in reading–in his text. The reader is invited to decide whether he will read figuratively or literally, just as Sancy chooses according to his whim or

---

[22]For instance, he excoriates the reduction of the divine to a priapic cult object in the following account: "les instituteurs de nos cérémonies . . . adore[nt] le Dieu des jardins en tant d'endroits de la France: tesmoin Saint Foutin de Varailles en Provence, auquel on desdie des parties honteuses de l'un et l'autre sexe formées en cire. Le plancher de la chapelle en est fort garni, et quand le vent le fait entrebattre, cela desbauche un peu les dévotions en l'honneur de ce Saint." *Sancy,* 634.

[23]". . . Ce livre qui est au rang des traditions, doit estre mieux creu que la Bible, car comme prescha ces jours le Curé de Sainct Gervais: les traditions sont plus croyables que le Vieux et Nouveau Testament, attendu qu'ils sont authorisez par les traditions, non pas les traditions par eux." *Sancy,* 646.

[24]Concerning this period of historical transition, it is possible to find indications of it in other authors as well. Pierre Villey, editor of the *Essais,* remarks in his prefatory comment on Montaigne that "il n'est aucunement question dans ce chapitre du 'peintre du moi,' et l'on remarque que les phrases où il parle de lui-même sont des additions postérieures à 1580, souvent de 1588." *Les Essais de Montaigne* (Paris: PUF, 1965), 11. This is the period in which d'Aubigné begins to write.

[25]Foucault, *Les Mots,* 15.

need. Sancy, for instance, approves the convenient mis-reading in the following anecdote:

> S'il trouve . . . qu'une . . . Dame de la Cour sent en son ame desolee qu'elle ne puisse passer d'une grande, catholique et universelle luxure, n'a elle pas pour se consoler comme Saincte Marie Ægyptienne, qui depuis douze ans jusques à l'aage du mespris, ne refusa homme (585)?

It is noteworthy that d'Aubigné ordinarily includes a preface which situates the authorial "I" in some context (cf. "Aux lecteurs" in *Les Tragiques* and the "Préface" in the *Avantures*). Here, however, to facilitate the technique of pronominal confusion he does *not* include a preface, but immediately begins to speak as an unspecified "on," and then as an unidentified "je" whose nature the reader must struggle to determine for himself: ("On n'a que trop debattu en ce temps . . . Mais je respons . . ." [580]; "Ayant deliberé de mettre en lumiere ma Confession . . ." [575]). This decision has implications for the articulation of a more complex self-image, resulting in an increasingly self-conscious writing style. Through the multiple voices d'Aubigné may speak with, or the innumerable roles he is thereby licensed to play, he displays his greater concern with "artfulness." The reader is thus required to enter into each of the roles, attend to all of these voices, in order to make sense of the work. A space between dogma and individual action is thus inserted, separating that which is decreed from that which one decides for oneself, through the medium of Sancy, into d'Aubigné's literary corpus. This creates the first major discernible rift between the Calvinist view of writing as mere exegesis and amplification, and d'Aubigné's ever more personalized model of literary expression. Rather than mandate a dogmatic, univocal interpretation of texts, d'Aubigné elects to display his *process* of writing, and concurrently compels the reader to re-enact it. The reader, through his involvement, consequently moves in and through d'Aubigné's text in an iconic movement: he grasps the polemic substance, but because of its complicated presentation he is also forced to envisage the writer behind the words, the consciousness textually miming itself in action, the complete sign rather than the signifier alone. D'Aubigné moves toward modernity in this respect for, as Rosamund Tuve notes, formerly

> coherence [was] imposed by the author's meaning, by subject and not by stuff . . . This recognition of author's interpretation as controlling subject must be distinguished from the modern author's portrayal of his own process in interpreting or feeling. . . . The earlier author's subject was different. . . . [It] was still "his meaning," not "himself seeing it."[26]

---

[26]Rosamund Tuve, *Elizabethan and Metaphysical Imagery* (Chicago: University of Chicago Press, 1947), 45.

The oscillation and interchange of subject and object, viewer and viewed established in *Sancy* by the ambiguity of voices that express, or comment upon, Sancy's stance produces a more open-ended reading than is customarily desired in polemic writing, which usually intends to solidify the reader in one position. It is clear that d'Aubigné himself, while willing this multivalence, must experience some questions as to his faithfulness as a Calvinist for, although the ultimate effect of the polemic is a negative reading of *Sancy,* the concatenation of various viewpoints is not always instructively unravelled for the reader so that at times it is not clear who is talking or how we are to construe his utterance. However, d'Aubigné may be creatively re-reading Calvinism here. De Bèze, for instance, indicates that the only possible purpose for debased humanity might be its ability to stand in utter opposition to Christ's life and, in that dialectical sense, to magnify his glory:

> J'ay tout gasté, j'ay tout destruit et ruiné. Et pourtant, ô Dieu, recommance ton oeuvre comme tout de nouveau, sois le créateur de cet homme intérieur, pour la seconde fois, desployant ta force qui pénetre jusques au fond de moy-mesme.[27]

By provisionally putting himself in the place of the shameful Sancy, d'Aubigné ultimately rights the balance, antithetically attesting to the Calvinists' rectitude. He shows how the Catholics resort to sophistry and an inauthentic presentation of self:

> Je di ces choses pour vous et pour moy, Monsieur, pour vous prier que les combats de nos consciences ne sortent point dehors, si la conscience pique pour esclatter, ne la pouvant rendre morte, il la faut pour le moins endormir (663).

He also demonstrates how Catholics put in place a strategy of textual mystification:

> Il y a trente ans qu'on laissoit desrober des greffes des Cours de Parlements tous les procés criminels desquels ce dangereux livre est plain, et vérifié. Mais aussi bien n'y a il pas moyen d'en estouffer la memoire, et faire conter telles choses pour fables tant que les tesmoins oculaires vivront? Que faut-il donc faire? Je suis d'advis que l'on choisisse quelque style bien fleury . . . de là, pour desguiser l'histoire. . . (654).

Because of the words d'Aubigné puts into his mouth, Sancy eventually appears as thoroughly reprehensible and untrustworthy, and the Huguenots, as a result, seem much more sympathetic than the Catholics: Sancy admits,

---

[27]De Bèze, *Chrestiennes,* 76.

d'autre part que les Huguenots, au lieu de faire mourir les hommes pour leurs erreurs en la foy [comme nous les ferions], s'amusoyent à prier Dieu pour eux (654-55).

The mutual relationship of, and eventual discrimination between, fact and fiction is what finally enables the reader to view Sancy pejoratively. Sancy is revealed to be a fiction, citing, for instance, the absurd and burlesque play contained in Book Two as "une piece . . . de Theologie moderne . . . digne . . . de tenir place en cette marqueterie" (623). In like fashion, his speech is inauthentic, altering always with his whims: "mais je change trop de discours en parlant du changement de conscience" (622). He epitomizes the Renaissance conception of fiction as lie or untruth (*feindre*). His statements are never realized, and he is incapable of establishing proofs for his assertions: "nous ne pouvons pas dire beaucoup sur le poinct de la Transubstantiation; car elle est plus malaisee à pouver qu'à prononcer" (620). He fills himself with others' lies and deceptions, and relies on mere appearance for his assessments: "Ceux ci sont pleins de discours agencés seulement pour l'apparence . . . les autres pour persuader" (648). In addition, he never reads completely. Rather, he chooses his authorities through a patchwork of citations removed from context: "tenez, je vous donne un petit centonnet que je desrobai à Lucain. . . . J'en faisois davantage, tout desrobez en divers autheurs. . ." (664). He misconstrues sacred text in a risible fashion:

> Daniel, comme dit son livre, preschoit à fenestres ouvertes, ayant la face tournee vers l'Orient: O que je vis un jour triompher M. le Convertisseur sur ce texte. C'est un merveilleux homme, quand il trouve un poinct de Matheologie propre pour ses allegories. C'est, disoit-il, que comme Daniel, pour faire ses prieres, tournoit sa face vers le Soleil levant, il faut toujours qu'un galand homme adresse tousjours ses devotions au Soleil levant, et aux grandeurs naissantes (636).

He is also guilty of literalizing, which leads to a misapprehension of meaning. In the following account, Sancy's reliance on the guarantees of relics leads him to misread or, at least, to inappropriately apply the relics' presence to the episode: Several court "mignons" are sporting with each other,

> pren[ant] leurs exercices accoustumez sur un lict, deux autres sur un autre lict . . .

when lightning strikes from heaven

> le foudre les partagea, car il en tua deux et laissa le troisieme à demi mort; à tous trois le coup entroit par le trou de la verge et sortoit par celui du derriere. Or voici de quoi faire dresser les cheveux à la

teste d'un Reformé, car les deux qui n'eurent point de mal avoyent chacun un chappelet . . . Je presuppose que La Passe (qui ne fut que demi mort deux mois) avoit perdu la moitié du sien. Voilà pour authoriser les reliques (609-10).

In addition, Sancy's family resemblance to Faeneste, who is dangerously credulous, preferring appearance over being, is borne out by numerous statements that are reiterated almost verbatim in the *Avantures*. He refers to the same "fable des estrons" (629) and, like Faeneste, he mutilates language so as to begin mass with a floating conjunction ("et") removed from context (631). Sancy's character is one-dimensional, like that of Faeneste. An actual, historical *personnage*, the Sieur de Sancy is here reduced to a puppet duplicating the experience of Jean de Sponde, another Calvinist turned Catholic. History is also, thereby, substantially fictionalized. A living person is reduced to a manipulable object. The "je" subject of *Sancy* becomes the true object of the narrative. Sancy becomes a sort of *prosopopeia*, a speaking allegory of betrayal who symbolizes the abuses inherent in theo-literary infidelity. His character is, at times, engulfed by his own words. Indeed, he disparagingly labels theology as "troulogie," reducing to mere "holes" (with their concomitant sexual connotations) the things of the divine. Sancy is characterized by a reductive mentality. In addition, he has no autonomy and, like Faeneste, no authority. He founds his actions and opinions on the words and writings of sources the text reveals to be unreliable ("et voici les passages que m'a donné M. le Convertisseur, pour m'asseurer en cette opinion nouvelle . . ." [580]), allowing himself to be swayed by the sham spiritual director's "paroles dorees . . . et couvertes" (663-66).

Although he appears to have a voice, Sancy's utterance is actually, ultimately, pre-empted by the collaboration between author and reader, who concur in imposing the Calvinist over the Catholic discourse. In *Sancy*, d'Aubigné follows the distinction between *verbum* and *logos* that Calvin emphasizes: the *verbum* reifies expression as a thing, while the Johannine *logos* clearly epitomizes a *process*, an intentionality and an interconnectedness. Sancy attends only to the outer semblance of an utterance (the *verbum*), omitting to penetrate to its true meaning (*Logos*). Just as Faeneste will later be revealed as a mere unmotivated image overwhelmed by the power of Enay's discourse, Sancy represents the Catholic tendency toward enclosure and consequent diminution.[28] For instance, he reduces the crucial doctrine

[28]Calvin treats Scripture as *sacrament* in its potency and unchangeability, because the divine inheres in it. Catholics separate that phenomenon, attempting to think *symbolically* in such a way as to make bread and God actually *conjoin* in the mass. All they are left with, de Bèze castigates them, is a mere *thing*; enclosure rather than connectedness, for by changing the "accidents" (attributes) of the elements, they rupture the role of the species as *signifiers* of the divine. Their God becomes, as Estienne puts it, "un Dieu de paste." *Apologie*, 122.

of transubstantiation in this way: "la Transubstantiation . . . Or voici les argumens que j'ay cherché de mon invention. Pourquoy soubs le nom de Dieu ne peut on changer la substance de toutes choses, veu que sous le nom du Roy on . . . fait tous les jours de si estranges Transubstantiations?" (620). Here fiction has a negative cast: it stands for insubstantial and shadowy sketches of reality which, somehow, never achieve life. The proliferation of words, unanimated by the Word, is ultimately both futile and deceptive. This enlarges the zone of tension within which d'Aubigné writes. If scriptural writing is the *logos,* and if Calvinism condones only writing that exposes the *logos,* then by incorporating secular considerations (the life of Sancy) into his text, d'Aubigné mingles divine considerations with profane substance. The fact that d'Aubigné here chooses the satirical genre only compounds the problem, for satire, employed customarily to unmask human deceptions or delusions, is purely a secular genre and one which, Calvinists hold, should not deal with religious matters. D'Aubigné needs to overcome the limits Calvinists such as de Bèze place on literary expression:

> Beza acknowledge[s] that humanism [and] humanistic knowledge is not an end in itself, but is to be used as an aid to Christian theology. . . . Errors and excess come from humanism when the humanist violates the divine boundaries of his discipline and devotes himself to vain speculation. . . . The message of *Abraham sacrifiant* [is] clear: as Abraham had been willing to sacrifice his beloved son, even so should Beza be willing to sacrifice his promising future as a humanist.[29]

However, it is paradoxically *through* d'Aubigné's fiction that Sancy's fiction is unmasked and demolished. By pretending to represent the Catholic, d'Aubigné constructs Sancy's existence as a feeble fiction, based on others' words and assessments, with no true coherence or core to his existence. Consequently, this resort to fiction on d'Aubigné's part is, in his eyes if not in the eyes of other Calvinists, *valorized* as a new, powerful tool in polemic warfare. Its enhanced status (due to its quantitative effectiveness, whether or not Calvinism approves of it) contributes to the permissions for literary creation which d'Aubigné is developing. The juggling act between authorial and invented *personae* is demanding, and attests to a great deal of self-awareness in d'Aubigné's writing as well as the need for constant guarding of the self lest he pierce through the pretext of Sancy. In fact, in one location d'Aubigné appears to "forget himself"; that is, he forgets that he is supposed to speak for Sancy, and inserts an explicit reference to *himself* as author, rather than Sancy as confessor, into the text: La Ruffie, a courtier, recounts to the King

[29]John Bray, *Theodore Beza's Doctrine of Predestination* (Nieuwkoop: B. de Graaf, 1975), 42.

Mais . . . [il] envoya ces recommandations particulierement à un
de ses compagnons. . . . Il [luy] faisoit souvenir . . . d'un sonnet
qui fut trouvé attaché sur le col de cette pauvre beste, au poinct que
le Roy arrivoit à Agen; si bien qu'il se presenta lui et son sonnet
que vous verrez ailleurs. *Il fit souvenir l'Autheur*. . . (597-98; my
emphasis).

The actual narrator is Sancy, "je," who refers to La Ruffie, "il." La Ruffie
speaks of *another* "il" who, we learn later in the text, is d'Aubigné himself.
La Ruffie may be referring to "l'autheur" of the sonnet or, in the vague
and indeterminate mention, to the "autheur" of *Sancy*. The two "il's" are
here oddly conflated, creating even further confusion. D'Aubigné's possibilities for creative manipulation of his text are thereby expanded.

That literary considerations are, indeed, at stake in *Sancy* is evident.
Sancy continually refers to patristic writings; his Convertisseur is constantly
bringing him new material meant to strengthen his conversion, and the
themes of reading and writing are incessantly rehearsed in the text.
D'Aubigné's polemic raises issues which are secondary to his professed
main concern. Additionally, the stylistic fireworks with which d'Aubigné
communicates his message–puns, *jeux de mots,* transposition of letters (e.g.
"garce" and "grace"), incorporation of other genres (particularly salacious
songs)–run counter to the typical Calvinist distrust of such resorts. Calvin
points out that the books of Scripture are

baillez sous paroles contemptibles, sans grande éloquence, de peur
que, s'ils eussent esté fondez et enrichis d'éloquence, les iniques
eussent calomnié que la seule faconde eust regné en cest endroit,[30]

indicating that all writing should attempt to be similarly free from contamination. It is also significant that a projected chapter of *Sancy* is omitted from
the published text.[31] The chapter is entitled "Des Escritz licentieux" and
is composed of satirical epigrams. The explicit linking of literary with
theological considerations in this chapter explains the probable cause for
its deletion, since Geneva, where the book is published, did not favor the
proliferation of licentious or secularly-based manuscripts. Since neither
sheds light on the *culte,* they were deemed worthless.

Thus, d'Aubigné chooses to write under the guise of a polemic, a genre
sanctioned by the heated contemporary religious climate. Within the genre,
as self-conscious and reflective author, he debates the nature of fiction.
D'Aubigné poses interesting problems concerning the nature of writing.
By subversively wearing another's *persona* with the aim of ultimately rendering

---

[30]Calvin, *L'Institution,* I.i.vii.

[31]The chapter can be found in manuscript form in the Archives Tronchin, coll. œ 151,
at the Bibliothèque de Genève.

the other untrustworthy, d'Aubigné explores the possibility that writing may be duplicitous, for it initially seems that we are to follow Sancy as his character develops through speech, rather than be on our guard against him. After all, he presents his text as a confession: Sancy begins in mid-stream, alerting us that he has "deliberé de mettre en lumière ma Confession," and invites us into his private existence: "oeuvre que je puis vanter n'estre pas *publici saporis*" (575). Baroque changeability of roles and protean metamorphoses are devalued throughout d'Aubigné's work,[32] yet here he sets up the very conditions which favor such changes. Also, by relating Sancy's story even while condemning it, d'Aubigné perpetuates it. He does so not to value it, however, but rather to contain it in an implicit "frame" just as Faeneste, in the *Avantures,* appears as an image dominated by Enay's encircling discourse. D'Aubigné employs such techniques constantly, with the aim of showing *certain kinds of speech* to be nefarious. It is actually d'Aubigné's writing, containing and parsing Sancy's duplicitous speech, that unravels the mystery and finally shows Sancy as insubstantial. Thus, through an apparent devaluing of writing's reliability–the incorporation of Sancy and the reader's temporary gullibility faced with his transcribed speech–d'Aubigné enhances its power. By resolving such textual contradictions, d'Aubigné is like Michel de Montaigne, who, in III, 2, acknowledges that his changeable nature is actually a continuum. Montaigne can embrace and reconcile his internal contradictions: "je ne peins pas l'estre, je peins le passage. . . . Je pourray tantost changer, non de fortune seulement, mais aussi d'intention."[33] Writing is the medium for the comprehension of the self. Writing's interiority, the private self, is privileged over Sancy's speech, the public self, which is always linked with deceitful action and deceptive interpretation: "là dessus avec une artificieuse et sacree prevarication il se laissoit vaincre d'une violence bien simulee" (619). Writing may only be publicly proffered once one has come to terms with the private conception of self: ". . . si particulier en usage, je me rend[s] public en cognoissance." Contrarily, Sancy's mentions of writing are always to expurgated and distorted versions:

> J'advoue pour traditions les livres corrigés par le Sacro-sainct Concile de Trente. . . . C'est un resultat du Concile de Trente, selon lequel estoit commandé à tous Imprimeurs de corriger les plus rudes passages, par lesquels les Saincts Peres ont barbouillé la croyance de l'Eglise, avec un catalogue des Sentences qu'il est bon d'estouffer ou restituer, afin que les Heretiques ne s'en servent (582).

Like Montaigne, d'Aubigné suggests that writing may be valued as an art, rather than as artifice, if self-comprehension is at its origin. This interplay of public and private self-presentation is a major theme of *Sancy.* The ability

---

[32]Cf. *Les Tragiques,* "Princes," vv. 713-864.

[33]Montaigne, *Essais,* III 2 805.

to "estre autre," and d'Aubigné's audacity in impersonating Sancy, arise from a multiple yet unified version of the self which d'Aubigné shares with Montaigne: "je puis desirer en general estre autre."[34] The strategy of temporarily assuming the other's voice is one which works toward an extension of the possibilities for language use. Two speaking voices have greater virtuosity than one, and the simultaneous meshings and gaps existing between the two foster a creative tension that enriches language. They also introduce a different, dynamic conception of time, in which Renaissance man, unlike his static medieval predecessors, evolves through his language. Texts, rather than didactic and definitive, become through the ludic proliferation of possibilities *open* to the future. As in *Les Tragiques,* d'Aubigné asserts his writing power through prophetic prediction: his *apophéties,* like God's glance, take in past, present and future. Similarly Sancy's shifting selves, through the time of the text, reveal him in his past, present and future over-determination. The high degree of self-consciousness in d'Aubigné's literary creation results in a sophisticated self-formulation. In fact, literary works are not only the vehicle for the expression of the self, but are indeed the actual self in a sort of intellectual consubstantiality: "Je n'ay pas plus faict mon livre que mon livre m'a faict . . . Aux fins de renger ma fantaisie . . . et la garder de se perdre . . . il n'est que donner corps et mettre en registre. . . ."[35] (Interestingly, the way that Sancy comes to believe in transubstantiation is through man's protean nature. This is a reduction of a divine subject to a human metaphor.) In the formulation of the self that Montaigne posits, however, the self must be coherent, unlike that of Sancy, for changes in the self will otherwise alter one's discourse. Of course, Sancy rationalizes that he has always been one and the same, because always constant in his changeability. The intention here is the reverse of Montaigne's tolerance of mutability as incorporating facets of one unified entity. Sancy says, "c'est n'est pas changer que de suivre tousjours mesme but. J'ay eu pour but, sans changer, le profit, l'honneur, l'aise et la seurté" (641).

The themes of writing and of misreading are thus important in *Sancy,* and will be in the *Avantures,* as d'Aubigné begins to elaborate a new perspective on literary creation. In his status of supplementarity to the Bible, and in his rejection as a Catholic of biblical phraseology,[36] Sancy's confessional speech is meant to demonstrate "l'insuffisance des . . . Escriptures" (577) but, through d'Aubigné's intervention, will actually

---

[34]Ibid., 813.

[35]Ibid., II 18 665. Cf. also d'Aubigné's preface to the *Tragiques* for his co-existence with the book.

[36]It is noteworthy that, in Sancy's parodic portrayal of Protestants, he always causes them to speak in language that is intensely biblical in nature. For instance, we find a Huguenot claiming "or il est dit: 'ma maison est maison d'oraison, mais ils en ont fait une caverne de brigands,'" *Sancy,* 628. D'Aubigné may be distinguishing himself both from the one-dimensional, superficial Sancy and from those cardboard-seeming Catholics here.

enhance their stature as well as that of d'Aubigné himself. This is indeed a battle of books. Scripture, the patristic writings, the "livres de l'Eglise" as opposed to the "canoniques Huguenots," are repeatedly referred to, and some events such as the Council of Trent are designated as being involved with censorship: "je dis qu'ils n'escrivoyent point hardiment en ce premier temps, et pourtant j'advoue pour traditions les livres corrigés par le Sacro-sainct Concile de Trente" (582). The very first chapter of *Sancy* introduces the question of books and authority as crucial to Sancy's conversion. Writing can be of two sorts, duplicitous and reliable. It is apparent, through the laughingstocks the text makes of such self-serving characters, that such sources, unbeknownst to him, are of the former quality. Writing may err, and must be rendered accountable:

> Qui pis est, quelques Docteurs . . . qui furent choisis pour cette reformation, se sont reformés eux mesmes, et ont confessé par escrits imprimez que l'un d'eux en avoit changé pour sa part six cents et tant de passages (583).

Unlike other Calvinist writiers, however, d'Aubigné does not ground the validity of writing in the authority of doctrine, but rather dares to found writing's legitimacy on a sure sense of the saved self. The self is dialectically redeemed from sin through the confession and catharsis effected in his writing. And, as Harold Bloom asserts, "a state of rhetoricity or word-consciousness . . . negates fallen history."[37]

Reading and Mis-reading

The self-conscious reflections about language found in *Sancy* testify to d'Aubigné's need to rationalize his personal use of authority. He needs to dodge the charge of textual tampering that other Calvinists might level at him. In their misapplication of Scripture, Catholics point to an abuse of writing. The Catholic church dares to expurgate the biblical text, interdicts access to Scripture ("mesdames les affetees, si je vous trouve entre les mains une Bible ou un nouveau Testament, je vous baillerai de mon fouet" [583]) and, at times, favors apocryphal books over canonical writing:

> Balize d'Anjou, qui menaçoit son fils d'excommunication, s'il sçavoit qu'il leust une ligne de la Saincte Escriture, notamment des Commandemens: enfin par l'intercession de l'Aubraye, bon Catholi-que, il lui fut permis de lire les Machabees (584).

D'Aubigné must take care not to emulate Catholic misuse of language, whereby Scripture is altered ("on feroit doubter s'il est permis de changer les paroles des Docteurs et quelque peu du texte des Anciens. Il faut

---

[37]Bloom, *Map of Misreading,* 138.

maintenir que ouy et que l'Eglise doit changer le vieil et le nouveau
Testament" [583]); preaching is fabulous and sensational rather than scriptural

> (ces choses semblent absurdes, mais elles font ce bien au peuple,
> qu'aprés elle il ne trouve absurde aucune absurdité. Et c'est pourquoi
> Sainct Paul appelle la prédication de telles choses la folie de la
> prédication [584])

and texts are misread so as to construct literary "indulgences" for misdoing

> (la légende des Saincts est le jardin des ames desolees, comme les
> images le livre des ignorans. . . . Un galand homme qui [vole]. . .
> s'il se trouve que son ame . . . ne puisse changer de vie, il y a en
> la legende au chapitre de l'Annonciation, l'exemple d'un Chevalier,
> qui voloit sans pitié pauvres et riches, et estoit quitte pour dire tous
> les jours une fois, ave Maria [585]).

D'Aubigné's reaction to Catholic misinterpretation appears strong, and
typically Calvinist, here. He seems to oppose the very permissions of which
he will avail himself when writing the *Avantures*. For instance, Sancy
defends the use of "contes grivoises" in preaching, for the purpose of
holding the audience's attention; he cites with approval the instance of the
"huyle d'amour" (584), a *topos* with distinctly scabrous connotations that
a priest associates with a religious matter. D'Aubigné employs syllogisms
to render Sancy's argument risible: "ainsi il a pleu à Dieu sauver les croyans
par la folie de la predication: la predication de la legende est folie de la
predication: Ergo Dieu veut sauver les croyans par la folie de la predication"
(585).

In similar fashion, d'Aubigné's style in *Sancy* seems plain, unadorned
and functional with few rhetorical flourishes, albeit a good deal of satirical
wit.[38] Even so, his style does not equate with the "plain style" by the very
fact of his espousal of Sancy's language and character in order to write the
polemic. The crucial distinction of, and empowering rationalization for,
this technique can be found in the schism between words and things. The
text becomes a battleground on which words motivated by truth, the Word,
suppress words motivated by illusory representationality, or images.
D'Aubigné is demonstrating, however, that such fictions, while not perhaps
at the time explicitly valorized, can be operative and can be positive,
depending on the end for which they are used. Fictions can dramatize
conflicts to be resolved and can lend impetus to the narrative. In the
distance they take from both author and reader, they may solicit involvement,
as well as interpolate an intellectual space within which the author may

---

[38]He distrusts additions and artifice: "quand donc ces Prélats voyent de telles inventions,
qui ne sont pas assez bien composées ou colorées, ils les doibvent raccoutrer, polir et faire
valoir." *Sancy*, 271.

reflect on his act of literary creation. Fictions construct a protective arena for the *essai* of the self. D'Aubigné would not trouble to include such a quantity of similar anecdotes, in such detail, both here and in the *Avantures,* were he not interested in experimenting with the functions such fictions may serve. Sancy and the Catholics are always equated with pejorative images, or fictions; they are unreflective and have no inner coherence. Like their doctrine, to d'Aubigné's mind, they simply *make no sense.* They are non-productive, passive entities upon whom d'Aubigné's word, animated by personal and religious considerations, proposes to operate. Descriptions of the Catholics are often made through word-plays or coarse epithets that d'Aubigné shares with the reader, implicitly signalling the Catholics' inability to read or discern that they are, themselves, the butts of these textual jokes.[39] Catholics misread because they have no critical capacities, d'Aubigné asserts. An example of the way in which Catholics mis-take words is found in the anecdote of the Bishop of Xainctes and the Abbess, who have a unique manner of performing pious works:

> l'Evesque et l'Abbesse de Xainctes,
> Pour faire oeuvres pies et sainctes,
> Vont au silence fort souvent.
> La plus finette du Couvent
> Y fait un trou, et les espie,
> Puis voyant presser flanc à flanc,
> Le roquet noir, le surcot blanc,
> Vit bien que c'estoit oeuvre pie.
>
> (617)

Sometimes, even worse, misconstruing words is actually *non*-reading: Sancy brags, "je luy ay appris à parler des Peres *sans les avoir leus*" (624). Catholics favor allegorical developments; M. le Convertisseur's absurd mis-reading of the book of *Daniel* to justify how quickly he switches political masters is one example (636). Along with spiritual and intellectual discernment, they lack any sense of attachment to the text at hand and are constantly corrupting Scripture. They do not read discriminately; in fact, the only use for books at the Sorbonne Faculté de Théologie is not for reading but rather for dropping on the floor to wake the audience (620). As Sancy notes, "il fait bon *lire* ce livre *sans l'examiner,*" (646; my emphasis) a contradiction in terms typical of his character. Catholic discourse is fractured, as misleading as the hiatus effected in the following anecdote:

---

[39]E.g. "Les Catholiques se roidissent comme beaux vits d'azes," *Sancy,* 635; "– à quoy on connoist aujourd'huy une belle ame?–Bel asne, mon ami." *Sancy,* 624. "– Voilà le Baron de Solignac qui passe.–C'est tout un: c'est un des mes porcs d'eslite.–Tu veux dires des Prosélites, fausse vesse que tu es!" *Sancy,* 628.

J'ay leu les sermons amoureux de Monsieur St. Panigarole, et ne croy point ce que les Heretiques disent de son bardache. Quant à sa maistresse, pour laquelle il commença son sermon ainsi: "C'est pour vous, belle, que je meurs," je ne reprouve point cette galanterie; car il adjousta quelque pause aprés, disoit Jesus-Christ à son Eglise (647).

If "allegorical characters are conventionally 'seduced' by images,"[40] these images in *Sancy* are seduced by allegories. Allegories tend to be secular in types and expression,[41] if not in motivation; even the popular *Ovide moralisé* upon which Catholics dote seeks to find divinity in the actions of men or in anthropomorphically-determined mythological figures. D'Aubigné is clearly expressing an anti-image bias which accords well with Calvinist anti-representationality. Images are a type of counter-productive mediation for d'Aubigné, who proposes to subvert them through the power of discourse.

Sancy, incapable of critical discrimination,[42] becomes a futile voice in the text. His speech is ultimately silenced and pre-empted by the progressive alienation d'Aubigné effects between him and the reader. His status becomes progressively anecdotal in the narrative; he is, despite his pretensions to a narrating role, a mere image upon which others act and comment. He becomes the tale others tell of him, as will be the case with Faeneste. An anecdote in *Sancy* that acts as a paradigm for the reversal of the subject into object, of the narrator into narration, is the dialogue between Mathurine and Perron:

M. . . . me feras-tu dire que ton frere te vendit à l'Abbé de Tyron? Veux-tu que je *conte de toy* et de ce beau parrain de l'amour sacré autant de sodomies. . . (626; my emphasis).

Sancy himself is like the possessed woman of whom he tells the story. This simple villager claims to be inhabited by demons. The local clergy determines that reading aloud from the Bible or the application of a crucifix to her body will cause Satan within her to cry out, if she is truly possessed. However, in the course of this test, one playful and skeptical priest decides to substitute his key for the cross, and to read a salacious tale in Latin instead of the Vulgate verses. The woman responds, nevertheless, as though the true test were made, screaming in agony at both the key

[40]John Guilleroy, *Poetic Authority* (Chicago: University of Chicago Press, 1985), 39.

[41]U. Milo Kaufmann, *The Pilgrim Progress and Traditions in Puritan Meditations,* vol. 163 of *Yale Studies in English,* ed. Benjamin C. Nangle (New Haven: Yale University Press, 1966), cf. pp. 6 and 162. John Bunyan, for example, "is an unusual Calvinist in that he reads Scripture as did the medieval church: to tap the world about him as a source of images and to use those images in the creation of realistic if fictive practice represents a deviation from the general Puritan practice" (171), and epitomizes the reasons for Calvin's distrust of allegory.

[42]Sancy also errs in attempting to reason "Par similitude." *Sancy,* 588. As Foucault observes, this is mistaken, for similitude is no longer the form of knowledge but rather the occasion for error, the danger to which one exposes oneself when one does not examine the obscure region of confusions. *Les Mots,* 51.

and the story (599-600). Sancy, similarly, has lost all sense of a signifying system. The signifier (the key, the story) no longer equates with signified (the state of being possessed), just as his narrative no longer conjoins with any reality. He unwisely bases his assessment on things rather than on words. Note that the woman in a sense made a misreading which led her to respond inappropriately, for had she attended to the *words,* instead of the image they created (this must be the Bible, therefore I must act possessed), she would have realized their substance does not correlate with their appearance. Similarly, Sancy "ferme les yeux à [sa] Bible pour les ouvrir à telles inventions" (599). Sancy effects a mis-reading of his own existence: his appearance, and apparent success due to his conversion, is revealed in the final chapter as illusory. In fact, the last chapter chiastically and obsessively takes up the very same issues, church and politics, that Sancy poses in the beginning of the book, underlining the failure of Sancy's confession to help him "parvenir" as he had hoped.

In the same way, Sancy's Catholic tendency to venerate the relics of saints rather than to rely on the efficacy of the Word reinforces his static, reified, object-oriented nature. D'Aubigné is intentionally bawdy in reacting to this particular delusion; the obscenities he uses not only inaugurate permissions and justifications for the more extensive "blasphemy" found in the *Avantures,* but also demonstrate d'Aubigné's intention to raise the word, both his and that of Scripture, to primacy over the image. He denigrates relics, showing the Catholics' mistaken reliance on appearance for revelation of being: images and impressions delude them:

> Une des choses qui m'esmeut le plus à desdaigner l'Eglise, fut la lecture de quelques livres . . . sur tout *l'Inventaire des reliques* . . . Ce livre confirme l'inventaire que fait Calvin . . . quinze ou seize testes à Saint Pierre, dix huit à Sainct Paul, sept ou huict corps à chacun, dix mille martyrs enterrez en la grandeur d'un coffre, les traces des pieds de nostre Seigneur et des Anges, la marque des fesses de Saint Fiacre en Brie sur une pierre . . . du linge salle de la Vierge ayant ses fleurs, . . . et un éterneument du Saint Esprit (604-5).

The insistence on not only vulgar but also minute enumeration demonstrates Sancy's attachment to things and images. The reduction in size demonstrates how attempted enclosure of the sacred–the way Calvinists perceive the Catholic definition of bread and wine at the mass–results in a diminution of it, and is to be avoided at all costs. For instance, the Virgin's nail parings are housed along with the Holy Spirit's sneeze "in una parva bursa satini rubri" (605). The diminutives, the precious italianate phrasing and the extraneous qualifying adjectives demonstrate this point. Images also mingle sacred with profane: "Ils nous ont appris à peindre nostre Dame à l'ancien modelle de Vesta, tenant en son sein Jupiter Bambino" (633).

While it might be argued that d'Aubigné is hypocritical in stating that he is opposed to such an admixture since it is he as author who perpetuates such imbrications by recounting these *contes grivoises*, it is more likely, given the overall intentionality he evidences in *Sancy*, that he employs obscenities, anecdotes and instances of improper usage to demonstrate the power of his discourse to contain and defuse them without suffering contamination. In this sense, d'Aubigné is making a case for the artist's freedom of expression and liberty to choose his tools, provided his intention is good. That is, the scandalous *appearance* of such episodes is *not* their reality.

Attentiveness to language as d'Aubigné employs it and as Sancy abuses it is crucial to an examination of *Sancy*. Sancy chooses to overlook the significance of words. Although he quotes the statement that "toutes les guerres ne sont nees qu'à faute de grammaire," (634) he immediately turns this into a misguided allegory, developing an image of *Grandem matrem* from "grammaire." He speaks of the need to purify preachers' language, but does so without taking in the sense of the words he prescribes:

> sa premiere reigle estoit, qu'on fist un grand retranchement de thresoriers, qui sont les participes, des interjections, pour oster les exclamations aux Prescheurs, de quelques noms et de plusieurs adverbes, comme corporellement, substantiellement, charnellement, et autres tels (634-35).

The vocabulary he favors is tainted by secular ambition and has little to do with religion, although he is not aware of this: "je lui appris encores à dire souvent, *maxime d'Estat, maladie d'Estat, periode d'affaires, interesser, prendre la garantie, faire fortune, courir risque, symboliser, jalouzer, ambitionner. . .*" (624). He does not even realize that the words he is banning are part of the approved Catholic vocabulary. Sancy's inappropriate use of words so that they no longer signify in a standard sense only further parallels the lack of equivalence between his being and appearance. Unlike Sancy, d'Aubigné is meticulous in his use of language, and shows a preoccupation with considerations of style and literary expression, whether it be explicitly his own (he forms neologisms to better express his thoughts: e.g. "onopatie" [584]) or that of his characters (solicitous of style, he notes, "apres ces contes le testateur eslevoit son style" [597]; he shows a desire to "corriger les plus rudes passages" [582]; and he defends against "mauvaises rimes" [624]).

Fact, Fiction and Textual Inscription

The adoption of an opponent's personality has complex ramifications when examined in the light of d'Aubigné's relationship to Scripture. God is the supreme Other against whose Word d'Aubigné must valorize his own work. In *Sancy*, d'Aubigné overwhelms Sancy's otherness by incorporating him into his discourse. He subordinates Sancy's ineffectual voice to the authorial word. He is able to do so because, despite Sancy's actual historical existence, in d'Aubigné's work Sancy is a fictional character. It is more difficult to so manipulate God. Because of his Calvinist beliefs, d'Aubigné may not attempt to subvert the revealed Word. Rather, he must move as a sinful creature through the Word, appropriating it as an aid in his own personal straits. Such appropriation creates tension between subject and object, since the Word, as Calvin construes it, relegates the human to the stance of mere listening ears, while authorship requires a speaking subject.[43] One strategy d'Aubigné uses to overcome the influence of the Word so that he may speak is that of allusion to the self he has established in previous texts. By quoting himself, he renders his self-expression canonical. This technique is more pronounced in *Sa Vie à ses enfants.* We can also see it in the personalized anecdotal outbursts, unmotivated by the explicated Psalm, in the *Méditations.* In the *Tragiques,* it appears in the dialogues between d'Aubigné and his conscience / consciousness concerning literary creation. Later, in another dialogic structure, d'Aubigné refers back to *Sancy,* an already-written text, in the *Avantures,* a text-in-process. This tactic establishes *Sancy* as an authority, since the previous text is quoted to substantiate the current text. It also sets up an interdependent relationship between the two and, through d'Aubigné's citations of himself, shows us the self-conscious author in action. All such interventions are acutely self-aware, and raise questions as to the relationship between authorship and authority.

Thus, in *Sancy,* d'Aubigné begins to articulate an inter-referential system among his works. First, episodes in *Sancy* are later appropriated to be more fully detailed or, even, revised in the *Avantures.*[44] Secondly, material from the *Avantures* is included, during a later editorial process, in *Sancy.*[45]

---

[43]Milton experiences a like problem: "Milton, who would not sunder spirit from matter, would not let himself be a receiver, object to a subject's influencings." Bloom, *Map of Misreading,* 126-27.

[44]There are many examples of borrowings from *Sancy* incorporated into the *Avantures:* (1) "Nostre Dames des Ardilliers," *Sancy,* 601, *Avantures,* 705; (2) The discussion of *Le Cose meravigliose de l'alma cita di Roma* and the "éternuement du Saint Esprit" *Sancy,* 604-5, *Avantures,* 716; (3) "la fable des Estrons," *Sancy,* 629, *Avantures,* 716; (4) the prayer which "commence par un *Et,*" *Sancy,* 631, *Avantures,* 699. The editors of the Pléiade edition note that "un certain nombre d'histoires ou d'anecdotes, primitivement racontées dans le *Sancy,* ont été alors versées dans le *Faeneste* et sont remplacées par un simple renvoi à cette oeuvre." D'Aubigné, "La Confession du Sieur de Sancy," in *Oeuvres,* ed. Henri Weber et. al. (Paris: Gallimard, 1969). All other references will be to this text.

[45]For instance, in *Sancy,* 625, we find mentioned a man who "parle des couleurs selon la nouveauté, et comme elles sont desduites dans le meschant *Faeneste.*" *Avantures,* 678-79; (2) "Il contoit aussi l'histoire du Marroquin et de Brillebaut, telle qu'elle est descrite au second livre de *Faeneste.*" *Sancy,* 596, *Avantures,* 724-25. Most of *Sancy* was written in 1599; the *Avantures* were not begun until 1617. "Les nombreuses références au *Faeneste . . .* s'expliqueroit par un simple remaniement postérieur." *Sancy,* 1277.

Thirdly, certain stylistic techniques begin to appear as typical of d'Aubigné, showing traits in common with expressions in *Les Tragiques* and *Sa Vie*.[46]

Finally, d'Aubigné textualizes himself, writing himself into his script as an actor who is spoken of as "other," perhaps to lend himself more credence (his affirmation cited in the third-person carries more weight than a first-person, subjective assertion). The characters he creates speak of him as though creator and creation are not of a piece. This effects a distancing phenomenon. Rather than labor under what Harold Bloom terms an "anxiety of influence"–most intense in the case of the Bible, but possibly prohibitive as well concerning powerful predecessors such as Ronsard–d'Aubigné circumvents divine authority to assert his independence. He does so by relying on textualized self-constructions for support for further self-assertions.[47] This gives d'Aubigné the

> true priority of interpretation, the powerful reading that insists upon its own uniqueness, and its own accuracy. Troping upon his forerunner's tropes, [he] compels us to read as he reads, and to accept his stance and vision. . . . His allusiveness introjects the past, and projects the future.[48]

Referring to past, present and texts to-be-written expands the author's capabilities in time. In the Derridean sense, the differentiations established also lead to *différance,* or a spatial and temporal deferring that sets up greater possibilities for the multiplicity of roles that d'Aubigné will play in his works, and a forced spacing, or critical pause, in the way the reader apprehends the text.

D'Aubigné's strategy of writing himself into the text also constitutes a strong and cunning sort of stylistic parody of the Catholic church's tendency to write glosses and commentaries upon authoritative texts (with the end result that the substance of the text is deformed by additional accretions). For example, Sancy reads a legend of a saint and confesses that "il y a encore un livre chez nous" in which he distorts the book's meaning "[en] fais[ant] de belles annotations" [584]). D'Aubigné ridicules the Catholic technique: bolstering an argument with cryptic references to external and decontextualized sources is obscurantist and fractures, rather than clarifies, language.

> il est porté au Canon qui commance, *is qui non habet loco illius,* etc.
> Il est dit notamment *in rubrica decreti quod non habet uxorem.* . . .
> Distinct. 34. hyper. de Var. Stud. Theolog. vol. libr. 4 cap. 5,
> Villavincent, ibid. cap. 4 . . . (631).

---

[46]In particular, the tendency already noted to biblical expression by the Protestants.

[47]Using a different strategy to a similar end, Milton "re-writes Spencer so as to increase the distance between his poetic father and himself." Bloom, *Map of Misreading,* 128.

[48]Ibid., 132.

Rather than follow this unintelligible model, d'Aubigné reverses it: he will not gloss another's text, but rather will comment upon his *own* constructions. He will thereby clarify his own authorial intentionality for the reader.

The inter-referential system is composed of a network of allusions to prior or projected texts, strengthening the impression of a literary universe that is self-sufficient and autonomous. There is no need to cite other authorities since d'Aubigné causes his other works to function as authoritative sources. Consequently, the quantity of references to Scripture that we find in the *Méditations* and the *Tragiques* diminish radically over the course of d'Aubigné's literary career. D'Aubigné comes to create from elements of his own creations – from himself.

The self is always apparent, although not always acknowledged by name, in d'Aubigné's texts. As mentioned earlier, the reader quickly becomes aware that Sancy is an unreliable narrator and, indeed, is the object of the narration rather than its subject. On the other hand, d'Aubigné's own reliability is brought into question by his initial ploy of speaking as though he were Sancy. Thus, most of the time we are compelled to seek out d'Aubigné's authorial expression behind the scenes. He inserts himself subtly into the text, so cleverly that, with all the confusion of pronouns and voices he creates, it is easy to miss him. Such "dissembling" serves two purposes. First, it forces the reader to discern the narrator for himself, then *choose* to trust him. This compels an active involvement in reading that amounts to a co-production of the text's readability. Secondly, d'Aubigné stresses his utter autonomy as a literary creator by actually intimately *writing himself into* his own text so that a text, by incorporating his essence, realizes autonomy. It has its own dynamism, and may even come to have an existence apart from the author. This is the case with the *Tragiques* for instance for, as d'Aubigné enjoins them to do in the conclusion, they continue to act in the world after his death. This technique occurs frequently in the *Avantures* and *Sancy,* and is predominant in *Sa Vie.*

The three specific instances in which such self-reference occurs are important, for they use d'Aubigné himself as an *exemplum.* The first instance is in the chapter entitled "De la justification des oeuvres," and is meant to show how true "oeuvres"–the Calvinists' attempts to aid the king–go unrecognized and unrewarded (594), or how Huguenots are the vessels of prophetic truth (in "De l'impudence des Huguenots"). D'Aubigné is summoned, as a character, to lend credence to the account. D'Aubigné the author does not acknowledge his identity with d'Aubigné the character. This forces the latter to function as an authoritative eye-witness whose credibility is unmarred by the possible bias of the author. Pronominal confusion prevails in both accounts. In addition, d'Aubigné is designated by a series of different names: "le compagnon" (579), "ce Huguenot" (651), "Aubigné" (spoken of in the third person singular [651-52]), and "ce rustre" (652). On one occasion he is referred to as "l'autheur" (598), but only as the writer of a satirical sonnet about how the king neglects his faithful dog (although this is possibly an avowal of the authorial voice behind *Sancy*). D'Aubigné's *Histoire universelle* is also cited as an authority (597). This exteriorization of the self, and the textualized self (in that d'Aubigné's identity is inscribed within his work), enhances the text's credibility as well as makes the author and his text two separate entities, related through mutual reference, that cooperate in the presentation of writing to the reader. For the informed reader, it also creates a delightful ludic scene, as though d'Aubigné is peering forth from a screen to reveal himself only to the initiated or to the elect. The ability to recognize d'Aubigné in such a guise indicates that one is reading correctly or fully. Such traces of difference result in d'Aubigné's self-definition. By commenting upon his own creation, within his text d'Aubigné acts like God who, in the biblical rendering, glosses his own Word. God, the original author,

> s[e] sépar[e] de soi pour nous laisser parler, nous étonner, et nous interroger . . . non pas en parlant mais en se taisant, en laissant le silence interrompre sa voix et ses signes. . . . L'écriture est donc originairement hermétique et seconde . . . déjà la Sienne qui commence à la voix rompue et à la dissimulation de sa Face. Cette différence, cette négativité en Dieu, c'est notre liberté . . . la possibilité de la Question.[49]

In the same way, d'Aubigné multiplies and distances himself from himself in order to attain greater eventual unity with his reader. However, his integrity is always maintained, as the text is not merely the vehicle of this separation but also, because of his inclusion within the text, the guarantor of reassemblage.

D'Aubigné's textual inscriptions in no way rely on images to convey their messages; each account describes a mini-drama in which d'Aubigné plays a vital role. These are not "portraits of the artist," but rather epitomes of the creative process. We do not *see* d'Aubigné but instead hear him *speak*. Thus, the true indicator of being–what one says and asserts–is emphasized over appearance, or how one *seems*. Three examples serve to bear out this point. In each, despite his stance as an actor, no description of d'Aubigné the *personnage* is given. Instead, he commands attention through his statements:

> (1) Un de ses compagnons, lequel trouvant un jour par les rues un vieux chien, nommé Citron, qui avoit accoustomé de coucher sur le lict du Roy, il faisoit souvenir ce sien compagnon d'un *sonnet* qui fut trouvé attaché sur le col de ceste pauvre beste, au poinct que le Roy arrivoit à Agen; si bien qu'il se presenta *lui et son sonnet* que vous *verrez ailleurs*. Il fit souvenir *l'autheur,* qu'apres avoir commandé

[49]Jacques Derrida, *L'Ecriture et la différence* (Paris: Seuil, 1967), 103.

long temps un regiment de dix huit compagnies, gagné un Gouvernment avec grands et hasardeux combats, il lui arriva d'estre porté par terre, et prins en une ambuscade. . . . Le Roy et la Reine firent telle depesche qu'il falloit pour le faire mourir, en haine de vingt cinq ans de fidelle service (597-98; my emphasis).

(2) Ce Huguenot replique [au Roy] impudemment: "Sire, le Roy de Navarre mon Maistre, a esté (à son grand regret) eslevé soubs ce fardeau; sans menaces, il hommagera tousjours sous Vostre Majesté, sa vie et ses conditions, mais de son honneur il n'en rendra hommage à Prince du monde, tant qu'il aura une goutte de sang et un pied d'espee" (651).

(3) [Il] fut à peine retiré de la porte par les honnestes Huguenots de la Cour. Aubigné fut si desvergogné, que le Roy lui faisant une honneste reception à Senlis, et lui ayant demandé familierement ce qu'il disoit de ce coup de cousteau que Jean Chastel lui avoit donné dans la levre, ce rustre repondit: "Je dis, Sire, que le Dieu que vous n'avez renoncé que des levres, ne vous a percé que les levres, mais sitost que le coeur renoncera, il vous transpercera le coeur" (652).

The emphasis on discourse (d'Aubigné's response cited authoritatively in full, where a paraphrase might have sufficed) and the identity insisted upon between d'Aubigné the character and his literary endeavors ("compagnon d'un sonnet"; "lui et son sonnet") show the dynamic, self-conscious tenor of these insertions. Also, by incorporating himself into the fictional fabric of his work, d'Aubigné implies that his text's existence is equal to fact. Just as his "apophéties," (cf. 682, supra) recorded retrospectively *as though* they are predictions in the future, encompass past, present and future, d'Aubigné's *literary* corpus turns fact (Sancy's historical existence) into fiction (his reified status in the narrative) and fiction (the pretense in the episodes cited above that d'Aubigné is *not* writing about himself) into fact (d'Aubigné as *exemplum* asserts the truth of his narrative). The unashamedly literary nature of d'Aubigné's writing asserts itself *beyond* his theological perspective. While in mystic writing[50] the self is abdicated to be possessed by the Other, here d'Aubigné subordinates the image of the other (perhaps a veiled figuration of the Other) by the power of his discourse.

Public and Private Presentation

The self of the other is unintegrated; it is reduced to the status of image because, since its essence is disparate, its language is shattered and

---

[50]Michel de Certeau, *Heterologies.* Cf. chap. 6, "Mystic Speech."

communication is not possible. Sancy's voice is, in fact, pre-empted by others. This work claims to be a confession. In a confessional statement, ordinarily the confessing subject is the only speaker heard. However, here Sancy is repeatedly interrupted by the voices of others, and the confession genre is abruptly transformed into a dialogue, or a disquisition by another speaker. Indeed, the first words of *Sancy* give greater emphasis to public opinion than to Sancy's private perspective: "On n'a que trop debattu en ce temps . . . ceux qui veulent . . . les uns disent . . . encore dit on . . . il alleguent. . ." (579). This textual strategy shows Sancy's inability to assert himself and consequent authorial impotence.

In a different way, the anecdotes framed within Sancy's confession that he does consciously introduce indicate the incomplete nature of his "self": he *needs* to supplement his own voice–which *never* succeeds in establishing a coherent, progressive narrative – with that of others. He is incapable of discussing issues through self-reference (as d'Aubigné does) but must rather rely on the statement of others.[51] The name-dropping of historical *personnages* in the text attests to Sancy's desire to bolster his fiction with their fact.

On several occasions Sancy refers to the work he is purportedly composing as a "marquetterie," a mosaic-like structure in which varying fragments are embedded, implying discontinuity and gaps in the presentation ("marquetterie"–"un ensemble formé de parties disparates"[52]). He claims something is "digne, à mon advis, de tenir place en cette marquetterie" (623), and refers to "la varieté et marquetterie de cette oeuvre" (659). Such "marquetterie" may be

> an emblem of a particular conception of the self that presupposes a personal identity fragmented as in a mosaic where the parts fit loosely together, but never perfectly, and with mysterious, dark gaps between the sections.[53]

It is in the intentionally-operated gaps between the sections that d'Aubigné's authorial presence may most clearly be discerned.

A double role for fiction is thus evolved through the greater permissions for literary creation that d'Aubigné devises in *Sancy*. Fiction may have a negative connotation. Sancy's existence, for instance, is reduced to mere fiction. However, through such a reduction, d'Aubigné demonstrates the ultimate *effectiveness* of fiction, wielding it as a tactic even more persuasive than polemic.

---

[51]For instance, he adopts Monsieur le Convertisseur's statements as his own: "Je remercie Monsieur le Convertisseur, et prenant son propos . . ." *Sancy*, 665.

[52]Paul Robert, *Le Petit Robert* (Paris: Société du Nouveau Littré, 1976), s.v. *marquetterie*.

[53]Daniel Russell, "Conception of Self and Generic Convention: An Example from the *Heptameron*," forthcoming in *Sociocriticism*.

5

Appearance and Being:
Fact and Fiction in the
Avantures du Baron de Faeneste

IN THE *AVANTURES,* THE RE-EVALUATION of fiction's role postulated in *Sancy* is carried to its logical conclusion. The *Avantures* is daring in that it claims autonomy and self-sufficiency as a literary work. It is established as such through the dual expanded techniques of inter-referentiality and self-inscription we have seen in the preceding chapters. At the same time, it contains the shadow of a biblical pre-text. That is, theological issues are mixed with secular and even scabrous topics, which are still a matter of concern for Calvinists.[1] Indeed, in the *Avantures* the structure of "argument" and ensuing text that d'Aubigné chooses recalls the "occasion" and "argument" format of the *Méditations.* In them, d'Aubigné constantly calls upon the reader to attend to the deliberate contrasts between his so-called exegesis and the biblical parent text. Rather than concede a superior status to the Bible, d'Aubigné causes it to function as but one more book in a network of discourses contained within his narrative. As a signifying system, the *Avantures* is a complete fictional universe. By incorporating and surpassing image, it is paradoxically liberated from representationality. Discourse prevails over description. In that sense, the *Avantures* remain faithful to the *oral* imperatives of the biblical Word.

Reading Emblematically

The Calvinists' fear of solipsism thus seems to be realized. Fiction, dangerous enough in that it refers to *any* fabrication and not to truth, is now freed to refer solely to itself: it does not necessarily need to mirror any reality. In fact, exegetical writing can itself be viewed as fiction, although writers such as de Bèze will never acknowledge it as such, for the commentary resembles endlessly that which it is commenting upon and which it cannot express.[2] In that space of inutterability, of divergence from the text to which it is supposed to conform, fiction may arise. Because of the original text's uniqueness, derivative text may even attain truth and

---

[1] D'Aubigné, however, intends that his work not function as a commentary, nor does he commit lèse-majesté by attempting to render the Bible a mere adjunct to his work but rather both works are valorized as independent entities.

[2] Cf. Foucault, *The Order of Things,* 41.

must remain tainted by fallen language. The medieval mentality we have deemed "imagistic," that of taking signs as presence, misreads fiction such as the *Avantures*.[3] For d'Aubigné does not propose to set his work up as the sign of a higher truth. Rather it is a human utterance that signifies itself alone. Its referent is clear, because it is interior.

D'Aubigné employs strategies in the *Avantures* that he develops thematically, in germ, in the works we discussed previously. He mandates a new kind of reading that intimately involves the reader's critical capacities. He then redefines authorship as an endeavor in which both reading and writing create conditions that favor the individual reader's enactment of his own salvation. He does so by valorizing both his word and that of God in a literary way that yet remains theologically faithful. In addition, he innovates a text that provides within itself the images that it glosses, showing images to be mere appearance while privileging his word as revelatory of true being. In such a manner, he establishes a creative, interpretative space between word and image, thereby dislodging the emblematic equivalence originally established. He causes discourse to prevail over image. Finally, through the opposition yet dialectical interpenetration of appearance (Faeneste) and being (Enay), d'Aubigné erects a new interpretative textual paradigm: an altered relationship between fact and fiction.

D'Aubigné's fiction is not gratuitous. He is very careful in the *Avantures*, as in all his previous works, to ground his narrative firmly in historical fact. He justifies his fictions' presence in a historical context: they are motivated by the context in order to act as palliative or remedy. Through the *topos* of the editor who is actually the author in disguise (as seen in *Les Tragiques*), d'Aubigné explains,

> On ne die pas . . . que les plaisants propos estoient dessaisonnez
> en un temps de guerre et d'afflictions: je dis . . . que lors les

---

[3]The defense of icons against the iconoclasts is that the icon, unlike an image of a saint, for example, does not encapsulate the divine. An entire iconographic system of signifying develops, with the intention of *suggesting* the divine, but not *specifying* it. For instance, a mandorla around a character's head indicates that he possesses attributes of transcendence. But there is no attempt to realistically or anthropomorphically portray God. Similarly, icons, unlike portraits or paintings, are not designed to be framed. This would be a containment of symbols of the divine. In instances where framing occurs, such techniques as a halo which extends beyond the boundaries of the painted border, or a bevelling technique to lessen the frame's impact, are employed. The distinction is also made that no icon is to be worshipped, rather it is to be contemplated. Catholics such as Faeneste distort the function of holy images by possessing them, by revering them as equal with the thing they represent. On the other hand, icons point *beyond* themselves. The Pseudo-Chrysostom even counsels that, when one stands before an icon, one should *close* one's eyes, the better to apprehend it. Rather than make pictures of God, "Icons are expressive of a mystical dogmatic reality open only to the eyes of faith in the context of worship." (Lecture delivered by Father T. Hopko, St. Vladimir's Orthodox Seminary, at Drew Seminary, Madison, New Jersey, November, 1986).

tristesses viennent aussi mal à propos que la peur dans les perils (669).

D'Aubigné asserts that fiction is not only a logical and helpful response to fact, it may actually facilitate the recomposition of the self brutalized by historical reality. Fiction here is allied intricately with the construction of selfhood: the self both writes, and writes to re-create himself autonomously: "un esprit, lassé de discours graves et tragiques, *s'est voulu recreer*" (671). Fiction surpasses fact in that it creates from its elements ("à la description de ce siecle") but moves beyond these pieces of a shattered reality ("quelques bourdes vrayes" [669]; contemporary history is defined as textual fragments) to re-structure them as part of an organic narrative.[4] History can only relate incidents. Narrative is required to link and evaluate them, while fiction may effect creative recombinations that open new perspectives.

Throughout the *Avantures,* the strategy employed to achieve narrative self-sufficiency is that of the creation of *textual images.* These are images that, like emblems, include their own commentary. Thus, unlike other Calvinists, d'Aubigné does not reject image, but rather uses it and moves beyond it. Its mimetic nature is revealed as an inferior accessory of the word. He thereby asserts his power as a writer: he is able to carry out the dangerous mixture of sacred and profane, image and word, without being contaminated by it. His work is autonomous because it need not refer to, or describe, any separate entity. Its references and descriptions are all self-contained. As *Sancy* proposes to fight the Catholics with their own weapons, glosses and polemic, d'Aubigné in the *Avantures* similarly adopts the predominantly Catholic emblem genre,[5] discerns proto-literary elements latent in it, and develops it into a mechanism by which it, and image, are ultimately subverted. *Ut pictura poesis,* the criterion for a successfully representative text in the Renaissance, calls for a text to refer to something external, other than itself, in its mimetic enterprise. Here, however, the text no longer needs images because the images are actually incorporated in its very words. In like fashion, d'Aubigné displays images of himself, propelled by discourse, which inhabit his text and valorize it as a medium of autobiographical expression that comes to full fruition in his final work, *Sa Vie à ses enfants.* In this way, he writes himself into the emblem.

---

[4]Paul Ricoeur makes this assertion in *Time and the Narrative,* I.214-16, as he evaluates Fernand Braudel's (in Ricoeur's view, unsuccessful) attempt to dispense with narrative history.

[5]Although most of the early emblem books in France were reworkings of classical motifs, later (around the 1580s) there developed a body of emblem books saturated with religious concerns (such as those of Georgette de Montenay). These often appeared as revisions of the pre-existing Catholic emblem writings. Catholic imagery tends to be more concrete and sensorial.

The *Avantures* open with the confrontation of Enay and Faeneste. Yet there is a dialogue between them also.[6] Faeneste is a young noble *parvenu* who, as his Greek name indicates, bases not only his assessment of others but also his own self-presentation on appearance. Enay, who at first seems to be Faeneste's antithetical opposite, represents "being," as his name translates; he is an older, probably Calvinist, noble who chooses to live apart from the court. By their very selection of geographic *cadres* in which to live, Enay and Faeneste set up a dichotomy between public and private domain that continues the theme developed in *Sancy,* in which writing epitomizes the true private self. Enay, in fact, functions more as a writer, a propagator of discourse, orality and textuality (he is "un homme consommé aux lettres" [673]) than does Faeneste, who, by minute attention to detail and the intricacies of the effect he calculates to make on the world, establishes himself as a static and reified image.

In the first sight we have of Faeneste, he is framed like a picture, *"enfermé* d'un parc et d'une riviere" (673; my emphasis). Similarly, he has no inner coherence, no sense of direction; he "se trouve esgaré . . . à Nyort" (674). In addition, as an image, Faeneste always functions as one who attempts to disrupt discourse. Enay is constantly reproving him, "ne rompons point le discours du Prescheur" (794); "vous rompez tousjours . . . nos propos . . . escoutez!" (809).

Thus, the fundamental focus of the *Avantures* is on the interplay of word and image. In this way, the work can be seen to arise out of a new notion of textual expansiveness: like an emblem, it contains the elements of both word and image. Unlike an emblem, however, the two parts are woven together in one medium and are independent as well as dialectically interpenetrated.[7] Both are distinct media—one representational, one discursive—which relate only in that they possess a common signifying goal. Separated from each other, they do not have similar impact. In the case of the emblematic textuality of the *Avantures,* however, the image upon which discourse comments is itself framed and expressed by that very discourse: the text *supplies within itself* all the elements necessary for a clear reading and a full interpretation.[8] The signifier and the signified can be found in the text itself. They do not themselves constitute a full sign, however.

[6]D'Aubigné originally labels his work "dialogues," and intends to include this term as part of the title (Cf. note in the Pléiade edition, 1350). However, he later drops this designation. This may be because true dialogue is not possible between types which represent "appearance" and "being," although a dialectic relationship in which "being" may incorporate and surpass "appearance" is possible.

[7]In Alciati's *Emblematum liber,* for instance, the pictures often seem to dominate the page spatially, while the moralizing commentary is then appended.

[8]In practice, the text of emblems often functions similarly. See Dan Russell, "Montaigne's Emblems" in *French Forum* (1985): 260-75.

Rather, the *text* is privileged as the sign to which signified and signifier, read critically and jointly, point. An emblem is established: the two components of picture (Faeneste) and moral or explanation (Enay) are provided by the text. This points to the need for a new manner of reading d'Aubigné's text that his former works, through their inclusion of, and numerous references to, other literary genres, foreshadow. The *Avantures* may be read emblematically, discerning imagistic structures framed within the narrative and finding the commentary that reflects back on them. In the *Avantures,* Faeneste may be seen as the object, while Enay is the subject. Reading must therefore cooperate with the writing process, becoming the

> *tertium quid,* the third term, the distributed middle, that mediates between subject and object and transforms binary opposition into the ternary form of *discordia concors.*[9]

The *Avantures* is thus composed of three parts, one of which serves as the synthesis of the other two. One element is pictorial: the description of Faeneste. The second component is discursive; Enay glosses the description of Faeneste and his world. The third factor is the act of reading.

In the initial encounter of Faeneste and Enay, it is significant that the apparent utter opposition of the two character types is actually a dialectic, in which both, as in the emblem structure, participate in one another's being. Enay, for instance, is not the limpidly straightforward fellow he claims to be, for he conceals something of himself, here symbolized by the dagger he hides in his doublet ("d'ailleurs j'ai une petite lame dans ce bourdon" [676]). This is not all that Enay conceals. He also hides his co-extension with d'Aubigné for, as discourse, Enay embodies d'Aubigné's eventual commentary on Faeneste. Clues in the text alert us to the mutual identity of Enay as discourse and d'Aubigné as writer (although d'Aubigné's "self" dialectically surpasses Enay and, as we shall see, in some ways incorporates that of Faeneste). For instance, Enay avows that "nous avons du commencement protesté de *bourdes vrayes*: nous n'avons rien dit en tout nostre discours qui ne soit . . . attribué à un mesme ce qui appartient à plusieurs" (726). This phrasing mimics that of d'Aubigné in the *Préface*: he proposes to compose from "bourdes vrayes," and the "nous" implicates Enay as complicitous with d'Aubigné. This is a key to presenting a new kind of readership: as Roland Barthes observes in *S/Z,*

> c'est une contre-communication; le lecteur est complice, non de tel ou tel personnage mais du discours lui-même en ce qu'il joue la division et l'écoute, l'impureté de la communication: le discours, et

---

[9]Wendy Steiner, *The Colors of Rhetoric* (Chicago: University of Chicago Press, 1984), 222.

non tel out tel de ses personnages, est le seul héros positif de l'histoire.[10]

When we read emblematically, accounting for both word and image rather than disregarding or privileging one of the elements, discourse ultimately prevails through the reader's act. In this light, it is important that the first encounter, while only the first of many occasions on which Faeneste describes himself or is described by others, is the *only* time in the entire work in which *Enay* is described. He is, therefore, to be interpreted through reliance on his discourse and not on illusory appearance which, indeed, is misleading in his case as well as in that of Faeneste, for he is garbed as, and mistaken by Faeneste for, a rustic peasant:

> La Baron . . . rencontre le bon homme Enay, vestu d'une juppe de bure et sans souliers à cric. . . . [Le Baron] a failli à faire une grande cagade, car le boyant sans fraise et sans pennache, [il] lui all[oit] demander le chemin (674-75).

Faeneste, however, is clearly constituted as an image. He is a picture observed by another. Like an image, he requires another's intervention in order to have or to produce meaning; his thick Gascon pronunciation renders reading difficult and epitomizes the opacity and incomprehensibility of images unmotivated or unexplained by discourse. His judgment is obscured by appearance. Appearance acts as an impenetrable screen blocking access to meaning. Faeneste explains, "assaboir que l'homme ne poubant juger de ce qui parest, toutes ces chauses se doibent contenter de parestre" (702). Appearance thus curtails man's insight and indeed represents his very short-sightedness. Even the words he uses and the actions he projects are never actualized: he fights a duel "à paroles, s'entent," (676) for instance. Faeneste is ultimately sterile and impotent: Enay asks Faeneste the result of all his efforts to shine in the world: "Et quels fruits de tant de fleurs?" Faeneste can only respond, "c'est pour parestre" (678). By not acting a part, but rather by *being* a coherent self, Enay prevails.

Another element of the first meeting between the two concerns the ability to call things by their proper name. Faeneste inflates things all out of proportion, calling them hyperbolically after their appearance. For instance, Faeneste is frustrated because he has been roaming, lost, for hours in what seems to him an enormous expanse. Because of his inability to recognize that he is deluded, he exaggerates. Enay restores things to their proper proportions and points up Faeneste's lack of discernment, instructing him that he has been walking in a mere "clos" rather than a "parc":

[10]Roland Barthes, *S/Z* (Paris: Editions du Seuil, 1970), 51.

E.–"Je ne vien pas de loin; je me pourmene autour de ce clos."
F.–"Comment Diavle, clos, il y a un quart d'ure que je suis envarracé le long de ces murailles, et bous ne le nommez pas un parc" (675).

His own delusions contaminate his ability to use language. In addition, Faeneste assumes that speech cannot be original but must be a citation, borrowed from another as he himself is derivative:

F.–"Encore ne coustera il rien de nommer les choses pour noms honoravles." E.–"Il serviroit encores moins qu'il ne cousteroit." F.–"*Et de qui est cecy?*" E.–"C'est à moi pour vostre service." F.–"A bous?" (675; my emphasis).

In the above example, Faeneste believes Enay is speaking sententiously, that he quotes to him some already-formulated truth in the words of another, just as Faeneste often cites others' comments to bolster his own insubstantial speech. Enay, on the other hand, *knows* words intimately and so is able to name them (and, as a result, to exert power over them). He recognizes that words appropriately name things but things may not, as is the case with Faeneste, predetermine their names.

The character of Faeneste is reified, through a plethora of description and his passive status, into a mere image upon which the Protestant paradigm Enay comments. Faeneste's entire existence appears to be composed of the recounting of tales, of himself and of others. He is incapable of self-animation, and his words lack autonomy. He says, "si je poubois parbenir à estre contai parmi les r'affinez, je serois vien contant" (689). In the pun on *conté* he becomes himself the object of narration. Consequently, he can be defined as an image, a tale others tell of him. Others do not hear him, but rather *see* him. Faeneste alerts us to this when he relates his primary mode of perception: ". . . comme je me *bis* en tren . . . 'Messurs,' di ye, 'tels que bous me *boyez* . . .'" (693; my emphasis). He is the image in the emblem; the active discourse of any narratizing "other" is the commentary. If we do not read the *Avantures* in such an emblematic fashion, however, we may err in interpretation, for it would not be difficult to mistake Faeneste, the more prevalent personage in the text, as the main, reliable character. When we observe the manner in which he is consistently "framed" by others' discourse, however, we perceive the need to rely on discourse over (albeit including) image. As Enay warns us, "nous sommes malades de parestre aussi bien aux affaires generales que particulieres" (687). He may be referring to the text itself which does not want to appear, but seeks to *assert,* a discourse.

The emblematic picture no longer exists *in relation to* words (as in Alciati's emblems), but rather *in conjunction with* words (the image can only be visualized through words, but an image *does* exist within the text as distinct from the commentary).[11] For instance, descriptions of Faeneste occur jointly with, yet separately from, Enay's reactions to them. The structure is not metaphoric, where the sense is embedded in the image, but rather is a structure of displacement and reference: metonymy.

Ultimately, through an emblematic reading the theo-literary nature of d'Aubigné's text is confirmed, for his fiction actually leads the reader back to God. An emblem is itself an icon, for it surpasses image through the inclusion of discourse which propels us beyond representationality. The process of emblematic reading implies a reference to something outside mere image and denies self-sufficiency to symbols.

> To put it in semiotic terms, "icons," or signs which resemble what they designate, are safe; they reinforce the chain of resemblances that ultimately leads to the arch-signifier and -signified, God. But "symbols," purely conventional signs, contain no such resemblances.[12]

An emblematic reading interprets the sign as an icon, as more than that portrayed. The sign thus possesses a transcendental point of origin. Thus, an emblematic reading such as that which the *Avantures* calls for uses the image only to undo it, and replace it with abstract discourse that leads to God's Word, that which cannot be reproduced.

Discourse and Image: The Self Revealed

D'Aubigné inscribes his "self" within his text as an image (his episodic self-descriptions or mini-dramas) joined with expression (through Enay's discourse). Such a formulation calls for an emblematic reading, one in which both word and image are accounted for, and one in which they may interact. This ultimately points toward transcendence, a synthesis of the purposes of word and image. So may the writing self be permitted. D'Aubigné's "self," along with the reader's "self," is imbricated within the text.[13] As we have noted, "l'imprimeur" is actually "l'auteur." Similarly, in some respects Enay represents d'Aubigné (although a full reading requires the dialectical reconciliation of Enay with his apparent antithesis, Faeneste). Just as the author avows his desire to divert himself with less serious

---

[11]Russell, unpublished comment, August, 1986. "The pictorial image in Renaissance poetry is different from the visual image in the kind of signals it gives to a reader. The pictorial image is coded in such a way that any reader from a more or less homogeneous pool will visualize in the same, iconographically standard way. Often these signals will include framing devices which set them off from the surrounding text. . . . The emblematic image in poetry is characterized by the message it is ornamenting or highlighting. The emblematic image is a support but not a vehicle."

[12]Steiner, *Colors of Rhetoric,* 222.

[13]We find such images of d'Aubigné as the following within the text: ". . . qui benez quauques en Cour abec le cul plat et le coullet ravatu, comme les Surs de la Noue et d'Auvigni . . ." *Avantures,* 678. All references in the text are to the ed. Weber, *Oeuvres.*

matters, Enay actively takes the opportunity to amuse himself at Faeneste's expense ("[Enay] qui prend occasion de la rencontre de Faeneste pour s'en donner du plaisir, et mesme en faire part à quelque voisin" [671]). In the tension established between Enay and Faeneste, the reader must invest his critical self to ascertain upon which character he is to rely for an interpretive guide. The reader finds that the image, or Faeneste, in the text is defined in opposition to the words that comment upon it.[14] The themes of disparities in perceptions of time, space and value between Enay and Faeneste point up Faeneste's confusion and unreliability.

In *Sancy*[15] we note that gaps, or lapses in the character as d'Aubigné presents him, are effective mechanisms through which the author's self may be disclosed. The character of Sancy, we observe, is a fiction. If d'Aubigné's factual, historical, as well as literary self can be shown through the medium of a fiction, fiction may be valorized to an extent. Fiction, while apparently duplicitous, may in reality be a means of conveying truth. In the *Avantures,* the case is similar, although more complex. Polemic is taken one step further. The Protestant polemic d'Aubigné expresses through Enay still requires Faeneste's fictive status as its motivating factor, for without the image of Faeneste to comment upon and disparage, Enay's discourse has no purpose in the text.

One arena in which the interplay of image and commentary is particularly evident is that of public and private domain. All that Faeneste is appears immediately, held up for public perusal. Enay, however, practices strategies of concealment that seem to facilitate coherence and self-expression. Enay retains a distance from Faeneste that enables him to be more astute and observant and, hence, more selective in what he divulges about himself. For instance, he never admits to Faeneste that he, too, is a nobleman and one who is familiar with court. He only acknowledges his identity to Cherbonniere, Faeneste's man-servant, an honest man who once knew Enay and who has the eyes, ears and disposition necessary to recognize him now (727). While Faeneste rebukes Enay for being close-mouthed ("Bous estes par trop discrets, bous autres, nous ne sommes pas si reteneus" [695]; "Bous ne me disiez pas qui bous estes" [727]), Enay's reserve and discretion confer more weight on the remarks that he does utter. In this, Enay is similar to d'Aubigné, who writes himself into his text in the third person singular without erasing his historical existence. Because d'Aubigné does not confess his actual reality, fiction, which paradoxically reveals him, is, therefore, more true than fact in the *Avantures.*

---

[14]That is, he defines himself against his perception of *others*: "Boilà des bostres prépaux, à bous otres." *Avantures,* 678.

[15]Cf. Chapter Four of *Les Confessions du Sieur de Sancy.*

The self evolved in concealment enters into a complex relationship with the publicly-portrayed self. The disavowal of one by the other is also inauthentic. The significance of the inclusion of both image and commentary in the same text is highlighted when one recalls the increased focus on the distinctions between public and private existence in the Renaissance.[16] These are exacerbated for Calvinists, who are called to private worship with their individual Bible, yet who are required to conform to public standards of interpretation.[17] This is why the act of fictional creation is seen by the epigones as reprehensible,[18] for it deviates from the established format. The poetics that d'Aubigné develops demands, therefore, a courageous reading: "a theory of reading as an act of courage–braving the gap between subject and object."[19]

Questions about public and private selves arise in the text when the reader notes that Faeneste, a fictional character manifested only through appearance, actually comments upon images of d'Aubigné inscribed in *his*, Faeneste's, image-saturated language. The dilemma of a fictional character's speech circumscribing a factual author's existence sets up a *mise en abyme* effect. Faeneste's intention is to reduce d'Aubigné to the status of an image similar to his own by means of containment and diminution. This is, however, negated through Enay's discourse, which reveals Faeneste's entire being as illusory. Enay thereby excavates and rehabilitates the miniature, denigrated d'Aubigné as actor within a fiction that d'Aubigné as author takes the chance of allowing Faeneste to describe. At the same time, d'Aubigné's images deeply embedded in his narrative are, like those in *Sancy*, actually depictions of *processes*; that is, d'Aubigné is always described in action, involved in literary endeavors or with self-presentation through speech. His self-depiction "n'est pas pour parestre," as even Faeneste acknowledges (678). This is even more the case in his autobiography, *Sa Vie à ses enfants*. Thus, the images of d'Aubigné, the despised Calvinist, which the Catholic Faeneste attempts to enclose and denigrate, in reality take precedence over Faeneste and assert their power as discourse. Faeneste deceives himself, through misreading, into thinking they are images. Here again d'Aubigné's intimate consubstantiality with his text is evident. As Enay is the commentary upon Faeneste's image, for d'Aubigné who comments–through Faeneste–upon

[16]John Guilleroy, "Dalila's House," in *Rewriting the Renaissance: The Discourses of Sexual Difference in Early Modern Europe*, ed. Margaret W. Ferguson, Maureen Quilligan, and Nancy J. Vickers (Chicago: University of Chicago Press, 1986), 109.

[17]Cf. Elizabeth Eisenstein, "Western Christendom Disrupted," in *The Printing Revolution in Early Modern Europe* (Cambridge: Cambridge University Press, 1984).

[18]Lauren Silberman, "Singing Unsung Heroes: Androgynous Discours in Book Three of the *Faerie Queen*," in *Rewriting the Renaissance*, 263.

[19]On misreading, cf. Jonathan Goldberg, "Marvell's Nymph and the Echo of Voice," in *Voice Terminal Echo*, (Ithaca, NY: Cornell University Press, 1985), particularly 277-328.

d'Aubigné's *own* image in the text, the text joins both image and commentary to provide an *emblem* of d'Aubigné's *self*. Authority consists in the maintenance of a hierarchical relationship between word and image, while true authorship, d'Aubigné asserts, consists in the ability to acknowledge both components and move beyond them. Authority requires the aping of a source of power (Faeneste decides, "il faut estre vien bestu à la mode de trois ou quatre Messurs qui ont de l'autourité" [677]), while authorship arises when the self is set up as a coherent entity capable of both imaged and discursive expression. An examination of the presentation of the *Avantures* reveals d'Aubigné's assertion of such authorship: deviating from the Renaissance tradition of *captatio benevolentiae* preliminarily founding a text upon classical or contemporary supportive examples in order to persuade one's audience that one merits attention, d'Aubigné plunges right into his text, including only a brief, informal preface that proffers no entreaty to read his text but rather assumes that the text is capable of standing on its own merit.

Textuality is a medium for the definition and expression of the self, even if it is not until *Sa Vie* that d'Aubigné dares to reveal and acknowledge his selfhood consistently. The two halves of the self must be reconciled through language, which is itself shattered, mirroring the schism between appearance and being. For instance, Faeneste in his status as image has *heard* of some words, but cannot place them in syntactical relationships. He reduces the discussion of "choses si hautes" to "chausses de la Cour" (699). Faeneste manipulates words as objects in his attempt to perceive words as things devoid of any grammatical resemblance. Enay, on the other hand, respects their differences and distinguishes among them. Faeneste does not play with words but rather becomes an object of their ludic proliferation. Enay, however, while using words, at the same time holds them in check, for their free play in the world is as potentially dangerous as is censorship. Faeneste creates his own words and terms, almost his own opaque dictionary (cf. his definition of "resolution": "Quand la chose est faite, il se faut resoudre à ne pas faire pis" [741]; cf. also the misuse of "r'affinez" [689]). He attempts to deform the meaning of words to suit his purpose or to disguise his lack of stature.

Enay distrusts new words, and acknowledges that context is required to verify them. Similarly, he judges the "parestre" by history's ultimate assessment-a *process* – while Faeneste evaluates appearance and its meaning by the unstable priorities of a misinformed social coterie, the court. For instance, Enay takes exception to Faeneste's description of how one "arrives" in the world. Enay finds that Faeneste's definition of social advancement is misleading, for some of those who seek to "parvenir" die in the attempt and, hence, cannot rightly be said to possess social prominence.

E.–"Excusez moi, mais pas empesché de parestre, car un de ceux là
ne parest plus." F.–"Bous boulez dire qu'ils sont morts, mais leur
renommee est immortelle, c'est un veau mout." E.–"Vous attendez-
vous que les Historiens facent mention de telle sorte de valeur?"
F.–"Je ne donnerois pas un estiflet de Roquemadour, ni un curedent
de Monsur lou Maneschal de Roquelaure, de touts bos Histoiregraphes,
c'est assez qu'on en parle à la Cour" (690).

Faeneste refuses to recognize the sense of the word "mort," preferring the
glamorous (and ridiculous, since conveyed through the vulgar play on
words, "veau,") illusion of "immortelle." Faeneste always reads literally,
while Enay is capable of comprehending both figurative and literal speech.
Faeneste brags, for instance,

Ye fis recontre d'un taquin . . . sans respect il jette la male men à
mon mantou, et de l'autre me porte une espee courte à la gourge,
si vien que n'estant pas sur mes armes, il falut lui avandonner lou
mantou, encores fut il si impudent de s'arrester à dix pas de moi
pour me regarder. Lors sans m'estonner ye criai: "Cabalier, il y ba
de boste haunur, car bous serez mon pourte-manteau."

He believes he thus saves his honor, but Enay, more adept with word usage,
turns the tables on him: "Ce fut bien dit, car au moins il estoit emporte
manteau" (741). The stories Faeneste relates of himself reveal his being as
mere appearance. He tells two sorts of stories about himself, one in which
he is the laughing-stock of a tale which, as he recounts it, turns back upon
him, and the other in which he only expresses the desire for, but not the
achievement of, his brand of success. He cooperates with illusion and
duplicity. Having made a serious theological error, for example, he seeks
glibly to cover it up. Enay reproaches him, "il valoit mieux confesser une
faute en Grammaire, que de la couvrir par les blasphèmes." We realize that
the stories Faeneste tells us of himself are like emblems set in the text
(they contain an image of him upon which others, including the reader,
must comment) that parallel, or prefigure, the false triumphs shown in the
tapestries with which the *Avantures* conclude.[20] What is revealed there is

a picture of extreme incoherence, systemic discontinuity masquerading
as continuous allegory . . . All the signifieds turn into signifiers
. . . deferred . . . by the writing.[21]

While the words Faeneste uses to describe himself and the world are
misleading, it is occasionally the case with the very words he uses that,

---

[20]Faeneste mentions "tapisserie" as early as the second book of the *Avantures*: Cf. 727.
[21]Silberman, "Unsung," 265.

instead of his defining them, they define him. In the account in which Faeneste "vrusle d'ambition" to be noticed by the king, he ultimately, literally, does just that: forced to stand too close to the fire as he holds the king's fire shade, Faeneste is aflame and, fearful of appearing foolish, remains silent and immobile (685).

Because Faeneste never looks beyond the "parestre," he never realizes that he becomes the butt of his language and of that of others. His very dialect renders his speech comic: the robber who comes upon him in the alley has, as Faeneste describes it, "la teste vessee." The obscene and bawdy connotations of "vesse" are readily apparent to everyone but Faeneste himself.[22] Elsewhere, Faeneste recounts the tale of a nobleman planning a voyage who seeks to "paroistre si bon Catholique." Faeneste is delighted that the nobleman will be accompanied by his apothecary. This latter rides upon a mule, carrying a douche syringe and a chamberpot on his saddle. Faeneste applauds this tableau, claiming that the apothecary is so accoutered in order to glorify noblemen (767). This absurd assertion further attests to Faeneste's inability to distinguish between appearance and reality.

In another episode, Faeneste tells a tale which describes the deflation of his own self-image. To mock him, his valets lift him high on their shoulders and, as he begins to exult in his triumph, from below they poke him full of pins, quickly deflating his delusion: "[ils] donnoient par dessus quauques foissades d'espingles."[23]

In addition, Faeneste has an utter lack of critical capacity. He recites a sonnet that amuses him, not realizing that it is directed against Catholics such as himself.

> Huguenots, confessez que l'Eglise Romaine
> Tient son giron paillard à tous venans ouvert.

(715)

He is distracted from the sonnet's meaning by its appearance, a sonorous surface. Similarly, Faeneste's "parestre" blinds him to any clues concerning Enay's identity. This is symbolic of Faeneste's utter inability to formulate or comprehend discourse. Because Faeneste is an image, he cannot "hear" discourse. Thus, when Enay casually mentions that he, this apparent rustic, one day "menai [quelqu'un] au cabinet du Roi de Navarre" (694), this hint passes unnoticed. Faeneste is thereby established as the paradigm of incorrect or incomplete reading, and appears in the text as a warning to the reader. While Enay judges appearance according to an interiorized conception of

---

[22]They also recall Epistémon's "couppe testee" in Rabelais' *Pantagruel*, in *Oeuvres complètes* (Paris: Garnier, 1962), II. 362.

[23]Such plays between literal and figurative meanings are characteristic of emblems.

God's will ("quand elle s'accorde à la regle du bien, . . . et au flambeau
de la verité," (700) Faeneste's criterion for determining truth is based solely
on appearances. He is, himself, a conglomerate of braggadocio and flimsy
pretensions. In developing Faeneste's character, d'Aubigné incorporates the
only biblical quotation of the entire work, setting up a revealing paradox.
In this passage, those who worship God are to appear as light to the world.
But the Greek term for appearance is one that *unites* appearance and being;
appearance is a truthful manifestation of being, and outward semblance
mirrors inward reality:

> enfants sans tâche au milieu d'une génération dévoyée et pervertie,
> où vous apparaissez comme des sources de lumière dans le monde,
> vous qui portez la parole de vie. . . (*Phil.* 2:15).

Faeneste's buffoonery and reprehensible vanity and greed signal the ironic
application of this term to him. He cites the above passage in order to
prove his long lineage and noble heritage; "faeneste" is Greek for appearance,
and Faeneste mistakes it for a *nom de famille*. He fails to perceive that
revelation, an inextricable meshing of appearance with the reality that
motivates it, is not a term applicable to him. The biblical word is intentionally
contrasted with Faeneste's inappropriate name throughout the narrative.

Elsewhere, through a false literalization, Faeneste misinterprets the
injunction "mettez en oeuvre vostre salut" as an incitement to "parvenir"
(812). He craves terrestrial advancement, feeling that honors in this world
must guarantee salvation in the next. Faeneste cherishes a small white
pebble, because it is the symbol in *Revelation* of salvation at the Last
Judgment. Enay, however, deflates this delusion by informing Faeneste
that the pebble is but a kidney stone. To drive home the point, this example
of Faeneste's blindness to meaning is followed by an attack on misinterpreta-
tions of the Bible and of doctrine.

Faeneste's failure to read accurately or fully—emblematically, accounting
for the configuration of all elements–is thus itself the emblem of the
unwary reader. When heedless readers attempt to communicate their misapprehensions, they distort a text, or write untruthfully. D'Aubigné warns
us that this will be the case, that there will be many who will attempt to
unravel the sense of his text, but that through delusion or inattentiveness,
they will not succeed: "Dieu sçait les gloses que les copieux feront sur ces
belles histoires, quand ils en auront sceu le secret" (820). (*Copia*, for
Calvinist authors as well as for a self-conscious writer who wishes to convey
his point of view *alone*, is not an ideal.) This is why d'Aubigné explicitly
attends to the reader through such remarks as "je me fasche bien d'alleguer
ces vers en ce lieu, pour ce que, depuis les trois permiers livres, on en a

imprimé en un recueil mais cela accourcit la peine du lecteur."[24] He hopes to find a "suffisant lecteur" who will perceive and complete his meaning.

The reader is again likened to Faeneste in Faeneste's credulous misconstruing of the "Enigme de filasse." Faeneste conveys the enigma to Enay as a form of disguised apocryphal prediction:

> ceci n'est plus du rang des railleries, il ne faut pas tousjours fadeger; c'est une prouphetie troubee aux ruines de Partenai lou Biux, abec une lettre que Nostre-Dame escriboit (747).

It is significant that Faeneste gives the enigma to Enay to read aloud. This symbolizes once again Faeneste's incapacity as image to do justice to narration or discourse. Interesting also is the emphasis on sight, rather than hearing, in the presentation of the enigma; it states, "je voi au premier beau temps . . . je voi [quelques] vieillards saturniens . . ." (749). The enigma contains, as well, the germ of its own demythification for, in its denigration of images and idols it renders itself and Faenestre inert: "les choses mortes, les spectres, les promptes idoles . . . des reliques" (748). Always concerned with how things appear, Faeneste is taken in by a false appearance. Once Enay reads the enigma aloud, he removes its written form from the public arena and retires into himself to meditate upon its meaning. Privacy is again associated with a coherent self, capable of a correct reading:

> E.–"Je demande loisir de repasser ceci à part moy" (748).

He determines that "de prophetie il n'y en a que le parestre" (749). Faeneste accepts the enigma as a thing–a full sign–while Enay seeks to scan it semantically, penetrate its syntactic structure, and from "un seul mot" alone, he grasps the secret. Faeneste remains obstinate in his attempt to view the enigma as an *object,* one that will yield its truth through examination of its appearance: "Bous me feriez vien estonner et mespriser les sabants hommes que y'ai oui là dessus, mais *boyons*" (749; my emphasis). Rather than take the enigma all of a piece, Enay parses it like a sentence, breaking it down into manipulable units of meaning upon which he then exercises the penetration of his discourse. This is paradigmatic of the way he fragments Faeneste's being through his commentary. Enay does not ask what the enigma *shows,* but rather what it *says,* reaffirming the text's preference for discourse over image: "l'Enigme *dit* donc. . ." (751; my emphasis). He states, finally, "le jeu des Enigmes est d'approprier les grandes choses aux pueriles comme cette ci" (752), indicating that the reader must realize that

---

[24]The editors of the Pléiade edition state that this is an unintentional interpolation by d'Aubigné in which a remark he makes in the margin of a printed copy is then incorporated into the text of the next printing (1393 n. 6). Regardless, such inadvertence only further strengthens the identity we have already posited between Enay and d'Aubigné.

Faeneste is doing the very same thing: trivializing the sacred to suit his profane existence, just as he elsewhere borrows the names of powerful princes to rationalize his own paltry conduct. While Enay sometimes makes predictions, Faeneste is utterly without the gift of prophecy. On one occasion he thinks that he has it: he has a dream in which he is the king, and denies advancement to one of his constables. He calls this dream "prophétique" (739). But *his* prophecy is, as Enay shows through his interpretation of the dream, after the fact: his man-servant has fled, taking with him Faeneste's sword and some of his valuables. The constable to whom Faeneste refused reward in his dream has seized it for himself. The dream is faulty and belated. For Faeneste, "si velles choses" will always "benir à rien" because of the "parestre" (753). Enay teaches Faeneste, and the reader, that correct interpretation must proceed emblematically, accounting for both word and image. Indeed, elsewhere Enay himself reads emblematically. Faeneste quotes a Latin tag to him (*Etiam nos, poma natamus*) and Enay retorts,

> C'est un emblesme d'une maison tombee dans l'eau, là où les estrons allant à nage avec les pommes *disent ce mot,* et les ruines des grandes maisons font nager les excremens les plus vils avec les meilleurs fruicts (716; my emphasis).[25]

He is referring here to the decline of noble houses through the admixture of bad blood and *poseurs* like Faeneste. Faeneste, on the other hand, has no idea what the Latin means, and is merely impressed by its sound. Enay accounts for both word and image, and thereby produces meaning.

Reading and Writing: The Occasions of the Self

The self that is sketched out in the space established by Enay and Faeneste's textual sparring manifests itself in a myriad of ways. In general, the text portrays historicized self, a self produced by theological reflection, an enamored self, and, finally, the self which subsumes them all: the reading and writing self. The emphasis that d'Aubigné places in the *Avantures* on the evolution and elaboration of a conception of self attests to his increasingly self-aware literary creation, and prepares us as readers of his entire literary corpus for the culmination of mutual textual- and self-identification in *Sa Vie.*

---

[25]In a similar instance of misreading, Faeneste misconstrues an insulting epigram (termed by Mario Praz the "literary form of an emblem" [*Studies in Seventeenth Century Imagery*, vol. 1 (Rome: Edizioni di storia e letteratura, 1975-76), 113]), thinking that it is a compliment. He says, "ye pense qu'il fut fait à nostre louange," not realizing that the epigram compares *parvenants* to Caesar, emphasizing Caesar's defeat: "lui et les siens sont des Césars, / Car ils sont vaincus eux mesmes." *Avantures,* 817. Enay must interpret the epigram correctly for Faeneste. Enay tells him: "si vous regardez bien à l'épigramme que vous prenez en faveur il y a de la malice" 817.

The question of the extent to which history predominates over fiction in the *Avantures* must, therefore, be addressed in order to determine the degree to which fiction renders the self possible. It is significant that, throughout the work, Faeneste is displayed as an epitome of his "siècle" (672) and all its cocomitant abuses: the distortion of history, which is demythified by Enay's discourse. It is also important that the emblems at the end of the *Avantures* portray history reified into allegories. D'Aubigné selects types that represent the static, misleading nature of human history, and displays them in apparent "triomphes" in which their evident progress in procession is actually negated. The tapestries' structure includes demarcations of history, seeking spatially and temporally to comment upon all ages of human existence:

> souvenez vous qu'à chaque costé de la salle il faloit trois pentes de tapisserie: la premiere, de ce que fournissoit l'Antiquité; la seconde, de ce que nous avons appris durant la primitive Eglise; la troisieme est des Modernes et de ce temps. Et cet ordre est observé par tout (621).

Elsewhere, the mixing of past and present time[26] signals the omnitemporality of both text and writer and heightens their status, as they are able, like God, to survey all of human history.

The Old French verb "tisser" originally applied to the weaving of tapestries and to the art of "making" a text,[27] so it is not surprising that the most striking emblems in the *Avantures* are pieced out on tapestries. The inclusion of tapestries in the text, as well as the text-within-a-text formed by the commentaries *written upon* the tapestries themselves, alerts us to the need for a new kind of reading. We have spoken of an iconic reading, in which mere representationality is surpassed in favor of a higher, transcendent interpretation. The "tapisseries" may be read in such a way. Indeed, from the fourth to the sixth century in Western Europe there existed *textile icons,* worked out on tapestries, which were designed for religious contemplation.[28]

In the "premier triomphe" the type of "Impietai" performs the descending motion associated with humans and the profane and, particularly, of Faeneste.

---

[26]Referring to Julien l'Apostat, d'Aubigné writes, "les meschants tapisseries l'ont tiré sur *un pourtraict de ce temps* . . . comme celui de Libanius a les traicts de M. le Convertisseur, comme aussi le Visage de Pepinau . . . est tout semblable au feu chancellier de l'Hopital . . ." (822; my emphasis).

[27]André Greimas, *Dictionnaire de l'Ancien français* (Paris: Larousse, 1968) Cf. "tistre," 629.

[28]Kurt Weitzmann, *The Icon* (New York: Georges Braziller, 1978),14. ". . . the story of Epiphanios of Salamis [shows him] tearing down a holy curtain with an image depicted on it."

Impietai's face is hidden for she does not have the clear conscience needed to raise it:

> Sur la place du derrier, plus haute que les autres, (comme il appartient à celle du triomphant) estoit un monstre en forme de vieille femme fardee. . . . Elle avoit tout d'humain pourtant, hormis qu'il lui estoit impossible de lever la face en haut, mais l'avoit ployee en terre comme les brutes; les oreilles lui pendoient comme à un braque, et la faisoient sourde par leur espesseur (820).

Like Faeneste, she is "sourde" to the Word, presented as an insentient image, and in this "triumphal" march lacks any self-mastery. Faeneste, however, continues to misread; he cries "bous boyez que l'Impietai vaisse la face, de pur de parestre, le parestre est donc propre de la Pietai" (821).

The self that is conveyed through historical commentary is one that must be excavated from the text and from history. D'Aubigné writes himself into both projects. He is inscribed in history through his literary creations: "le chariot a pour pavé force livres polemicques . . . et l'*Histoire* d'Aubigné" (824). Because history purports to be self-evident, fiction must necessarily oppose it, in order to be a corrective. D'Aubigné notes that on the tapestries "la bordure des grotesques est d'escriture en chiffres que personne n'entendoit" (820). He is alerting the reader to the imperative of a careful examination of the text. It is notable in this regard that as d'Aubigné, the creator, inscribes himself into his work, Faeneste, the supposed observer, also finds himself written in, in a less favorable light. The *devise* of Faeneste, we are told earlier, is "une fenestre en incarnadin d'Espagne, et la divise: *Entre comme lou vent*" (788). Symbolizing Faeneste's lack of discernment and self-coherence, the *devise* finds itself reworked in the manner in which the tapestries are displayed. Beaujeu, who narrates the tapestries, observes that "l'entrepreneur . . . vid la grand salle, qui ne se pouvoit tapisser à moins de douze pieces, trois de chaque costé, *separees* par les *fenestres,* et d'une bande par la cheminee" (820; my emphasis). It is interesting that, to the extent that the linked tapestries constitute an emblematic text (cartoon and marginalia), their syntactical arrangement is interrupted by the semantic void, the "fenestre," which recalls the symbol of Faeneste's lack of identity.[29] Also, a window is a *frame*, not even itself a complete image. It opens on to everything that passes it, but is utterly passive and without being of its own.

The self that is developed through religious consideration is done so in the space that Enay attempts to maintain between sacred and profane,

---

[29] Lewalski, "*Paradise Lost,*" 111. Lewalski notes that "interpretative frames" produce "scenes of closure which . . . point up how partial, inadequate and incomplete is any single frame – even the biblical one."

but which Faeneste constantly violates. D'Aubigné inserts an interactive space between the components of word and image. The reader is asked to place himself, as does d'Aubigné, in this space as mediator. That is,

> the interaction of fiction (pure language with . . . systemic or ideal meaning) and image (reference to the perceptual world) [pushes beyond the confines of representation] in order to produce clarity, to reveal the real. This triangulation between language system and thing system is the way of . . . all . . . dialogic prose.[30]

Just as for Calvin faith plays a mediatory role, acting as a "kind of tension,"[31] an emblematic reading of the *Avantures* establishes a tension, which it then works through and resolves. In some ways, Faeneste is representative of d'Aubigné's daring act of mixing fiction with theology; however, the resemblance is only superficial, for Faeneste's motivation for doing so is gratuitous, while d'Aubigné feels that he can better witness to transcendence by exemplifying its ability to subsume, and not be contaminated by, the profane. Through participating in the process of reading emblematically, we move beyond superficial appearance to the ultimate reality to which the text has been pointing all along: not unlike God's ability to absorb evil yet remain inviolate, d'Aubigné's text incorporates image but is not contaminated by it; the text prevails.

In the chapter "Entree de table, attaque de religion," Faeneste initiates the discussion of doctrinal matters while seated at table. By insisting on holding theological discussion in what Enay feels is an inappropriate context, Faeneste epitomizes pollution of the sacred by the profane. Enay admonishes him, "nous ne ferons pas de la Theologie un propos de table" (692). Faeneste trivializes the Word through its imprisonment in secular form, when he refers to the Holy Spirit's sneeze, preserved as a relic for Catholic adoration (700).[32] However, Enay undoes such entrapment of the divine in the human, of "être" in "paraître":

> le profit [de ce] discours est qu'il y a six choses desquelles il est dangereux de prendre le Parestre pour l'Estre: le gain, la volupté, l'amitié, l'honneur, le service d'un Roi ou de la Patrie, et la Religion (726).

---

[30]Steiner, *Colors of Rhetoric,* 116.

[31]Selinger, *Calvin against Himself,* 211.

[32]A similar problem obtains for the depiction of the divine in images. Jaroslav Pelikan, *The Christian Tradition: A History of the Development of Doctrine,* vol. 2 (Chicago: University of Chicago Press, 1974), 115. "Either an image of Christ assayed to picture him both with his divine nature and his human nature, or it contented itself with picturing him only in his humanity. If it were to claim to be doing the former, it would be maintaining that the divine nature was susceptible to being circumscribed in a portrait."

While Faeneste claims to have "seen" all the ramifications of theology ("je bus donc bous conbertir aprés soupai et bous faire parestre que j'ai beu toute la theologie moderne" [692]), Enay insists that it is *content,* and not form, that is essential: "l'estoffe est plus que la façon" (692). Thus, the self that fears to meditate upon the significance of theology is a superstitious, ill-defined self, and the revision of Calvinism that d'Aubigné must effect in order to write is actually seen to be more faithful to Calvin's original intent than the expedient of blind acceptance. That is, the hermeneutic tradition of Calvinism that requires the recognition of the limitation of the reader's abilities in the presence of the Word paradoxically forces a *knowing of the self* so that such limitations may be discerned within the self. As a result, d'Aubigné surpasses permissible reiteration to rework and rewrite, ultimately creating his own work. Making the same sort of distinction, Enay contrasts mere "saying" with "understanding" the prayer one offers. He finds that the expression of Faeneste's self in prayer is inauthentic, for he is too much in the world.[33] As an image, Faeneste does not attend to discourse. Hence, his communications are unclear and truncated. He begins the *Ave Maria,* for instance, in the middle of the prayer, thereby allowing no contextual development and rendering the prayer incomprehensible:

> F.–"Mais j'ouvlie de bous expliquer ma priere c'est: Et les vien heureuses entrailles de Marie qui ont pourté le Fils du Pere eternel." E.–"Comment? Vous commencez par un Et?" F. – "Pour bous dire, il y a debant. . . . Mais je ne di jamais gueres le premier pour accourcir" (697).

Because for him words are devoid of meaning, it is all the same at what point he begins his prayer. The mingling of Faeneste's secular self with sacred expression results in a senseless phrase. Enay attempts to sort out the jumble by pointing, as does d'Aubigné, to the need for theo-literary interpretation: the prayer can be understood if certain *grammatical* points are rectified:

> Il faut que ce soit Dieu aie pitié des entrailles ou qu'elles aient pitié de nous. F.–On n'ezamine pas ces chauses à boste mode; nostre Theolougie n'a que faire de la Gramaire, car aussi vien ce *mais* debroit contredire et ne le fait pas (698).

Faeneste resists Enay's attempt at syntactical salvage; the more mystifying speech is, the more it translates the effects of miracles, Faeneste believes:

---

[33]For instance, he attempts to prove his intelligence through his *secular* education, failing to acknowledge the need for a theological formation: "Oy da, j'ai esté de la première au college de Guienne, et de la Philosophie à Poictiers, où nous paressons bien escouliers" (697).

"Il semvle qu'il n'y a pas grand sens à cela, et c'est ce qui faict tant de merbeilles" (698).

D'Aubigné's decision to treat the entire Catholic-Calvinist controversy as though it is entirely motivated by incorrect grammar attests to his desire to incorporate the sacred into his literary vehicle. His insistence is, like Enay's, on the demystification of words so that things may be fittingly labelled, and so that the superstitious will not rest their faith on sham. To this point, Enay recites the following epigram. He chooses a *literary* genre to discuss the sacred, in an attempt to right the perception of what may properly be called "holy":

> Que dites-vous, disoit n'agueres
> Le bon Curé des Ardilieres,
> Des miracles qu'on faict ceans . . .
> –Je responds qu'ils sont invisibles.
> –Vous estes, dit l'autre, terribles,
> Si vous ouvrez encor les yeux,
> Si vos oreilles ne sont sourdes,
> Tant de bourdes de ces boiteux
> Qu'en dites-vous? Ce sont des bourdes.

(705)

The play between presence and absence (in this case, the misnomer "miracle," since abandoned crutches do not necessarily indicate a miraculous cure),[34] is carried further by the contrast between Faeneste's stress on the "bisivle," while Enay points to the "invisible."[35] Taken literarily, the theological sign that Faeneste claims is presence is, in fact, absence for, as Enay notes, the apparent sign must always, dialectically, point to something beyond itself and function as a signifier. Thus the theological discussion leads us to read texts, as well as miracles and purported eruptions of the divine, like icons. In the final tapestries of the *Avantures*, for example, "estre" is opposed to "parestre." In the tapestry showing the martyrs of the Protestant church, the biblical meaning of the word "parestre" is employed to show the persecutors *appearing* to triumph, while in fact this image's true sense is eschatological; the martyrs who presently *appear* to suffer will be redeemed at the Last Judgment (825). Faeneste errs in restricting the painting to two-dimensionality, while Enay causes it to

---

[34]Enay comments, "je m'y menois pour demander un miracle qui fut vray et vrayment miracle. Je les ay trouvez invisibles, et c'est le poinct où je m'accorde avec vous pour demander le parestre." *Avantures*, 688.

[35]Similarly, the apparent presence of Faeneste's bodily hygiene is in fact an absence, for, as his valet alerts us, in keeping with the "parestre," Faeneste "est propre comme un chandelier de bois aux choses qui paressent; pour le reste . . . ." he is not. *Avantures*, 728.

function as an icon (which might be called the emblem of emblematic reading). An icon is not representational in intention. All lines of direction in an icon disrupt perspective and point-of-view, forcing the viewer out of the image. A painting, on the other hand, is designed for a frame, facilitating its perception from a particular angle, and allowing it to be contained and analyzed as a static object.[36]

Enay moves beyond the explicit potential of warp and woof to a transcendental reading of the tapestry. Iconic language is

> "tensile" . . . in its . . . simultaneous existence as physical object and as intellectual referent to something other. . . . The physical and spiritual [Calvin realizes] [can] not *be* one, but in language they [can] be *at* one.[37]

Language is thus paradoxically, through d'Aubigné's revision of Calvinism, privileged both as a medium for the revelation of the sacred and for the development of the self. Writing, when it is faithful to the self that motivates it, and even fiction, when it contains inscribed within it the self which devises it, is expressive of "estre" rather than "parestre": it is not idle display, but essential communication. Writing, properly disciplined, may reveal truth:

> F.–"Et comment jugerez-bous que l'intention est vonne?" E.–"Quand elle s'accorde à la regle du bien . . . ce que nous demanderons au jour et au flambeau de la verité" (700).

It is true that d'Aubigné may still feel some ambivalence concerning this point, which he nevertheless surmounts by completing the *Avantures*. At one point Enay does state that "jamais le mensonge n'édifia la vérité" (687). It is, consequently, d'Aubigné's task throughout the *Avantures* to move toward a way of valorizing fiction and showing it is not a lie. He does so

---

[36]Puttenham, *Art of Englishe Poesie*, cited in Lewalski, *"Paradise,"* 181. Puttenham gives icons their *usual, non-theological* definition by terming them "resemblance by imagerie or pourtraict," "a visible representation of the thing [the painter] describes." However, icons as religious objects *read literally* function somewhat differently. The qualities of hieratic depiction, progressive dematerialization and spiritualization of representation indicate the painter's hidden agenda which elicits a move *beyond* concrete portrayal to an *abstract pattern*, a deeper sense. As the picture disintegrates, fractured by multiple points of view, an effort at reassemblage is required on the reader's part, which is analogous to the act of reading. Examples may be found in Weitzmann, *The Icon*. For instance, a disturbingly altered spatial representation characterizes Ohrid's *Icon with the Annunciation* (Weitzmann, 126, œ 44); a temporal oscillation in which the reader begins with the central point of Christ but is compelled by the mandorla structure to refer continually back and forth between Christ and the other figures is found in the *Paris Mosaic Icon with Transfiguration of Christ,* (no. 28); the arresting eyes of most of the icons create the impression of being drawn *out* of the picture, while multiple lines of direction then move the viewer *through* and *beyond* mere representation.

[37]Selinger, *Calvin against Himself,* 176.

through the unique strategy of writing himself into his text and thus standing as a guarantor for his words. Ultimately, writing must be a *scripture of the self* that reveals authenticity: by inscribing a factual self into a fictional work, the work is attested to and legitimized. On the other hand, much of Faeneste's expression, including any writing he does, is merely derivative: he does not speak his own words, but only those of others. He must rely on the creations of others, which he reifies and delivers second-hand. Enay observes of Faeneste, and of other Catholics, that "ils emplissent leurs lettres des pas et des paroles des plus gens de bien du pays, en destournant toutes choses de leur droit sens" (762).

This parasitical experience of the world prohibits an authentic formulation of the self, as the description of Faeneste's amorous adventures demonstrates. It is a common classical and Renaissance *topos* that love is associated with writing, for the romantic inspiration lends impetus to poetic expression. However, in Faeneste's case the recognized relationship is distorted. Not only does Faeneste not succeed in writing of his love episode, he cannot even succeed in speaking of it coherently. Rather than possess a love object, he becomes the object of the futile narration he fails to articulate. He does not even possess a style of expression unique to himself but parodies that of others. Here, as in his historical and religious existence, he is derivative. His amorous serenade of a lady on a balcony ends in a denial both of the "parestre"–his extravagant attire and inflated lyrics fail to impress her–as well as the "estre"–his protestations of heart-felt love are revealed, in his sudden spite, to be superficial:

> Comme nous finissons ceux dux vers: "Sois de douceur la fontaine, comme tu l'es de beauté," me boila une terrace pleine de pissat, abec quauque bilanie parmi . . . Mes compagnons se mirent à injures: l'un l'appella fontaine de merde, l'autre fontaine de pissat (713).

Faeneste is, as always, portrayed as an image, the object of his own failed attempt at speech: his "vers" are abruptly silenced by *another* external agency–the love object that gives proof of more dynamism than does Faeneste himself–and the confused structure of the phrase "me boilà une terrace pleine de pissat" not only frames Faeneste in filth, but "me boilà" almost implies that he himself becomes that very space that filth invades.

Similarly, despite all his efforts to achieve the spectacular "parestre," Faeneste finds himself in incongruous positions when he tries to speak of love. Faeneste is often described hung upside down due to some ridiculous miscalculation on his part. He also sympathizes with like predicaments that other characters in the tale experience. For instance, Brilbaut, a courtier, is sent to a whore before whom he is to impersonate the king, thereby relieving the king of his promise to sleep with her. She unmasks him and calls for help. In his fright, Brilbaut falls out of the window[38] and hangs from a tree limb, "la chemise troussee sous les esselles, les bras enveloppez dedans, le voilà pendu" (725). Similarly, Faeneste is found with his shirt over his head and his nakedness revealed; Cherbonniere relates that

> mon maistre ne fut pas si heureux à Paris, que deux Sergens emmenerent, lui donnant du pommeau de la dague dans le croupion pour le faire aller. Il fait . . . le brave au commencement, et puis se coiffe de sa chemise (735).

Enay alerts us that all those who seek to appear but have no internal coherence will be subject to a like fate: he recounts the tale of a pious doctor who dons a cassock to make an imposing pilgrimage. Watched by all the gaping villagers, he suddenly loses control of his mule who, it turns out, is an "heretical" mule (that is, a Protestant). The doctor is found hours later, in the same reversed position as that which Faeneste and Brilbaut experience: "enfin la lune estant levee, lui virent le cul le premier" (737-38). The reversal and insistence on a descriptively descending movement has implications for the discussion of the paradigm of reading that the *Avantures* suggests.

All Faeneste's attempts at the "parestre" through the pretext of love are negated. His disguises and costumes are shown to be more substantial than he himself:

> Quand je fus debenu amoreux de la Dame, [un magicien] me changea un yor en un escaveau, surquoi Ferbaques s'assioit prés d'elle; le rivaut me fit ploier les rens en se laissant choir sur moi; et pris plaisir d'entendre de lurs amours; par fois ils disoent mal du praube Varon de Faeneste: en fin, mon gouberneur s'abisant que les yamves de l'escabeau plioient, et suoit, à grosses gouttes, il s'en bint dire au Maneschal: "Si bous boulez estre au Coucher du Roi, il est temps,' et ensi il me delibra d'un pesant fardeau" (722).

The tale of love that Faeneste attempts to tell is rapidly silenced by the actual, physical heft of those of whom he tries to speak: Fervaques causes Faeneste to fold in half beneath his bulk, and overwhelms Faeneste's narration by forcing him to hear himself spoken of mockingly. Faeneste is powerless to put an end to the physical suffering that is brought on him

---

[38]It is tempting because of the prevalence of images of windows in the *Avantures* to speculate that they may be strewn throughout the narrative to remind us of Faeneste's revealing *devise.* "Faeneste" itself may be a pun on "fenestre." Faeneste is, indeed, often displayed framed by windows. He states, for instance, "ye recevois toujours quauque affront abec ces Nourmans. Un yor ye les ouis rire par une fenestre qu'ils me regardoient marcher par le rue." *Avantures,* 716.

by his attempts at narration; he must wait for another, the magician, to relieve him.

The "je" of another always prevails over that of Faeneste, revealing his credulity, his lack of substance, and his readiness to be manipulated through description or deception. In the following episode, Faeneste's desire to impress his lady and, simultaneously, to amaze the court is unexpectedly effective:

> un soir [le magicien] me mena vien bestu, et quand ye fus dans la salle, tout lou monde me prenoit pour nud . . . En nous retirant au soir, ye m'abise d'un vrabe trait: "Cette dame," di ye, "me met la men sur les chaussses en debisant; ne me sauriez-bous mener là dedans tout nud, et que je semvlasse vien bestu?" (722-23).

The magician grants Faeneste his wish to appear dressed despite his actual nudity. But since others, unlike Faeneste, are able to discern appearance from reality, he is, as it were, abruptly exposed. Having surrendered himself passively to the magician who "[le] mena" before the court which "[le] prenoit," Faeneste has no authority over himself and cannot regulate either his appearance or being. Unable to comprehend words, he is discussed as though he were an image in a frame; he is "monstré" before the court (recalling the pejorative emphasis Calvinists give to the Catholic term "monstance" in contemporary pamphlets), and after experiencing the humiliation of having all eyes at court upon him Faeneste then voluntarily reframes himself in another setting: "ye saute en la salle comme un lion . . . Aprés quauques essuyades, ye gagne la garderove où ye *m'enfermai*" (723; my emphasis). He is *structurally incapable* of anything but an illusory "parestre"; always presented, by himself and others, as an image, he is inevitably deceived by the discourse of both himself and others. In fact, the preparation for Faeneste's exposure before the court is contained from the very beginning as a warning in his transaction with the magician, for if Faeneste knew how to hear, read and understand, he would be aware that the gnomic formula he is instructed to recite is actually a mockery of his own credulity. The magic spell, to be understood, has to be read backwards; that is, removed from the context of "parestre," which reverses all things, and re-reversed in the truth of "estre." "Tassius ei," mouths Faeneste devoutly, confessing, unbeknownst to himself or to the unwary reader, "je suis sot" (722). Even after the incident, however, Faeneste still fails to realize how completely befuddled he is by the magician's illusions and the "parestre"; he insists that the only reason the spell does not work is because, in his haste to assay it, he omits the magic utterance: "l'excuse fut que nous abions failli aux mouts" (723).

Enay notes that as Faeneste has no self-integrity or coherence, "l'Estre et le Parestre tomberent d'accord en [son] accident" (723). The episode itself is a model for how Faeneste's character is to be apprehended for, with its interplay between presence and absence, visibility and invisibility, it shows clearly that Faeneste is absent even from himself, is an unreliable narrator, and is ultimately subordinated as image to the narration of others and to the text itself. Faeneste in love is shown to be no more than the illusion of any ability to achieve his amorous goals.

Text, Tapestry and Transcendence

Because the *Avantures* is constituted explicitly as a text that consciously contains, and strategically employs, both image and word, it calls for a new kind of reading in which the two may be played off against each other dialectically. In this respect, the *Avantures* is a textual figuration, or emblem, of sin and salvation through which d'Aubigné must move in order to create literarily. Faeneste, the image, is devalued just as sin is, yet ultimately is paradoxically necessary to salvation (one must be saved *from* something). A new way of reading is thus likened to the dialectical process through which salvation is obtained, and both theological and literary considerations are thereby linked in this *apparently* profane piece of fiction. It is, consequently, important that we examine the particulars of this innovative manner of reading.

Certain clues alert us that such a different pattern of reading is required. We have already observed that the figure of Faeneste functions as the image that Enay glosses. We note also that examples of emblems are themselves frequently incorporated into the text.

Faeneste describes the criteria that he believes writing should fulfill. He obviously opposes any writing that requires critical sifting, preferring books that function as images. In fact, most of the types of books he favors contain a quantity of images.

> Il seroit de besoin pour l'Eglise qu'on ne s'accoustumast point à tant de subtilitais, et qu'on fist vrusler tous les libres qui empeschent la debotion par leurs abisements. Il ne faut libres que de la croix, des hures à l'usage de Jean le Cocq et à la moude . . . si bous boulez des sermons, çus de Varletta et Menotus; *La Legende doreye* de la bieille impression: car tous çus qui les ont corrigeais se sentent en cela de l'Huguenot (817).

He opposes the act of reading, as he alerts us when he cites what he considers to be an authoritative text: "pour les saboir lire y'ai troubai un excellent libre fait par la Chaume Guinart qui s'appelle *l'Art d'Aprenmolire*" (817). We may construe this as the act of learning to "molire," or to be softened and weakened in one's intellectual faculties as well as in one's capacities for faith.[39]

If Faeneste is the antithesis of writing or of apprehending in a literary mode, Enay epitomizes both the reader and the writer. In the *Avantures,* he speaks of "un de mes voisins" who is working on a novel that is remarkably like the text we are reading: "le corps est d'un Baron de ce pays, qui comme Don Quichot[40] voyagea pour remettre la Chevalerie errante . . . Il lui arrive des accidents . . . ." The text even echoes some of Faeneste's statements in the *Avantures*; for instance, the character in the "novel" mimics,

> l'hoste propose que le train estoit un peu trop modeste et de trop peu d'esclat pour une si haute entreprise, pource, disoit il, que sans parestre vous ne pouvez garder vostre authorité (768).

Enay, upon hearing Faeneste's inquiry, professes himself able to relate "et le commencement et la fin," having already "leu [le livre] deux fois" (764). He thereby establishes himself as the authorial voice behind the novel, for before that he has been insisting that the book is not yet finished (765). He goes on to give a synopsis of the novel, and several excerpts from it in the form of oral anecdotes. The significance of Enay commenting *within* the *Avantures* (which is in process, through our act of reading) on the composition of the *Avantures* itself (as though it is not already written) serves two purposes. First, it confers a great deal of authority upon Enay himself who is now, we realize, capable not merely of commenting upon Faeneste's image, but also of intervening in the very text of the *Avantures* to influence its outcome. Secondly, it creates a *mise en abyme* effect, in which the current text is, as it were, inscribed in the third-person within itself. This recalls two of d'Aubigné's strategies: that of the inter-referential system and that of self-inscription. Because the text refers to itself obliquely as an *exemplum within itself* (Enay's book contains themes in common with the *Avantures*), we are reminded of the manner in which, within the over-arching structure of d'Aubigné's literary corpus, all his works refer back to each other and intersect at different points to create the impression

[39]The editors of the Pléiade suggest that the title is, rather, an abbreviation of "l'art d'apprendre-mot-lire." *Avantures*, 1398. If this is so, it still supports the contention that the word "mot" is being truncated in the title, as Faeneste in his image-oriented way disregards the importance of verbal and written communication.

[40]Faeneste resembles Don Quixote in that his adventures designate him as a reified sign, incapable of participating in the dynamics of metaphoric resemblance and thus existing contrary to language. His entire being is composed of nothing but stories others have told of him. Cf. Foucault, *Order of Things*, 46.

of a self-sufficient literary universe.[41] By commenting upon each other, his works function both as text and as gloss, and therefore need no supplemental outside authority. The technique by which d'Aubigné writes images (albeit *dynamic* ones) of himself into his text is recalled because it, too, is a *mise en abyme* structure.[42] We see d'Aubigné watching himself as he operates inside, and outside, his text. Thus, by referring to the *Avantures* as his work-in-progress, Enay strengthens the case for the authority of his discourse since he thereby likens himself to d'Aubigné and thus to historical reality.

Enay, therefore, is the reliable narrator who will instruct us in how to read his work. Faeneste is paradigmatic, as we have noted, of the credulous reader. Yet the text itself is complicitous in creating confusion. The typography of the text wilfully confounds the two speakers at times, soliciting the reader's discernment to unravel its true sense. For instance, in the chapter "Theologie de Surgeres, querelle du Baron," Faeneste speaks the last line of the tale Enay is narrating; it should be Enay who completes the tale he tells (720).

Image and word must be read jointly for this text to make sense. Enay, and the reader who mimics him, must therefore bestow signification on the empty signs of the narrative. Faeneste, as image, threatens to rupture discourse. However, constricting Faeneste through his commentary and thereby, in an act of "textual cannibalism," incorporating him, Enay finds *within himself,* (unlike the Anglican Vaughn who, in *Silex scintillans* finds *outside*) "hyeroglyphics quite dismembered / And broken letters scarce remembered",[43] which he may then reassemble. We as readers participate in this act of restructuring. In that discourse itself is composed of word-pictures, the *Avantures* approximate oral speech and presence more nearly than any of d'Aubigné's other works. Consequently, in its fictional status, it may be perceived as more threatening to Scripture, the written form of

---

[41]In the *Avantures,* for instance, we find a mention of the character Sancy on page 823: ". . . comme faisoit Sanci au massacre d'Orléans en tuant son hostie." The "Imprimeur au Lecteur" recalls that of the *Tragiques,* with the parallel drawn between "livre" and author's "enfant"; "l'autheur avoit condamné au feu ce dernier livre . . . [mais] je trouvai moyen d'en desrober une grande partie . . . [et] il a esté constraint de faire comme la bonne mère ne pouvant voir son enfant mi-parti" (672). Other instances may be found in the Pléiade edition on the following pages: 671, 699, 700, 704, 716, 724, 766, 790, 811, 826 and 828.

[42]It is illuminating to compare this strategy with a similar one effected to a different purpose by the Puritan Thomas Traherne. In his "Fourth Century" he attempts to "move beyond the limitations of personal experience and to grasp the essential principles of a life lived in the presence of God . . . . He attempts to project an ideal image of his best possible self, and he speaks of this self *as if it were another person* . . . . The dominant mode of this writing is thus in *the third person,* as contrasted with the intimate autobiography of the 'Third Century'–and the personal 'I' is always breaking through to make it clear that 'the friend' and 'He' are ideal projections of the man who has revealed himself in the previous Century." Louis Martz, *The Paradise Within* (New Haven: Yale University Press, 1964), 97; my emphasis.

[43]Martz, *Paradise,* 18.

the oral *logos*. Yet, "in the case of *logos*, words [are] supposed to be the vehicles of meaning independent of the imaginative appreciation of referents."[44] Here, fiction rejoins *mythos*, valorizes itself in its own right as *verba* but not *verbum*, permits sensorial apprehension, and begins a course that is parallel in self-sufficiency to that of the Bible. In *Sa Vie* this strategy will be fully realized when, through "formal meditation upon the individual's past experience, autobiography become[s] assimilable as *logos*."[45] Self-inscription is an exteriorizing of the self in a pure literary beginning.[46]

Enay calls for attention to the text in all its ramifications. He attempts to teach truth, dialectically, through Socratic dialogue, a process of faulty formulation (Faeneste) and subsequent correction (Enay). When, for instance, Faeneste reproaches him with the tedious quality of Calvinist preaching and writing, Enay invokes a standard of fidelity to the Word which Faeneste is incapable of grasping, for his imagination only finds appeal in disjointed, sensual imagery. He only understands fractured, imagic discourse in which tableaux alone are presented (for instance, theological explication becomes for him a mere matter of adoration of images: "la chapelle est pleine de si veaux tableaux qu'on y est tout rabi en debotion" [805]). Enay, on the other hand, approves only *textually-motivated* discourse. He observes that the Calvinist preaching style is wholly other:

> F.–"Il faut abouer que le style et la feiçon de nos Prescheurs sont bien otres chouses que celles de vos prouves Ministres, ausquels on ne permet ni Allegories, ni Paravolles, ni Favles, ni gentillesses, ni livertez qui biennent quequesfois vien à proupos, quand ce ne seroit pour resbeiller lou puble. . . ." E.–"Non, on ne permet pas ces gayetez à nos Ministres, mesmes on leur defend les Allegories, tant qu'on peut, pour les attacher à leur texte sans eschapper" (792).

Enay requires context and completeness for textual comprehension, denigrating the inadequate impression that derives from truncated words or syntactical hiatuses:

> Panigarole, commençant par ces mots: "C'est pour vous, belle, que je meurs," en appliquant ses yeux sur une galande . . . le peuple tout estonné de cette entree, se rasseura quand . . . ce bon Docteur suivit: "dit nostre Seigneur à l'église" (792).

---

[44]Kaufmann, *Puritan Meditations*, 11.

[45]Ibid., 24.

[46]Jacques Derrida, "Violence et métaphysique," *L'Ecriture*, (1967): 169. As Derrida notes, "l'inscription est l'origine écrite tracée et dès lors inserte dans un système, dans une figure qui ne commande plus."

He mandates that unrelated or extraneous images be extirpated when he counsels Faeneste: "y mettez du vostre le moins que vous pourrez" (794).

On the other hand, Enay still holds out the possibility of "inventio," and does not choose solely to epitomize the "plain style," for such a language would be counter-productive: "a language in which all meanings are systems would be a language precluding the necessity of speech."[47] Thus, false "inventio" contrasts in the text with opportunities for permissible "inventio." Enay even dares to include an occasional salacious anecdote in his narration, if it is illustrative of his message: a wronged husband in a tale Enay recounts demands of his wife and her lover:

> Vous, comme Procureur de l'ancienne maison, et vous, comme estant le tige feminin, je veux que vous presentiez à justice, de vos deux mains unies ensemble, les parties nobles offensees par enorme contusion, et que vous vous rendiez parties, pour voir aujourd'huy torce et arrachee la racine et l'organe par lequel devoit pululer l'illustre germe (770).

Enay then concludes, "voilà comment succeda le remede aux desordres de la France," showing that he employs this example for a purpose.

Incorporating Enay's instructions about writing and reading into a fictional narrative, d'Aubigné distinguishes between the opposing kinds of "inventio." One is associated with Satan, for "les diables eurent recours à l'invention" (795) in their struggle with God. Such corrupt inventions are to be removed from the literary vocabulary. We find this concern epitomized in the following account of the fate that befalls the illustration of a too-well-endowed devil hung above a church altar.

> A ce rustre de Diable pendoient deux gros et immenses testicules où bon frippon de peintre s'estoit esgayé. Cela fut trouvé de mauvais exemple, et le Chapitre assemblé pour y adviser, pource que cela scandalizoit les Dames et faisoit rire les Huguenots. Le débat fut grand, si on pouvoit toucher à estropier un tableau sacré . . . enfin, le plus de voix porta que le Diable n'engendroit point, qu'il seroit chastré par le peintre, qui eut charge ainsi d'abbaiser de couleur de marbre . . . trop enluminez (804).

The painter's individual contribution to his work might be legitimate, the anecdote seems to imply, in a secular context. Viewed theologically, however, it is a distortion. Distinct valorization of the self through such additions is not acceptable in a theological context. Note that it is indeed the individual invention–the painter's decision to emblazon the devil's

---

[47]Steiner,*Colors of Rhetoric*, 101.

testicles–rather than the overall subject matter–the appropriateness of the devil himself–which is at issue with the perturbed priests.

The problem of distinguishing between acceptable and unacceptable "inventio" is crucial for d'Aubigné's use of fiction. A historical change in point of view must be acknowledged in order to address this question. That is, common assumptions about the manner in which to view a work of art exist in the sixteenth century, in which clearly delineated areas are blocked out to govern the placement of viewer and viewed. Interaction is limited, and the degree to which the viewer can "enter into" a painting is blocked by two-dimensional representation as well as framing devices. In the above description of the painting of Satan, the image, despite its subject matter, is potentially unalterable simply because "elle est image consacree dans l'Eglise" (805); the priests debate "si on pouvoit toucher à estropier un tableau sacré." They allow form to prevail over content. Not only that, but when they finally do dare to castrate the demon, they *literally* attribute to him much greater power than a *figurative* image may have, explaining that they castrate him so as to ensure that "le Diable n'engendroit point." As Faeneste assumes elsewhere,

> on ne doit pas seulement saluer le Sainct ou la Saincte [qu'un tableau] représente, mais pource qu'elle est image consacree dans l'Eglise. . . . L'Eglise ne sauroit vien parestre sans images (805).

D'Aubigné, by establishing his art in a literary rather than painterly medium, and by encouraging the iconic movement in and through the text which we have described elsewhere, opens up greater permission for "inventio" and the entrance of the self into the work. He simultaneously demonstrates a shift in the relationship between viewer and viewed.

The significance of the constant dialogic interplay between Enay, Faeneste and, in the fourth book, Beaujeu, is that speech is never crystallized for long into mere static description: while Faeneste is always an image, Enay, Beaujeu, d'Aubigné and the reader conspire to create space in which they move freely in and around his image, commenting upon it from varying angles. Thus the would-be viewer may sometimes become the viewed, as we have noted is the case with Faeneste. The viewer may repudiate that which he views, as Enay does at times with Faeneste, or may develop a complex pattern of interaction with the viewed through which he gradually assimilates the latter. Images of d'Aubigné inscribed within his text cause us to question whether he is the viewer or the viewed. When the reader finds the imperative of his own textual involvement[48] mandated by the *Avantures*, his status as viewer or viewed is also problematic

---

[48]The very first words of the *Avantures* show this role: the "lecteur" is defined specifically as "lecteur qui *cherches*" (674; my emphasis).

and provocative. Such questions will be fully resolved in d'Aubigné's autobiography.

In the *Avantures*, the mixture of viewpoints leads us to the suggestion that it may be possible to combine theological and literary considerations in the same work. How may this be effected?

While Enay disparages the mingling of sacred and profane apparent in Faeneste's conversation ("quel meslange d'affaires en la teste de ce pauvre Baron" [707]), he and Beaujeu nevertheless valorize the emblems at the end of the *Avantures*. There, a *secular, allegorical* medium is used to portray theological issues. In fact, in that Enay is only half of a dialectical entity which will be formed once he assimilates Faeneste, Enay fittingly expresses some of d'Aubigné's ambivalence about theo-literary writing. In addition, it is possible that the presence of Faeneste in the text acts as a repository for d'Aubigné's mixed feelings over literary (and especially fictional) creation.[49] While Enay scolds Faeneste, "il y a trois sortes de gloire: la divine, celle du cavallier et celle du barbier. De la divine, il n'en faut point parler en nos causeries" (779), that is nevertheless exactly what he goes on to do.

Theology and literature may conjoin if *the act of reading* itself is correctly directed. Of course, we have already recognized that Faeneste is absolutely incapable of such critical perception. Faeneste, parallel with the reversed postures we have seen him in elsewhere in the narrative,[50] *reads in reverse*[51] and, hence, lacks comprehension. Because he cannot understand content, context or even form accurately, he resorts to the purely unmotivated permission of the imagination to decide that any given element may be construed in any way that *seems* useful. Enay labels *this* sort of invention when he associates it with spies:

oui, mais ce mestier [d'espion] veut une grande dilligence, dexterité, invention, impudence, et avec tout cela il n'est point sans danger: car quand l'espion n'a rien de vrai à produire, il faut qu'il entretienne sa boutique de faussetés (762).

[49]A certain degree of ironic sympathy for, or even identity with, Faeneste can be seen on d'Aubigné's part in the "Imprimeur au lecteur": while d'Aubigné calls Faeneste a "baron en l'air," he also refers to Enay as a "faux Poictevin." Similarly, Faeneste is a Gascon, and d'Aubigné includes a mini-*éloge* of Gascons. *Avantures*, 669.

[50]"Il n'y a qu'une chose qui me fasche en ce mestier. C'est qu'aujourd'huy n'est pas tenu pour Gentilhomme qui n'est toujours voté et esperonné. . . . Les vottes failli à ruiner principalement quand je boulois m'arrouser au bet à trabers d'une palisse, mes esperons se prenoient aux espines, et je demourois pendu par les pieds: toutesfois il faut ovéir à la mode" (774).

[51]Cf. Chapter Three on *Les Tragiques*, where God's book is read in reverse, and where d'Aubigné suggests the possibility of reading his text in reverse.

Faeneste's ability to be deceived through his misreading is actually written into the concluding emblem as the figure of Ignorance:

La Dame est toute nue . . . les yeux petits . . . elle lit par contenance dans un Breviaire, *de bas en haut* . . . s'esclatte de rire en y lisant, comme y trouvant la matiere plaisante et delicate (823; my emphasis).

While Faeneste and Impietai read improperly, Beaujeu instructs us as to how correct reading may proceed. In so doing he makes a case for literary invention. The emblems with which the book concludes are consequently pieces to which the interpreter must continually return in his search for meaning in the otherwise apparently picaresque and fragmented puzzle of words and images that make up the *Avantures*.[52]

The tapestries upon which the emblems are pieced out do indeed consist of word (on the tapestries: "d'escriture en chiffres que personne n'entendoit," [820]; and, projected into the future, "les gloses que les copieux feront sur ces belles histoires" [820]) and image ("ces grotesques" [820]). Their importance is highlighted before we may even examine them, for it is clear at the outset that they are produced during a scene of *semantic confusion* similar to that which Faeneste epitomizes:

Puisque vous allez à Lyon, dit la Dame, je vous prie de me faire une patisserie (je voulois dire une tapisserie) de quelque nouvelle invention. S'il se peut, qu'il y ait des bresmes?–Qu'appelez-vous des bresmes? dit le poete.–C'est, répond la Dame, de cela qu'il y avoit en la tapisserie que Le Roy osta à Madame . . .–je voi ce que vous voulez dire avec vos bresmes: ce sont des emblesmes. . . . Vous prenez des mots que vous n'entendez pas pour mots de cuisine (819).

In addition, the tapestry is not meant merely to be contemplated, as Faeneste would prefer to do, but to be attended to, to be *heard* as revealed truth; it is a "Prophetie en tapisserie" (830). This "prophécie" contrasts starkly in both method of presentation and interpretation with the would-be prophecy Faeneste claims to see in his *énigme*.

The emblems portray not historical "triomphes" but ultimate eschatological triumphs. Significantly, the book of *Revelation* itself is customarily construed in the sixteenth century as emblematic in structure, "a sequence of emblematic scenes or pageants requiring interpretation."[53]

Without interpretation, contemporary events *seem* against the Huguenots. Yet, both d'Aubigné's and the Bible's emblems assure us, the outcome will

---

[52]A similar pattern of suggested reading may be seen in Spenser's *Faerie Queen,* which opens with the "iconic, tapestry-like description of the Red Queen and the Dwarf." Lewalski, *"Paradise,"* 182.

[53]Lewalski, *"Paradise,"* 225.

ultimately be favorable to them. The emblems demonstrate this by borrowing elements from history and reworking them in an expectant, soteric context. The "triomphes" show a world set *à l'envers* so that divine restoration may ensue. Fiction is here the medium for the restoration of this expression. History, normally construed as fact, is reversed to the status of fiction which the Last Judgment reveals to be mere appearance. If fact can be so debased, why, then, can d'Aubigné's fiction not be exalted as possessing a status commensurate with that of divine history? Fiction, that is, may actually be fact, and it is only an inadequate reading that prohibits a recognition of its merits.

The elaborate system of presentation breaks history down into three epochs. The pictures are built upon textual artifacts from each period, stressing the connection of truth with writing; these books are truthful yet are being trampled underfoot temporarily by such misreaders as Impietai, Ignorance and Superstition.

> Pour le pavé du chariot, vous y voyez les Evangiles, les fueillets d'Eusebe, et autres bons livres de ce temps. . . . Le chariot a pour pavé force livres polemicques, *l'Institution*. . . . De ce rang sont la *Sepmaine* de Du Bartas, les livres de du Moulin, *l'Histoire* de d'Aubigné (822-24).

The only two aspects of historical thought that are valued are those that in no way participate in the "parestre": writing, and the martyrs (826). This suggests an equivalence between literary and theological witness. The emblems are themselves composed artistically as is a *literary* work, with license granted to the author to include or omit details as he feels necessary: "plusieurs tragedies de France, d'Angleterre, d'Italie, de Flandres et d'ailleurs, sont en si grand nombre qu'elles ne peuvent trouver la place, et ne sont mises ici que *par abregé*" (822; my emphasis). Each tapestry is not self-evident in its "parestre," despite Faeneste's insistence that it is so. Rather, each is a separate signifying system that must be interpreted both separately and in conjunction with the other tapestries to determine its true meaning, its "estre." "Nous aurons encor besoin de l'explication du Poete," Beaujeu concedes, emphasizing the literary interpretation the primarily theological content will be given. The "estre" must be diligently sought for, as the "parestre" will mislead the reading ("si la semblance ne me trompe . . ." [821]). Finally, one area of the tapestry, that which hangs over the chimney, is left blank: "cette cheminee donc reste pour les propheties, et la variation des modes" (830). In this way, the *Avantures,* as well, is left open-ended as an organic work[54] to which only the reader may write the conclusion,

---

[54]D'Aubigné also acknowledges this open-endedness in the last words of the *Avantures*: "Adieu jusques à une matière qui pourra servir de cinquièsme livre à Faeneste" (830).

because "il y a force choses que le Poete n'a pas interpretees" (830). Through the emblems, and through the *Avantures,* the reader may learn that appearance is not being; the fictional cloak of the text disguises a hidden truth; sinfulness may be transmuted into salvation:

> Or ça, M. le Baron, vous voyez la diversité de ces tableaux: de quelle bande aimeriez-vous mieux estre? F.–"Cap Sant Arnaud! J'aimerois vien mieux parestre dans le triomphe et dans le felicitai." E.–"Et moi y estre veritablement" (830).

However, we note that the pattern of discussion is altered in Book Four, so that while formerly Enay commented upon Faeneste, now Faeneste comments upon the image Beaujeu displays before him. Why? This is Faeneste's final opportunity for choice. He refuses, or is unable, to surrender his image-based self-presentation and perspective, repulsing thereby both word and Word. Faeneste, the unwary reader, thus loses his last chance at correct interpretation, the literary equivalent of salvation.[55] Enay, on the other hand, now recognizes the usefulness of images as long as they do not seek to overwhelm or supplant discourse. Implicitly, fiction is accorded a similar acknowledgement in its relationship to theological writing.

In such a way, d'Aubigné legitimizes his writing, weaving himself into the text/tapestry by, for instance, depicting Ignorance's chariot rolling over a pavement composed of the *Histoire universelle.* So does Enay inscribe himself and us, through our participation as readers, into the discourse of salvation, the perfect correspondence of "estre" and "parestre" that results from the incorporation, evaluation and surpassing of the image by the word.

---

[55]We may note the instructive parallels between this section of the *Avantures* and book eleven of *Paradise Lost*: "when the pageants . . . elicit erroneous interpretations from Adam, Michael engages him in rigorous dialogic exchanges, teaching him to read history as a sequence of moral emblems manifesting the ravages of intemperance and vainglory." Lewalski, *"Paradise,"* 256.

6

Sa Vie à ses enfants:
the Scripture of the Self

THE TENSION BETWEEN PUBLIC and private *persona* that d'Aubigné develops in *Sancy* and the *Avantures* informs the structure of *Sa Vie à ses enfants* and creates a fundamental dualism in the perception of self. This can be seen in the two conflicting traditions within which d'Aubigné's autobiography is contained: that of the spiritual autobiography and that of the moralizing *exemplum*. *Exempla* are the more common form in the later Middle Ages and the early Renaissance. These are directed *outwards,* toward the public, and are designed to elucidate a moral assessment of the self in the world that may be applicable to all men. In this light we recall Théodore de Bèze's *Chrestiennes méditations,* which refuses all autobiographical indulgence and is characterized by an opaque universal presentation. The precedent for spiritual autobiography is established by Augustine's *Confessions.* There, Augustine speaks of the self as an individual entity, evoking his battles with sin and describing the struggle for self-legitimation.[1] *Sa Vie* is unique and rich because it utilizes elements of both modes.

D'Aubigné wishes to rework and surpass the standard writing of *exempla.* He expresses his distrust of *exempla,* pointing out that they are too open to ambiguity, too easily distorted by misreading:

> je ne vous soupçonne pas, haissant la lecture comme vous faictes, d'avoir amassez les mauvais exemples que vous avez recitez. . . . [Vous voyez que vous ne pouvez] prend[re] l'exemple de ces Princes [que] quand vous leur semblerés de condition (427).

Elsewhere, he notes that "estant commandé de dire franchement [il] commença par la detestation . . . de . . . telles histoires . . . 'Ces exemples,' (dit-il) 'Sire, sont . . . inutiles pour vous'" (426). As the individual is increasingly distinct from others, the universality and applicability of the *exempla* become more problematic.

Generic manipulation is a conscious stylistic tool that d'Aubigné employs to this end. By incorporating different genres, permitting different points of view, and subordinating them all to the direction of the authorial "I," d'Aubigné in his text suggests totality and transcendence. He thereby

---

[1]For Augustine, the soul may be found only in God: "Thou has created us for Thyself, and our heart knows no rest until it rests in Thee." *An Augustine Synthesis,* ed. E. Przywara (New York: Harper and Row, 1958), 95.

strengthens his self-permissions for authorship. Such a strategy results in the production of the iconic form of reading we have discerned in other d'Aubigné texts. In this regard, Paul Ricoeur instructively associates narrative, and especially fiction, with iconicity. He explains that

> far from producing only weakened images of reality–shadows, as in the Platonic treatment of the *eikon* in painting or writing (*Phaedrus*, 274e-77e) literary works depict reality by *augmenting* it with meanings that themselves depend upon the virtues of abbreviation, saturation and culmination, so strikingly illustrated by emplotment.

The icon is produced by a dialectic in which images are employed but are ultimately surpassed:

> metaphorical reference, it will be recalled, consists in the fact that the effacement of descriptive reference–an effacement that, as a first approximation, makes language refer to itself–is revealed to be, in a second approximation, the negative condition for freeing a more radical power of reference to those aspects of our being that cannot be talked about directly,[2]

such as, in d'Aubigné's case, the nature of transcendence.

As opposed to a contemporary tableau in which there is generally an intentional single point-of-view[3] (I except those that employ anamorphosis, a phenomenon analogous to the baroque), the baroque multiple perspectives cause multivalent directions of vision and of reading, creating a polysemous text and requiring an alert, critical reader who participates intimately in the re-assemblage of textual elements of meaning. "What is written is what can be interpreted, where interpretation is not finding the text's meaning but appreciating the plural that constitutes the text."[4] Such a text is properly "iconic." It is a process, rather than an object or image.[5] "It aims less at restoring the author's intention behind the text than at making explicit

---

[2] Ricoeur, *Time and Narrative*, vol. 1, p. 80.

[3] Lewalski, *"Paradise"*, 111. Lewalski notes in book four of *Paradise Lost* that Eden is portrayed like a picture, in which the point of view is Satan's. Because it is framed like a picture, and because there is one perspective only, the picture of Eden may succumb to manipulation.

[4] Mary Bittner Wiseman, "Texts of Pleasure, Texts of Bliss," in *Text, Interpretation and Theory*, ed. James M. Heath (Lewisburg, Penna: Bucknell University Press, 1985), 53.

[5] We may contrast with such a text one in which there is no plural "because its meanings are given by fixed and single relations to other words. This absolutely readerly text could hardly be *read* in any sense of 'read' worthy of the name. It could only be 'gazed at.'" Wiseman, 54.

the movement by which the text unfolds, as it were, a world in front of itself."[6]

Generic alterations may also signal periods of stylistic transitions that parallel changes in the conception of the self. Mikhail Bakhtin, for instance, observes progressive "novelization" in mid- and later-Renaissance due to two factors which *Sa Vie* and d'Aubigné's other literary works evidence: "multiple genres, including extra-literary kinds, that create multiple perspectives upon the subject and the valorization of process"[7] are a part of this program.

Thus, claiming a utility well matched to the Calvinist aesthetics of applicability (that is, only the useful or the didactic is praised), while he surreptiously permits the individual's voice, d'Aubigné constructs within a kind of tension of selfhood the drama of subjectivity in writing. A spiritual autobiography, unlike an *exemplum,* gives equal emphasis to the actions of God and the reactions of man, while the *exemplum,* intending to empty out the self, focuses all on God. D'Aubigné will further develop the balance found in the spiritual autobiography so that the writing act is a privileged creation. While portions of his autobiography are clearly motivated by God (for instance, his attempt at suicide is, he is sure, divinely thwarted[8]), these are circumscribed with his *own interpretation.* Such generic transformation is a theo-literary strategy: "the literary manifestation of the action of divine grace."[9]

This presentation is even more compelling because it is elaborated between two books: *Sa Vie* itself, and the *Histoire universelle.* Straightforward, factual historical reporting and autobiography (which purports to be factual but which in fact, due to its subjective nature, may contain elements of distortion, over-emphasis or fiction) are both opposed and dialectically joined within *Sa Vie.* Thus, two differing descriptions of rationalizations for the self and its role in the world obtain. It is incumbent upon the reader to effect the operation necessary to reconcile the two so that complete reading may be achieved.

The reader must penetrate the problem of the suspect narrator. D'Aubigné begins the work with a preface to his children. This introduction seems

---

[6]Ricoeur, *Time and Narrative,* vol. 1, p. 81.

[7]Mikhail Bakhtin, paraphrased in "Issues and Approaches," *Renaissance Genres: Essays on Theory, History and Interpretation* (Cambridge: Harvard University Press, 1986), 3.

[8]D'Aubigné, "Sa Vie à ses enfants," in *Oeuvres,* ed. Henri Weber, Bibliothèque de la Pléiade, 206 (Paris: Gallimard, 1969), 390. All other references will be to this edition and will appear in parentheses in the text. "Il passa la teste vers l'eau pour passer ses larmes qui tumboyent en bas, il luy prit un grand désir de se jetter après elles, et l'amas de ses desplaisirs l'emportoit à cela, quand sa bonne nourriture luy faisoit souvenir qu'il falloit prier Dieu devant tout action, le dernier mot de ses prières estant la vie éternelle, ce mot l'effraya et le fit crier à Dieu qu'il l'assistast en son agonie."

[9]Lewalski, *"Paradise,"* 230.

transparent and without pretense. He claims that his autobiography is written solely for the edification and benefit of his progeny:

> Mes enfants . . . voicy le discours de ma vie. . . . Je desire que mes heureuses ou honorables actions vous donnent sans envie l'emulation pourveu que vous vous attachiés plus exprés à mes fautes, que je vous descouvre toutes nues (384).

His writing, he asserts, is motivated not by authorial ambition, but rather by their "requeste raisonnable" (384), and takes place "en la privauté personnelle" (384). Why, however, if this is to be an intimate and even paradoxically secretive work ("J'ay encore à vous ordonner qu'il n'y ait que deux copies de ce livre: vous accordants d'estre de leurs gardiens et que vous n'en laissiés aller aucune hors de la maison," [384]) does he take such pains throughout *Sa Vie* to justify himself theologically and politically? Why, further, is his narrating voice deceitful? Rather than begin the body of the autobiography by continuing to speak in the first person singular as he does in the preface, he switches, influenced by the genre of the *exemplum*,[10] to the third person singular. Later, however, he unconsciously appears to slip, reverting to the first person singular and, occasionally, first person plural for brief stretches of the narrative after which he corrects himself and returns to the neutral third person singular. The focus of the work is on the "je," but the "je" is usually not acknowledged, attesting to some tension with the strictures of historical self-depiction. That is, as the predominant third person singular voice shows, the "je" is always unavoidably in some ways determined by the actual people and events around him. However, the manner in which he chooses to shape himself internally may, although not bruited abroad publicly, differ privately. D'Aubigné must devise strategies in *Sa Vie* to overcome the dilemma Benveniste elucidates:

> the "I" in discourse exists only by virtue of its relationships to the categories of third-person (the person that is not a person) and the . . . plural privileges inscribed in the "we." Hence, this text does not say "I," but emerges buried in the otherness to which it consigns [the author]–and itself.[11]

A similar phenomenon obtains in Calvinism, where the "I" is always subordinate to its Creator. Hence the importance of the reader as complicitous

---

[10]Similarly, he obeys generic imperatives when he situates himself genealogically, naming his father, mother and birthdate, and explaining the significance of the name Agrippa. He proceeds, in addition, in the customary chronological manner.

[11]Emile Benveniste, paraphrased by Goldberg, *Voice*, 129.

co-producer, enabling a multi-voiced discourse that expands its authorial possibilities.

Sa Vie, begun in paternal fondness and plain speech, is more ambitious than it admits: by speaking primarily in the third person singular, it dares to set itself up as *history* rather than mere autobiography and thereby constitutes itself as "truth." Two factors may contribute to this development. First are constraints of the era, which generally prefer historical reporting and which emphasize the importance of public events over the insignificant private existence: witness the proliferation of *mémoires* like those of Blaise de Monluc, which contain a minimal amount of personal description and intervention. Of course, Montaigne is a notable exception. A second factor is the comparable position of Calvinism, which, as we have already discussed, holds the self suspect and sinful. Indeed, d'Aubigné acknowledges this latter stricture in a letter to Simon Goulart, the minister of Geneva, in 1616, lamenting that he (d'Aubigné) labors under the imperative of strict factual transcription and is discouraged from poetic or fictional creation: ". . . il a pleu au Synode de Gap de changer mon delectable à l'utile . . . me reduis[ant] à l'Histoire."[12] It is interesting here that he apparently perceives history as a step *down* from fiction. This is atypical of the respect that is accorded to historical recounting during the period.

At the very beginning of the preface, d'Aubigné indicates that his autobiography may, perhaps, be legitimized because it is like *exempla,* associated with the patterns established by the great men of history: "Mes enfants, vous avez de l'antiquité de quoy puiser dans les vies des Empereurs et des Grands exemples et enseignements" (384). Further, he evinces an ambivalent attitude toward the value of the expression of his private self, for what will be contained in *Sa Vie* are those events that he does not deem *worthy* of inclusion in the *Histoire universelle* (or so he claims–at this point): "[J'y ai] cach[é] ce qui en l'*Histoire universelle* eust esté de mauvais goust" (384). Such concerns privilege history over self-scripture, implying that the private self is not only of dubious merit but also may be saturated with sin. (This is why the self is never *explicitly* discussed in his previous works. Now, however, the taint of sin is effaced; even the "fautes" he avows, he does so vaingloriously: "là il faisoit valoir sa faute d'avoir osé commander avant que l'aage lui eust donné autorité," [393] he confesses, actually highlighting his precocious success.)

Thus, from the outset of *Sa Vie* d'Aubigné seems to subvert the program of his entire literary *corpus* to this point. All the strategies he has been devising to overcome the interdiction of the self and of permissive and even fictional writing are apparently forsaken here. The autobiography appears as a mere adjunct to the *Histoire universelle,* a suspect, supplementary

---

[12]D'Aubigné, "Lettre a M. Goulard," in *Lettres,* 474.

trace that may only be sanctioned in that it refers to another work posited as a transcendent model. This hierarchization recalls the primacy of the biblical text, beyond which exegesis alone may progress, the parasitical grafting of feeble human expression onto the font of all expression, the divine Word.

Fact and Fiction Reversed

However, this apparent disavowal and undoing of the self is a ruse. In fact, d'Aubigné's "fautes" and sins are the very source and substance of his literary expression: ". . . que vous vous attachiés plus exprés à mes fautes que je vous descouvre toutes nues, comme le point qui vous porte *le plus de butin*" (384; my emphasis). In addition, Sa Vie has much more integrity and strength than it at first seems, for it contains the possibilities of at least two different kinds of reading. In the first, *Sa Vie* would appear as a gloss on the *Histoire universelle*, one in which minor details and, perhaps, abject confessions of sinful doings are included. The reader may, if he so chooses, approach the text from such a perspective. Such an attitude would be analogous to the misreadings of which Faeneste is guilty, however, for it does not account for the multivalence of this unusual autobiography. It does not adequately excavate the self-revelations buried in *Sa Vie*. In the second paradigm of reading, *Sa Vie* may be seen as the medium which both subsumes and transcends history, reversing the role of text and commentary so that it attains superior status. This occurs when the reader becomes aware that, although there are numerous references to the *Histoire universelle* embedded in *Sa Vie* (to the point that it seems the autobiography is unreadable and does not make full sense unless the "source book" is consulted for crucial material[13]), these references are, in reality, unessential. *Sa Vie* is coherent and creates its own sense without them. In addition, the references to the *Histoire* usually do not contain information that is particularly enlightening, and occasionally merely repeat or amplify the assertions of the autobiography. It is interesting that this strategy differs from its application in d'Aubigné's other works, where he borrows sketchy indications of narratives and then fully develops them in his later works (as we discussed in the interaction between *Sancy* and *Avantures*). Here he alludes tersely, usually by chapter only, to an episode which he then declines to discuss. These allusions are framed by d'Aubigné's discourse in *Sa Vie*. By giving the reader permission to look them up, d'Aubigné asserts his authorial powers: it is still *he*, writing within *Sa Vie*, who directs the reader.

Sa Vie is meant to be the *true* "source book," for it is by reading it that the reader may learn the truth behind the deception of the *Histoire* (or the

---

[13]References to the *Histoire universelle* are found on the following pages in the Pléiade editions of *Sa Vie*: 391, 393, 397, 401, 402, 404, 405, 406, 408, 410, 411, 412, 413, 417, 419, 420, 422, 424, 425, 426, 428, 429, 431, 432, 434, 435, 436 and 454.

lacunas of the *Histoire*: often d'Aubigné makes such confessions as "nous n'avons pas aussi specifié en l'*Histoire* . . ." [405]). For instance, d'Aubigné enumerates many episodes in the *Histoire* where he performs an important act under an assumed name (e.g. ". . . Aubigné, comme aussi les actions despeintes soubs un nom caché. . ." [412].). He does not lift the veil and properly reveal his identity until *Sa Vie,* which thus becomes the necessary "key" to truth. We know from his personal correspondence that d'Aubigné is not telling the "full truth"–does not *allow* himself to tell the full truth–in the *Histoire*. He feels obliged to maintain an impassive, "objective" mask: for he is hampered by the generic format of history. For instance, he writes to le père Fulgence in 1624,

> Je vous supplie vouloir faire venir entre vos mains mon livre d'*Histoire*. . . . Vous verrez comment entre les loix que j'ai receues des meilleurs maistres, j'observe de ne descrire que les pures actions sans donner ma sentence au lecteur. Je ne luy fais present que de premisses, et luy laisse la façon de la conclusion.[14]

He pushes this purported objectivity to such a point that it becomes downright duplicitous: ". . . que pour eschantillon de ma modestie j'ay descrit la Ste-Bathelemi sans avoir usé mot de cruauté."[15]

The *Histoire* becomes the *incomplete fiction* (assumed identities, inadequate descriptions), while *Sa Vie* becomes the transcendent, truthful text. The relationship newly established between history and the story of the self (formerly considered as unreliable and even fictitious) is a fascinating one. Through it, d'Aubigné daringly subverts the conventional conception of fact and fiction. By privileging the private self over public manifestation, d'Aubigné simultaneously permits subjectivity. A personal perspective is, in fact, essential to the comprehension of events. By compelling the reader to search for clues concerning d'Aubigné's personal interventions in history and in *Sa Vie,* d'Aubigné involves the reader in a process that validates d'Aubigné's subjectivity. This effort is strengthened by the obvious program or schedule of writing that d'Aubigné sets for himself. His authorial interventions are increasingly apparent in *Sa Vie,* and attest to certain judgments he consciously makes as to the formulation or arrangement of his work. We find apparently arbitrary assertions (because unexplained to the reader) which underline d'Aubigné's power over his text. He decides, thus, that "il est temps de dire . . ." (458) a particular episode, or again, "il est bon . . . de vous conter . . ." (458) a certain occurrence, showing a specific narrative time-table to which he intends to adhere. When he notes, "à ce discours j'en veux joindre un autre" (436), the reader senses an active,

---

[14]D'Aubigné, "Lettre au père Fulgence," in *Lettres,* 312.
[15]Idem, "Lettre à M. de Louvenie," ibid., 475.

thoughtful textual assemblage occurring in the narration. The interplay between *Sa Vie* and the *Histoire* is equally intentional.

These dual possibilities for reading create a new spatial-temporal expansiveness within the written structure. The reader may opt to read *Sa Vie* straight through, without pausing to look up references. If, however, he searches out the indications in the *Histoire,* he opens *Sa Vie* (as d'Aubigné intends). *Sa Vie* comes to enfold the *Histoire* within the spatial movement and temporal lapse needed for the reader to consult one book, turn back to the other, and then reconcile the two. Those events "signified" in the *Histoire* point back to *Sa Vie. Sa Vie*'s role as the signifier of the writer and of the text is thereby enhanced. The autobiography signifies the self-sufficient scripture of the self (*Sa Vie* may stand alone), and designates the supplementary status of purely factual narration (the *Histoire* is misleading unless read in conjunction with *Sa Vie*).

The play between public and private, fact and fiction, poses the question of interiority and exteriority. In both works, d'Aubigné practices the technique of self-inscription we have already discussed. However, in the *Histoire* he deliberately chooses to inscribe an incomplete and, hence, untruthful simulacrum of himself. That is, in a work claiming to be historical fact, he includes a locus of subversion. In *Sa Vie,* a less trustworthy genre, he displays truth. He thus renders the *Histoire* a fiction: he becomes a character, a *personnage* in what now is mere drama, while by revealing his true self in *Sa Vie,* he causes it to be a historical vehicle. He is *inside Sa Vie,* integral to it, and moves beyond it to comment upon the inadequate articulation of the *Histoire.* He is also *outside Sa Vie,* through the strategy of a multiple narrating voice. When he speaks in the third person singular, he is a character and an actor in the tale of his own life. This may in fact be a prerequisite for the later shaping and presentation of his real self. An actor functions in a role; a role becomes a *form* for the self. When d'Aubigné intervenes as "je," or invites our complicity as "nous," he reveals himself as the active authorial voice behind the narrative. The result of this rich and multi-faceted narrative structure is that fiction and fact interpenetrate dialectically. In order to grasp fully the significance of the *personnage* inscribed in the *Histoire,* we must refer to *Sa Vie.* "Fact" is subordinate to "fiction." In order to augment the conception of the *personnage* d'Aubigné includes in *Sa Vie,* we may, but need not, consult the *Histoire.* "Fact" is still unessential; "fiction" prevails, in this system, as the privileged medium of truth, because the fictional narration shapes the self. Finally, in order to attain a full reading of each text, we need only turn to the explicit directives and explanation expressed by "je" in *Sa Vie.* "Fiction" contains all truth.

At the same time, the discussion of *exempla* as opposed to spiritual biography is resolved, for it is apparent that the two genres interpenetrate in d'Aubigné's unique vision of autobiography. *Exempla* are shown to be inadequate, just as the public presentations of self (under a pseudonym) in the *Histoire* may provide an *apparent* mold to which the reader may conform. He would be mistaken in so doing, for the truthful motivation for that model as, ultimately, for all exterior human actions, may be found only in the examination of the spirit. In such a way, the *Histoire* and *Sa Vie* may be likened to word and image in the *Avantures*: the representation of d'Aubigné in the *Histoire* becomes the insufficient image upon which the word of *Sa Vie* comments and, ultimately, builds to achieve an independent status. Indeed, as we shall see, d'Aubigné devises a formulaic introduction for all his references to the *Histoire*. It is, generally, "vous voyez descript," or "vous voyez despeint" (410) or some variation that attests to the *visual* apprehension of an image. The *Histoire* is treated as a collection of images.[16]

Through writing, d'Aubigné articulates a new conception of the self. This self has the characteristics of both continuity and contiguity. While d'Aubigné describes himself in rudimentary fashion through episodic events in the *Histoire*, he then fills the gaps between them with the self-revelations integral to *Sa Vie*, necessarily constructing a narrative, rather than a chronicle, in order to do so. Through a baroque multiplicity of viewpoints[17] in which he portrays from many angles his self-construction, he ultimately arrives at one sure and certain focus within which the self stands as psychologically and literarily legitimized. This project is confirmed, as it is in *Les Tragiques*, through the textually-inscribed death of d'Aubigné as a historical figure, leaving the author written into his work, a voice as assertive in its directorship as was the actual, physical presence of d'Aubigné.

Strategies of Self-Inscription

Because *Sa Vie* is an autobiography, it appears immediately to be a significant document of the process of self-conscious literary creation, and of the drafting of the self, that we have been discussing. There are many ways in which the articulation of the self appears in *Sa Vie*. One of the earliest to be mentioned is the intimate involvement between personhood and writing. D'Aubigné's literary identity is the very first manner in which he defines himself:

---

[16]It is, then, significant, that in *Sa Vie* as in the *Avantures*, images are associated with death. For instance, d'Aubigné recites this quatrain in which "meurs" and "tableaux" are linked:

Paris te dresse un vain tombeau,
A Geneve un certain hyménée . . .
A Paris tu meurs en tableau,
Ici, vis . . .   (457)

[17]These are the viewpoints of the reader of the *Histoire* and *Sa Vie*, respectively; the viewpoint of the audience inscribed within the *Histoire* and within *Sa Vie* (the court, his children . . .).

> A sept ans il traduisit avec quelque aide de ses leçons le Crito de
> Platon, sur la promesse du pere qu'il le feroit imprimer *avec l'effigie
> enfantine* au devant du livre (385; my emphasis).

This first image *en abyme* of d'Aubigné the writer incorporating within his
text a smaller, younger, textualized vision of himself alerts us to his strategy
of self-inscription within the text to insist on its veracity: he thus functions
as the "tesmoin" he claims to be in the *Tragiques*. This strategy is further
developed throughout the text, with d'Aubigné's literary self-identification
becoming progressively stronger. He is truly an "inventeur" of himself,
shaped through his "parole" and, especially, his textually recorded speech:
"[à la cour] . . . leurs mascarades, balets, et carousels, desquels Aubigné
seul estoit inventeur . . . il se rendit cognu . . . par ses bons mots" (398).
At times d'Aubigné embeds other literary pieces of his own making within
the over-arching structure of *Sa Vie,* increasing the inter-referential network
of his literary *corpus.* Similarly, d'Aubigné identifies himself as the author
both of the *Histoire* ("il acheva l'impression de ses *Histoires,* tout à ses
despens, tint à grand honneur de les voir condemnees et bruslees au College
Royal à Paris" [450]) and of *Les Tragiques.*[18]

In addition, writing becomes a dangerous and heroic enterprise, for
the truth of d'Aubigné's utterance is not always favorably regarded by his
audience: "le mesme Prince fit envie au duc d'Espernon de lire *Les Tragiques*;
et luy ayant exposé les traicts du second livre, comme escripts pour luy,
fit jurer la mort de l'autheur" (445). Several instances of this tactic deserve
particular notice. In one, d'Aubigné creates a sonnet addressed to the king,
reproaching him for his abandonment of his faithful lap-dog, Citron. This
sonnet, by the addition of a final *pointe* to the detailed image given first,
becomes emblematic of d'Aubigné's personal feelings of ill-treatment at
the hands of the king. Through a literary composition, d'Aubigné shows
himself best able to convey these sentiments:

> Le fidele Citron qui couchoit autrefois
> Sur vostre lit sacré, couche ores sur la dure:
> C'est ce fidelle chien qui apprit de nature
> A faire des amys et des traistres le chois: . . .
> Courtisans, qui jettez vos desdaigneuses veues
> Sur ce chien delaissé, mort de faim par les rues,
> Attendez ce loyer de la fidelité.

The incisive eruption of the authorial voice (the series of imperatives) in
the formerly anonymous sonnet clearly signals d'Aubigné's literary role,
and separates the "pointe" from the description, the word from the image.

---

[18]He also refers to "les *Epistres famillieres* qui s'imprimeront" (448).

Elsewhere, d'Aubigné dramatizes the impermanence of spoken words, privileging their written, indelible transcription. His writing is acknowledged as important and self-definitive throughout, for even when he momentarily loses his powers of speech, he is able to *write* about that very phenomenon, filling the absence with a textual presence: "Aubigné veillant dedans son lict . . . il veit . . . une femme fort blanche. . . . Morel arrivé le trouva ayant perdu la parole" (385). D'Aubigné's writing is always associated with permanence and perfection, an evolved state of the self-consciously honed self. He is proud to be chosen to draft a declaration for a religious council and relates in *Sa Vie* that his work issues forth spontaneously, already in a state of near-perfection:

> quelqu'un proposa . . . qu'il seroit plus aisé de corriger sur l'escrit que sur les paroles qui s'en alloient en l'air. Aubigné choisy pour cela, demanda trois jours de terme, et des lors sortant de l'Assemblee, prit du papier, et sur la memoire fresche esbaucha sa besogne, et puis ayant consideré qu'aprés y avoir pensé plus long temps, il rentre dans la compagnie, blasmé de n'aller pas travailler à sa besogne. Il la leur mit sur la table, et dans demie heure rappellé, aprés la censure, trouva qu'on luy avoit troublé une silable seulement, et a tousjours estimé cest escrit le plus heureux de tous les siens (437).

His experiences naturally give rise to a literary expression that both reflects on an event and moves beyond it to claim a purely literary status. For instance, when d'Aubigné fears for his life, he prays to God for help. He then turns his thanks for the answered prayer into an epigram. It is significant that he does not choose to write a hymn, song or canticle but rather an epigram–a uniquely *literary* genre: "En l'extremité de son péril, il fit une prière à Dieu, laquelle le lendemain, se voyant délivré, il tourna en une epigramme que vous verrez entre les siens" (422). The transformation of theological supplication into literary form is indicative, further, of the theo-literary strategies we have noted throughout d'Aubigné's work. This sort of change of form for the same content results in a new kind of *exemplum,* one in which theological experience *embraces,* rather than rejects (as does de Bèze in his *Chretiennes méditations*) literary expression. D'Aubigné calls his epigram "un exemple notable de sa foy" (422). Finally, d'Aubigné literally makes his mark upon the world through writing. While his singularity is signalled elsewhere,[19] it is emphasized through his writing acts.

Images of defenselessness work to this effect. D'Aubigné's adversaries are always fully clothed and well-armed, while d'Aubigné himself surmounts

---

[19]D'Aubigné is singled out, for instance, in this way: "la Royne de Navarre estant retournée à son mari se reconsilia avec tous, hormis avec Aubigné" (419).

impossible odds to win military engagements half-dressed, thus confirming his unique strength (and integrity). At a very young age, for instance, he flees from his tutor:

> [il] se devala par le fenestre par le moyen de ses linceulx, en chemise, à pieds nus [pour se joindre à l'armee]. . . (390).

D'Aubigné always finds a way to comment literarily on his physical state. Joining the army in a naked, defenseless condition, he writes "au bout de sa sedulle, 'A la charge que je ne reprocheroys point à la guerre qu'elle m'a despouillé, n'en pouvant sortir plus mal equippé que j'y entre'" (391). He thereby emphasizes his unusual bravery. He also enhances his writing act as the agent expressive of his daring, and guarantor of his continued courage in the future. This insistence on nakedness also demonstrates d'Aubigné's willingness to yield himself, without artifice or deception, to the reader's gaze: his is not appearance, but being. "En pourpoint" possesses this figurative connotation. It may be found in other contemporary texts, such as Montaigne's *Essais,* with the same intentionality: "sans resources, ou proprement sans manteau."[20]

In another *mise en abyme* formulation, d'Aubigné the author describes d'Aubigné the *personnage* as he strides forward before the nobles to, literally, *inscribe himself* on marble, daringly imposing his (unpopular) discourse on the court:

> Aubigné gagna le devant, s'arresta à un marbre noir de sept pieds de carré, qui servoit de tablettes à ce bon homme. Là, ayant trouvé les pinceaux, et ce qu'il falloit, Aubigné en prit un, et oyant qu'ils disputoyent des fardeaux, escrivit. . . (414).

This dramatic act of literary self-expression is clearly delineated as a scene of self-distinction. It opens with d'Aubigné's arrival, centers on his writing, and closes when he pulls the curtain, giving a prophetic cast to his act.[21] He is acclaimed by others for his audacity, which he articulates literarily: "M. de Candalle dit au Roy, 'Voivy mes tablettes'; mais les ayant descouvertes et leu le distique, il s'escria par deux fois: 'O il y a ici un homme!'" (414). D'Aubigné the author is so pleased at this acknowledgement he has earned as the character d'Aubigné that he allows his authorial mask to drop momentarily: "le Roy ayant repliqué, 'Tenez vous le reste pour des bestes?'

---

[20]The definition is that of Pierre Villey, editor of the *Essais.* He is commenting on a passage from III.xii.1045: "je pensay desja estre entre mes amys, à qui je pourrais commettre une vieillesse necessiteuse et disgratiée, après avoir rodé les yeux partout, je me trouvay en pourpoint."

[21]By painting his graffiti into a permanent fixture and addressing it to the king, d'Aubigné may be comparing the purpose and intent of his writing to the (apocalyptic) words written on the wall in the book of Daniel.

pria son oncle de choisir à la mine celuy qui auroit faict le coup: sur quoy il y eust d'assés plaisants propos, auxquels *je* m'amuserois trop" (414; my emphasis). Significantly, the perpetrator of the inscription can *not* be identified by his physiognomy.[22] In *Sa Vie* d'Aubigné alerts us that identity is established literarily, not visually through appearance.

Emblematic of this emphasis is the youthful d'Aubigné's extreme reluctance (almost anxiety) to leave his schoolroom when he and his household are forced to flee during the massacre of Orléans:

> les massacres et les bruslements qui se faisoyent à Paris ayant contrainct aprés de trés grands dangers Beroalde de s'enfuir avec [d'Aubigné] et sa famille, il fascha bien à ce petit garçon de quitter un cabinet de livres couverts sompteusement . . . si bien que . . . ses pensees tirerent des larmes (386).

D'Aubigné shapes for himself an exclusively *literary persona*. It is interesting that he participates thereby in a historical phenomenon then in process: the definition of the self by opposition to the other (in this case, the military man as opposed to the man of letters) such as we noted in *Sancy*. Contemporaries demonstrate similar aims although not with the extreme degree of literary self-consciousness that permeates the economy of d'Aubigné's narrative. For instance, Robert Cottrell observes that

> the biography has as its center a radiant paragon, an ideal, unique and yet exemplary: it defines an Object. The memorialistic passages have at their center a Renaissance man who . . . "désigne d'un main sa poitrine, comme pour indiquer que c'est bien lui qui importe, et nul autre." They define a subject. Two mental structures are thus juxtaposed: one oriented toward the Other, the second oriented toward the self. The first is essentially medieval, while the second, essentially Renaissance. Furthermore, each mental structure is characterized by certain stylistic peculiarities.[23]

At the same time that he arrogates to himself the permission of self-definition, d'Aubigné recognizes the need for a participatory audience in order for him to accomplish his goal: "il se faisoit admirer à toute la compagnie" (386); "la Duchesse de Ferrare les receut avec son humanité accoutumee, mais sur tous Aubigné qu'elle fit trois jours durant asseoir sur

---

[22]Our case opposing appearances is made even more plausible in that d'Aubigné elsewhere accords to himself skill in reading physiognomies. Cf. p. 474. If, here, he stresses literary identity over one's ability to discern truth through appearance, he does so in order to hierarchize the arts of divination and self-definition, subordinating all processes for determining identification to that of the literary signature.

[23]Robert Cottrell, *Brantôme: The Writer as Portraitist of His Age* (Geneva: Droz, 1970), 80.

un carreau auprés d'elle pour ouir ses jeunes discours sur le mespris de la mort" (387). Thus, beyond the readership of his children for whom he ostensibly writes, there is a need for another implied reader. D'Aubigné's instructions to his reader are meticulous. Yet, presumably, his well-informed children would have little need of such extensive clarification. For instance, he thoroughly details not only what material is to be read, but also the required *disposition* of the reader:

> je vous convie donc à lire ceste entreprise tout au long, au commence-ment du susdit chapitre, où il y a des notables instructions; et en suivant celuy d'aprés, vous verrés la prise des armes, et puis au sixiesme, la prise de Montaigu jusques à la fin du chaptire, où vous verrez les employs et perils de celuy que nous descrivons; mais sur tout au chapitre dixiesme du mesme livre, lisez fidelement l'entreprise de Blaye (410).

While such listings may at first resemble a table of contents, we soon note that the chronicle of events contained in the *Histoire* is directed for a specific purpose, that of focusing on the actions of the d'Aubigné *persona*. We are told to read these events not to ascertain how they fit into the historical account, but rather with the intent of determining the intention, nature and effect of "celuy que nous descrivons."

The animation of the *persona* thus depends on the insightful act of reading. The "vous" is essential to the internal construction of *Sa Vie*, and not merely to its external reading, for *Sa Vie* is actually formed as a dialogue between the directive, although veiled, author, and the reader. Indeed, *Sa Vie* derives its impetus from the potential reader; it is only written at the request of its future readers, d'Aubigné's children: "c'est ce que je fays en ottroyant vostre requeste raisonnable: et voicy le discours de ma vie" (384). The text is not merely inter-referential to itself and to the *Histoire*, it is indeed a triangular interaction which elicits a coproduction of meaning from the reader. The *Avantures*, with its emphasis on the reading process, prepares this development which finds its fullest realization in d'Aubigné's final work, *Sa Vie*.

The constant solicitation of the reader, "vous" (e.g. 410), is paralleled in the text by d'Aubigné's sensitivity to the effect his words and writing have on others. He incessantly spies out others' reactions, stressing at the same time the manipulative power his discourse wields; "le Roy," for instance, is so affected by d'Aubigné's written word that he "changea de couleur en lisant . . . [l']escrit de [d'Aubigné]" (408). The speech of others is powerless to impose itself when confronted with the superior force of d'Aubigné's self-assertion. For instance, the king of Navarre repeatedly summons d'Aubigné, who ignores his injunctions "qui toutes furent jetees au feu en les recevant. . ." (409). D'Aubigné's self-construct stands above his king's entreaties and commands.

The logical extension of d'Aubigné's literary potency is that, as elsewhere in his literary *corpus,* he begins to mix theological with literary considerations, proclaiming his *apophéties.* Most of these *apophéties* have already been proclaimed in *Les Tragiques* or in *Sancy,* and so contribute to the organic *réseau* d'Aubigné's individual works established among themselves. In addition, the *apophéties* are stamped adverbially and adjectively with the marks of supreme self-assertion. That is, he describes himself formulating these statements, portraying himself in a bold and favorable light. For instance, he makes a prediction as a young man in order to dissuade his relatives from stealing his lands: "il leur predit qu'un jour ils luy feroient homage." He takes them to court shortly thereafter, and soon alerts us of the success of his prophecy:

> son exorde fut si pathetique . . . que le juge regardant d'un oeil furieux ses parties, ils se leverent de leur place, et s'estant escriés qu'autre que le fils d'Aubigné ne pouvoit parler ainsi, luy demanderent pardon (394).

The fact that this prophecy is purely personal in nature, while the others are theologically motivated, shows that d'Aubigné considers his personal, literary and theological *personas* to be of a piece.

The second *apophétie* is a theological prediction motivated by Henri de Navarre's religious compromises:

> ce fut là où se dit un mot qui a tant couru: car comme le Roy monstroit sa levre percee au flambeau, il . . . ne print point en mauvaise part ses paroles: "Sire vous n'avez encore renoncé Dieu que des levres, il s'est contenté de les percer; mais quand vous le renoncerez du coeur, il vous percera le coeur" (431).

The *apophéties* play a complicated role in the fabrication of d'Aubigné's identity. They are written in the present, here in the text, but expressed in the past as though they had not yet occurred. D'Aubigné's unavowed retrospective knowledge is not the element of the *apophétie* most apparent to the reader: rather than perceiving it as a "prediction after the fact," the reader believes in d'Aubigné's prophetic gifts (as, indeed, d'Aubigné himself does). Through a literary strategy of hidden hindsight, d'Aubigné's claim to a theological mission is strengthened. The literary factor is crucial in d'Aubigné's utterance of the *apophétie* for, as in the above instance, many of the *apophéties* seem to arise in metaphoric expression: d'Aubigné could merely be constructing a literary analogy when he equates the piercing of the lips with the wounding of the heart due to faithlessness. Nevertheless, if this is the case, he later turns around to claim a hidden prescience in his words. The tense confusion of the *apophétie* works to the same effect, giving d'Aubigné time and space in which to maneuver narratively. It has been observed that similar contemporary

> historical prophecies deriv[e] some of their considerable power from the fact that they emplo[y] *history* as a predictive *fiction*–once again purporting to describe events taking place in the future while actually chronicling developments from the past.[24]

As we have observed elsewhere, the *apophéties* are permissions for narrativity. Paul Ricoeur defines narrative sentences as "refer[ring] to at least two time-separated events though they only describe (are only about) the earliest event to which they refer . . . this 'retroactive re-alignment' of the Past [is] brought about by the properly narrative description of action."[25] He sees temporal fluctuation as the enabling factor in the movement from history to fiction:

> Indeed, the inserting of history into action and into life, its capactiy for reconfiguring time, brings into play the question of truth in history. This question is inseparable from what I call the interweaving reference between history's claim to truth and that of fiction.[26]

D'Aubigné is at great pains to legitimize his oracular voice, explicitly reacting against the "ennemis d'Aubigné [qui] pour rendre inutiles ses prevoyances, dirent qu'il les avoit aprises du muet, et par tel soupçon rendirent vains ses salutaires advis" (448). This is because his religious self-definition is inevitably expressed literarily. D'Aubigné dedicates himself to God. That is, the self of its own volition and action *chooses* God: a bold move that recalls the dialectical resolution of the sinful creator. He decides to "relever l'enseigne d'Israel" (420), calls himself "celuy que Dieu a choisy pour instrument" (405), and utters God's pronouncements: "aprés avoir mis deux fois le genouil en terre, et prié Dieu, il luy commanda sur toutes les vérités qu'il avoit autres fois aigres, mais utiles en la bouche" (431).

There is an interesting tension between d'Aubigné the authorial *persona* and d'Aubigné the worshipping *persona,* for while d'Aubigné pays lip service, as above, to the divine mission to which he is called, he devotes the majority of his prose to detailed, personal discussions of his daily and literary life, and does not seek to bludgeon the reader with his piety. This tendency is suggestive of the manner in which the *Histoire* and *Sa Vie,* as juxtaposed texts, may be treated, for, similarly while d'Aubigné accords some recognition to the *Histoire,* he does so only where straightforward historical narration

---

[24]Ibid., 81.

[25]Ricoeur, *Time and Narrative,* vol. 1, pp. 145-47.

[26]Ibid., 93.

of *events* is concerned. The more important, intimate psychological insights are the integral fabric of *Sa Vie*. He de-emphasizes references to the *Histoire* by brushing past them: "je n'ay rien à y adjouster" (419). The only occasions upon which he does choose to intervene in the *Histoire* interpolations are when he wishes to point up or elaborate a trait of his personal character. He does so when he signals us that he is acting in the *Histoire* under an assumed name: "J'adjousterai seulement . . . que ce Capitaine, que le Conte de Lude envoya querir, fut Aubigné, comme aussi les actions despeintes soubs un nom caché sont à remarquer estre de luy" (412). While maintaining a distance between himself as writer ("je") and himself as actor ("luy"), the insistence on clarifying the issue of identity effects a *rapprochement* between the two. It seems d'Aubigné experiences some degree of uneasiness concerning the elaboration of his private *persona*. He writes that the stuff of *Sa Vie* is that "qui ne valoyent pas l'*Histoire*" (404). Yet he takes the trouble to write an extended autobiography composed of that very substance, and is at pains to disclose to his reader episodes of which he is obviously proud:

> Vous avez à la fin du chapitre du tome 3ᶜ, un discours notable soubs tiltre d'un Gouverneur de place, estimé violent partisan. C'est Aubigné qui monstra par là comment sa violence aux affaires des Reformez ne le faisoit point consentir aux iniques moyens (434).

Text and Gloss: Pronomial Confusion and Inter-referentiality

It is provocative to speculate on the literary formation of a self-concept. First, there exists within the work a dislocated typography of personal pronouns. D'Aubigné refers to himself alternately as "je," "il," "luy," "nous," and occasionally calls upon "vous." He acts under the sobriquets of "Aubigné," "le Bouc du désert" (432), and "le bon Compagnon," the latter two seeming to possess the biblical resources of the Old Testament scapegoat and the New Testament Christ. Secondly, the work oscillates between its own presence and the absence of another, the *Histoire*. The references d'Aubigné makes to the *Histoire* are generally broad and unspecific, requiring that one read the entire chapter, thus acquiring a general picture rather than a detailed *aperçu*. The authorially directive "je" does not display the *self* as do the impersonal references to the d'Aubigné *persona* in *Sa Vie* which actually provide a good deal of intimate information, but rather indicates the *process of reading* necessary to ultimately excavate the references to the self. D'Aubigné therefore employs "je" throughout whenever he wishes to make a historical observation (e.g. "J'adjousterai encor à ce que dit l'*Histoire* . . . . Voilà ce que j'adjouste au discours du premier livre, tome 3ᶜ. . . . Icy veux je seulement specifier que Aubigné. . ." [405-21]). The richness of detail given by the impersonal narrator in *Sa Vie* contrasts starkly with the terse, almost neutral wording of the information given, paradoxically, by "je" as regards the *Histoire*. We may compare the two:

Sa Vie:

. . . qui ne valoyent pas l'*Histoire*, l'une se voyant seul de la trouppe avoir des brassars, il les despouilla avant la charge: l'autre, qu'au milieu du peril, ayant dans le bras gauche un brasselet des cheveux de sa maistresse, il mit l'espee à la main gauche pour sauver ce brasselet, qui brusloit (404).

Histoire universelle:

Vous le voyez descript à la fin du mesme chaptire, soubs mesme titre assés au long . . . (404).

It seems that by referring to the "facts" in the *Histoire*, d'Aubigné is licensed to do some self-portraying, or self-magnifying, in *Sa Vie*. In the episode above taken from *Sa Vie*, for instance, d'Aubigné appears as a chivalric hero, jealous of his honor and solicitous of his mistress's favor. He begins to glorify himself as he is unable to do in the *Histoire*. In so doing, he distorts, and moves toward fictional characterization. However, since we as readers by now accept *Sa Vie* as his revealed autobiography, the "true story," we take him at his word. The fledgling fictionalization becomes plausible, for it gives shape to the self. An unusual analogy is thereby set up in which history stands in the same relationship to a life story as does exegesis to the Bible. D'Aubigné converts fiction into truth, and fact into its accessory.

In similar fashion, d'Aubigné relies more on the literary vehicle than the historical medium for his self-depiction. We notice that this is a highly *literary*, rather than documentary, piece. There are constant references to texts, both those of d'Aubigné and those of others. The inclusion of multiple genres and, in particular, citations from personal correspondence within the text, cooperate in d'Aubigné's project to expand the role of fiction. Claudio Guillèn, in "Notes toward the Study of the Renaissance Letter," makes the observation that

the letter, as écriture, . . . begins to involve the writer in a silent, creative process of self-distancing and self-modeling leading perhaps, as in autobiography, to fresh knowledge and even to fiction.[27]

---

[27]Claudio Guillèn, "Notes Toward the Study of the Renaissance Letter," in Lewalski, ed., *Renaissance*, 78.

As d'Aubigné applies it, this appears textually as another *mise en abyme* tactic, for the reader views d'Aubigné the writer contemplating d'Aubigné the *personnage,* amplifying d'Aubigné the *personnage* by inscribing, within his speech, written guarantors of it. These are, necessarily, witnesses that d'Aubigné the *personnage* also, at times, sits down to write. This returns us chiastically to the primary authorial figure, and emphasizes d'Aubigné's power over his text.[28]

There is a veritable profusion of letters quoted in *Sa Vie.* This strategy is designed to heighten the identification between self and textuality. Letters epitomize a fascinating fusion of public and private self. Written as private communication, they are nevertheless a recognized form of acting in the world, and particularly at court. Conceived in a state of limpid personal expression, they are nevertheless guarded, and composed with art. It is also interesting that d'Aubigné chooses to cite his letters in detail in *Sa Vie.* On the other hand, he chooses to send his reader to consult the *Histoire,* and does not quote from the *Histoire* in *Sa Vie.* He is, again, thereby privileging the expression of the self over the mere recounting of events.[29] Finally, these letters establish a near-symbiosis with the reader:

> What is more important, the reader is an accomplice. Will not the letter be read by numerous persons for whom the information was not intended? . . . [This demonstrates] the double intentionality of language. The words of a dialogue are really meant for three, at the very least.[30]

By *inviting* the reader into the universe in which he sculpts himself, d'Aubigné proposes a dialogic situation contrary to the normal, epistolary scene of reading. While d'Aubigné also at times cites his actual speeches in detail, the feeling and the intentionality are not the same. The impression of penetrating into the inner recesses of private being is reinforced by the

---

[28]Other contemporary writers of similar theological perspective literarily enact such *mises en abyme.* Edward Taylor's *Meditation 50,* for example, displays a series of boxes which dwindle in size while increasing in impact:

> O! Box of Truth! Tenent my Credence in
> The mortase of Thy truth; and thou in me.
> These mortases, and Tenents, make so trim,
> That They and Thou and I ne'er severed bee.
> Embox my Faith, Lord, in Thy truth a part
> And I'st by Faith embox Thee in my Heart.
> (II. 50, 15-50)

Mason Lowance, Jr., *The Language of Canaan: Metaphor and Symbol in New England* (Chicago: University of Chicago Press, 1980), 104.

[29]Guillèn, "Study of the Renaissance Letter," 99. "The classical radical of presentation [history] . . . [is] not sufficient for the writer willing to confront ample regions of human living and feeling."

[30]Ibid., 105.

voyeuristic gaze at a letter originally sent to another addressee. Another movement occurs within the text as well. Upon comparison of his spoken and written communication, we realize that d'Aubigné's speech mirrors his word, that the two are equally reliable and, in that sense, participate in the "plain style." For example, we find a speech and a letter in close proximity to one another on the same page. D'Aubigné's oral diatribe is certainly direct and to-the-point; he audaciously accuses Henri de Navarre of misusing him:

> Vous avez donc, Sire, peu penser à la mort de celuy que Dieu a chois pour instrument de vostre vie, service que je ne vous reproche point, non plus que ma peau percee en plusieurs endroits mais bien de vous avoir servi, sans que vous avez peu faire de moy, ni un flatteur, ni un maquereau. Dieu le vous veille pardonner. . . (405).

The letter is equally provocative; it is written to a nobleman, daring him to a duel:

> Monsieur, je vous fay resouvenir de ma franchise d'avoir contre tous advertissemens marché sur vostre parole qui est d'avoir mis l'advantage de l'appel à mon costé . . . si le Sieur de la Magdelaine a envie de fournir sa poincte, il y a beau sable entre ci et Nérac, dans lequel je prendray telle heure et telle place que vous voudrez assigner sans autres cautions (405).

Of course, the fact that personal intervention or clarifications by the author of *Sa Vie* into the text of the *Histoire* are, as we have observed, always expressed by "je," and that these letters, of similar stylistic directness, are also written by "je," also serves to establish further d'Aubigné's identity as the universal authority in an entire system of self-construction scaffolded upon *Sa Vie,* the *Histoire,* and the letters and speeches transcribed in *Sa Vie.* Thus, what might be a suspect literary construction actually vouches for original speech. D'Aubigné's selfhood is constructed as integral and possessing integrity.

　　Often d'Aubigné uses the letter as a springboard to further textual inventions. The account of Citron and the resulting sonnet that we discussed earlier arises, for instance, from an acrimonious letter d'Aubigné writes to the king (407). Whether he employs the letter as a device to amplify his arguments, or whether he textually intertwines the authorial self of the over-arching work with the correspondent self of the letters, it is significant that d'Aubigné devises a structure wherein his text may function *both* as text *and* as gloss. In this light, it is noteworthy that there are no biblical interweavings in *Sa Vie*; the extensive biblical quotations of the *Méditations,* the paraphrases from the *Tragiques,* progressively diminish in number and importance. The Bible remains for d'Aubigné the primary theological text.

But his *own* work demands recognition as a self-referential and self-sufficient *literary* entity.

Reading the Text and Writing the Self

The affirmation of literary selfhood is thus achieved. D'Aubigné revalues private expression by mythifying it, reaching toward a form of fictionalization. In order to elucidate this process, it is important to assess the types of experience and expression he deems appropriate for an autobiography. He seems to compose his "self" from fragments of recollections, textual traces such as letters, verbal transactions and, finally, from a notation of his reactions to other people and experiences. To a modern view, d'Aubigné's autobiography at times appears *décousu,* not, surprisingly, because of his copious references to the *Histoire,* but rather because he at times incorporates material which, at first glance, has nothing to do with the articulation and elaboration of his individual *persona.* For instance, he devotes several pages to the discussion of a notorious "prophetic" villager, the "muet":

> Or est-ce chose assez merveilleuse, pour à ceste occasion vous faire cognoistre ce muet. C'estoit un homme (si homme se peut dire, car les plus doctes l'ont tenu pour daemon enchanté) qui se monstroit aagé de dix neuf à vingt ans, sourd et muet, l'oeuil tres horrible, la face livide, qui avoit inventé un alphabet par les gestes et par les doigts, par le moyen duquel il s'expliquoit merveilleusement. Il a esté quatre ou cinq ans dans le Poitou . . . admiré de tous pour deviner tout ce qu'on luy proposeroit. . . . On luy amenoit quelque fois trente personnes, auxqueles il contoit toute leur genealogie, les mestiers des bisayeulx, ayeulx et grands peres, combien de mariage chacun, combien d'enfants, et enfin toutes les monoyes piece à piece que chacun avoit en sa bource. Mais tout cela n'estoit rien au prix des choses avenir et des pensees les plus occultes, desquelles il faisoit rougir et paslir chacun, et sachent Messieurs les Theologiens (de qui la censure est à craindre en cest endroit) que ce furent les Ministres les plus estimés en ce pays qui donnerent cognoissance de ce monstre à Aubigné: estant arrivé en sa maison il fit deffences á ses enfants . . . sur peine de punition de ne enquerir le muet sur les choses à venir. . . . Il faudroit une histoire à part pour vous dire comment cest homme là monstroit . . . (447-48)

Upon closer examination of this unusually detailed and apparently unrelated account, we realize two things. We see that d'Aubigné posits the "muet" as a second author, a type of creator or predictor, whom d'Aubigné anxiously seeks to neutralize so that his own text will predominate. In addition, we find that one strategy d'Aubigné employs to this end is that of fictionalization:[31] the "muet" is portrayed in super-realistic terms; he is a horrific, threatening yet fascinating figure.

In the first instance, it is notable, in light of the surrounding context of this ostensible textual anomaly, that d'Aubigné is seeking to defend and justify his own role as a seer: "Voilà où Aubigné s'estoit fait sçavant en predictions, et importun par elles, et non pas pour avoir eu chez luy le muet qu'on luy reprocha," constitutes the initial border of the episode, while "or la verité est qu'il observa religieusement de ne demander jamais [au muet] une seule chose avenir; mais son employ aux affaires et sa longue experience luy faisoyent dire ce qu'on a senty depuis" (448) completes the frame. Such a framing scheme is conventionally employed to highlight a particular incident or observation:

> Renaissance optical perspective implies a viewer and projects a scene from a specific standpoint. It is a way of relating the viewer to the painting, since it posits a specific viewing position by which the scene depicted achieves its organization.[32]

And, indeed, not only is this description set aside from the main body of the account, it is also distinguished by the intricate degree of (unnecessary?) detail it provides the reader. It is, in fact, the *single most* vivid description of the entire work. At the same time, the framed narrative acts to solicit and emphasize the role of the reader. Why, for instance, are all these specifics required if it is true that the intended readers of the text are to be d'Aubigné's children, when we know from the account that the children have already seen the "muet" for themselves?

We noted earlier that the children's function is that of "containers"[33] or guardians of the authorized text. This is shown to be d'Aubigné's hope in his injunctions to them in the preface to guard his manuscripts carefully. However, his desire is thwarted in the scene of closure with which *Sa Vie* ends: Constant, d'Aubigné's ironically-named and rebellious son, is an unworthy container. His rejection of d'Aubigné and of the text compels an end to the narrative. The termination of the text prefigures d'Aubigné's own death: "le vieillard pour garentir sa personne des puantes actions de

---

[31]Another similar, apparently unrelated episode that has miraculous and fictional elements is found on page 451: "le Pasteur de Sainct-Léonard le conduisant à Confogien, le destourna pour luy faire voir en un village le miracle d'une femme de septante ans, de qui la fille estant morte en couche [comme était la mère de d'Aubigné lui-même] elle pressa son petit fils contre son sein, s'escriant, 'O Dieu, qui te nourrira?' A ces mots l'enfant empoigna un des bous de sa grand mère, et les deux mamelles furent à l'instant pleines de laict, duquel elle l'a nourri dix-huict mois parfaitement bien."

[32]Steiner, *Colors of Rhetoric*, 60.

[33]Elsewhere, children are accorded this same role: "ses enfants seront songneux de garder les pièces justificatives de tout ce que dessus" (454).

son proche . . . ne laissa pas de se resoudre de quitter tous autres desseins, pour chercher dans Geneve une honorable mort" (463). Also, significantly, the text closes with the same concerns with which it begins: the question of a place of safe-keeping for the *persona* d'Aubigné unveils. In the beginning, he stresses the need to guard closely the two existing copies of the manuscript; in the end, he is anxious to "garentir sa personne des actions de son proche" (462). The two preoccupations underline the close relationship between text and self.

The text, a faithful repository for the self, supersedes biological offspring and remains a literary artifact which the reader, not d'Aubigné, must now reactivate. Why is the reader's attention so strongly called to order in the incident of the "muet"? It is because d'Aubigné is allowing his point-of-departure, his concern over the rival claims to the productions of truth the "muet" makes, to lead him more afield. He is himself mesmerized by the unique qualities and gifts of the "muet," so much so that he not merely describes him physically, but goes on to spin tales of situations in which the "muet" practices his powers of divination. But such digressions on d'Aubigné's part (he actually demurs, "il faudroit une histoire à part pour vous dire . . ." when he in fact has already given us that story) removes d'Aubigné from the primary focus of a work that is supposed to be about *his* life. The "muet" momentarily usurps the rightful status of d'Aubigné within his own text. We realize that this is so when d'Aubigné is so expressly at pains to command that his offspring have no dealings with the "muet"; temporarily at loss as an author, d'Aubigné insists on the observance of his paternal authority.

The "muet" acts as an author does: he is omniscient, defined by his speech which is always congruent, miraculously, with truth. Like the creator of fiction, whatever he asserts is, somehow, magically realized. Indeed, his predictions are recorded in writing, reinforcing this authorial perception of the "muet": "Il leur marqua tout ce que fait . . . et plusieurs autres choses que vous pourrés voir dans les *Epistres famillieres* qui s'imprimeront" (448). Gradually, however, d'Aubigné is able to reassert his discourse by characterizing the "muet" fictionally: he is elaborately pictured ("sourd," "muet," "l'oueil tres horrible," "la face livide"), he acts as a catalyst for the fertile fears and beliefs of the superstitious ("l'ont tenu pour daemon enchanté"; "merveilleusement," "occultes," "monstre") and he has visionary powers that, by framing this threatening image and making it an object of his tale, d'Aubigné re-appropriates and goes on to assert through his own *apophéties,* other forms of fictional permission.

Thus, within his autobiography, d'Aubigné provides us, in miniature, with a model both of the motivations of, and the techniques for, fictional writing. Coming at the culmination of d'Aubigné's literary career, the "muet" epitomizes the process of fictionalization toward which d'Aubigné works throughout his literary endeavor.

The "muet's" embedded authorial characterization serves as a reminder that the act of reading is a factor of primary importance for d'Aubigné as he writes. There are many instances in which readership is discussed in *Sa Vie*. Misreading is also linked with distortion and danger. The King "haissa la lecture" and so is easily swayed by ill counsel. The Duc d'Espernon is told by Condé that he should read the *Tragiques* and, having done so, "et luy ayant exposé les traicts du second livre, comme escripts pour luy, fit jurer la mort de l'autheur" (445). This is why d'Aubigné is so careful to give the reader detailed instructions for the interpretation of *Sa Vie*.

Consubstantial with the text, the self must, thus, also be read, not merely viewed. D'Aubigné intentionally creates pronominal confusion, forcing the reader to discern the truth of d'Aubigné's identity with the text.

It is possible that fiction may be a better way to show *process,* one of d'Aubigné's obsessions throughout his work. Fictionalization may be a medium that allows a *moveable text,* a sort of sliding plate to bring the world and the self into relation. Biblical exposition does some of these things, bringing in contemporary events or related incidents from other areas of the Bible, so it may be viewed as d'Aubigné's point of departure for fictional creation. However, while the situation of d'Aubigné glossing his own texts recalls the relationship that biblical commentators have with Scripture, it actually points up d'Aubigné's greater independence: he has no parasitical dependence on an external work, for his works provide both source and commentary. Similarly, by employing different pronouns, d'Aubigné creates a space into which the reader may enter, and within which he pivots, from one pronoun to another, as he shifts point of view with their altered directionality. Ultimately, he is brought in a full circle, as it were, *around the self,* perceiving it exhaustively, in a multi-dimensional fashion. In like manner, d'Aubigné's identity is truly circumscribed in the chiasmus effected between his literary and his actual existence, for *Sa Vie*'s termination is, within a few years, the date of its author's death. *Sa Vie* completes d'Aubigne's selfhood, just as the *Histoire* and *Sa Vie* mutually, textually, complete each other.

7

Conclusion
Strategies of Overcoming

THE CALVINIST MODEL OF STRICT BIBLICAL EXEGESIS and rejection of fictional creation is itself a structure resulting from misreading. While Calvin's theology contains implicit elements of anti-fictional polemic, he does acknowledge the looser form of theological explication, exposition, and recognizes the contribution classical and humanist authors can make to Christian doctrine when their statements are properly selected and applied.[1] However, Théodore de Bèze and the epigones, by intensifying certain emphases of Calvin's thought, altered the presentation of his theology in the world in such a way as to make predestination and determinism its predominant characteristics. The Calvinist theologian John Bray notes that de Bèze, the highly influential successor to John Calvin as pastor of Geneva and the head of the Genevan Academy during Calvin's tenure, deviates from and transforms Calvin's thought. While both share an emphasis on Scripture, de Bèze is more rigid in his belief system. "Calvin [teaches] theology primarily by means of biblical exegesis, but Beza [feels] the need to clarify and systematize the passages in question."[2] De Bèze repudiates his licentious adolescent writings, the *Poemata* (1548), along with pure humanist learning, finding that

> humanistic knowledge is not an end in itself, but is to be used as an aid to Christian theology. . . . Errors and excesses come from humanism when the humanist violates the divine boundaries of his discipline and devotes himself to vain speculation or to self-glorification.[3]

Hand-in-hand with this shift is a distrust of literature as a force tending to lead the believer away from the Word, and of fiction as a misrepresentation of truth.

---

[1]François Wendel, *Calvin et l'humanisme* (Paris: PUF, 1976), 64. "Il suffit de parcourir les ouvrages publiés par Calvin au cours de sa carrière de réformateur, pour se rendre compte que la rupture avec l'humanisme a été moins complète qu'il ne se l'est peut-être imaginée lui-même. Sa méthode éxégétique . . . est celle des humanistes."

[2]Bray, *Théodore Beza*, 33.

[3]Ibid., 42.

Hence, a concept of "self" threatens Calvinists. It opens a spatial zone for potential error in the massive block of their faith. When one analyzes the writing of men such as Agrippa d'Aubigné, who was schooled during his formative years in Geneva; remained in close correspondence with de Bèze and Goulard, his successor; borrowed heavily at times from John Calvin's work; and was well informed of the nature of de Bèze's anti-literary program as outlined in the *Abraham sacrifiant,* it becomes apparent that French reformers actively endorse the theological formulations of their Genevan prototypes and counterparts. Indeed, in order eventually to write such works as the *Avantures,* d'Aubigné has to surmount extraordinary obstacles, for literary creation is, under this system, tantamount to confessing (and rejoicing in) one's fallen state.

Other French and Genevan writers do not overcome such obstacles. Jean de Sponde never attains the innovative, fictional quality of much of d'Aubigné's later work, for instance, while Jean Crespin's prose demonstrates a lack of narrative continuity typical of the reformers' writings,[4] with the exception of their polemic (not a literary genre). By the 1580s, during which time d'Aubigné's literary career is really beginning, Calvinist preachers are, as Enay describes them and as Thomas Hall, a mere fifty years later in England, experiences the phenomenon, descrying fiction as a dangerous dilution of doctrine:

> preachers [are] proclaiming that the Arts, Sciences, Language etc. are Idols, Antichristian, the Smoak of the bottomless Pit, Filth, Froth, Dung, needlesse and uselesse for the right understanding of the Scripture.[5]

The elaboration of a conception of selfhood is closely tied to the notions of fiction and invention. The self is a construct that may interpose itself between God's Word and the soul; it is a worldly excrescence that emblematizes man's sinful nature. Focus on the self detracts from appropriate meditation on the divine. The issue is then, as Barbara Lewalski phrases it, that

> Poets writing out of an emerging Protestant aesthetics [have] to engage the question of how a poet using biblical materials [for] models can find his own artistic stance and release his own poetic voice through these materials . . . [since] laying claim to any kind of merit or desert for one's works is a dangerous sign of reprobation.[6]

---

[4]William Nelson, *Fact and Fiction,* 14. For the time-period, Nelson notes that the "rejection of stories that may mislead is a rejection of the verisimilar as a narrative mode. For if a tale resembles the truth–takes the form of history–it must be judged as history."

[5]Thomas Hall, *Vindiciae litterarum* (London, 1655), 68.

[6]Lewalski, *Protestant,* 11.

D'Aubigné reworks this mentality, subverting it through a creative re-reading of John Calvin that actually brings him closer to Calvin's thought and enables him to circumvent de Bèze and the epigones. Calvin implicitly acknowledges the value of sin in motivating his own writing; since he writes to enlighten sinners, sin is thus paradoxically necessary to the articulation of his written expression. Acknowledging his status as a sinful creator, d'Aubigné is able to work in and through the iconic theory of reading he ultimately develops. In this formulation, then, the portrait of fallen man, in Calvin's original theological explanation, is not meant to be the sole image upon which one's inner gaze is fixed, but rather is a stepping-stone that must be recognized, yet that leads beyond itself to an affirmation of God's grace. Indeed, while de Bèze promulgates the doctrine of predestination,[7] emphasizing damnation of certain souls, Calvin's focus is on the *dual* nature of predestination,[8] tallying up the total number of the elect who will be saved. The dialectical nature of sin and salvation–the one cannot exist without its opposite80is, for Calvin, a doctrinal reality from which d'Aubigné extrapolates literary ramifications.

Since sin is necessary for salvation, in furnishing the imperative of God's grace, literary creation, associated with the fall and the confusion of language at Babel, may be linked, ultimately, with redemption. Fiction may be as truthful as fact if it contains its own guarantor. D'Aubigné establishes himself as a faithful witness in the earlier stages of his literary career. He then progressively liberates himself from the constraints on fictional creation, employing several strategies in order to do so. We may observe the increasing permissions for fiction–and for the self–in the straight-forward chronological evolution of his writings. They move from exposition (the *Méditations*), to epic (*Les Tragiques*), to polemic in which he adopts an adversarial *persona,* radically altering the generic conventions of polemic so as to make of it a literary work (*Sancy*), to fiction in the *Avantures* and, finally, to an unabashed avowal of and focus on the self in *Sa Vie.*

It is evident that selfhood, as actualized through the literary coproduction of writing and reading, is a crucial construct in d'Aubigné's literary endeavor. In all his texts, we find images of himself inscribed *en abyme.* These may be veiled or explicit, but they always serve the purpose of rendering his work, even if fictional, credible. They also tie in closely with specifically literary considerations concerning the creation of a text. D'Aubigné does not gratuitously solicit the reader's response. The reader is, in fact, essential to the revivification of his texts in the world, the medium through which

---

[7]Bray, *Beza's Doctrine of Predestination,* 70. "With Beza, predestination becomes a form of philosophical determinism hardly distinguishable from the Stoic doctrine of fate. It is Beza, and not Calvin, who becomes the father of the hyper-Calvinism of Reformed theology."

[8]Ibid., 46.

praxis may take place. Correct reading may lead to salvation. In this sense, theological and literary conceptions are mutually reinforcing. While d'Aubigné, as a Calvinist, rejects works as instrumental in attaining redemption, he does not classify his texts as works, for they are, rather epitomes of his "self." Paul Ricoeur deems *praxis* the third step in actualizing mimesis.[9] While d'Aubigné certainly does not seek, through literature, to reduplicate the world (he would perceive that as a Catholic intentionality), he uses fiction iconically, forcing the reader to examine the world and then to make certain directed choices–within their religious framework–about it, in the same way Enay and Beaujeu challenge Faeneste's misapprehensions in the *Avantures.* D'Aubigné needs the reader, for it is only through the reader's reaction that d'Aubigné may observe his textual effect and, consequently, be assured of the redemptive role of the self.

Just as man is offered a choice between sinfulness and righteousness, d'Aubigné accords the reader choices among different paradigms of reading. The reader is not meant to stay within the text, fictional or otherwise, but rather to learn from it and move beyond it, in an iconic fashion. An icon forces a distinction between mere viewing, and active reading and interpretation, for the wholeness of what it represents is always beyond itself: it is always the signifier and never the signified. An icon is the *phenomenon* (appearance) that points beyond itself to the *noumenon* (being).

The close dialectical relationship between that which the text, image-like (*eidolon*), exhibits, and that which the text, icon-like (*eikonen*), directs us toward, is uniquely resolved by d'Aubigné through the technique of an elaborate, inter-referential network among his texts. While always signaling beyond itself, each individual work's designating function nevertheless remains within a closed literary universe: ultimately, no transcendental reference point (e.g. the Bible) is required, since all of d'Aubigné's works converse in and among each other. His texts thus contain signifier and signified, attaining the status of self-sufficient sign.

The significance of d'Aubigné's strategy of writing himself into his own texts is, thus, that he thereby achieves a textually mediated integrity of the self, using sin to secure salvation. He similarly inverts the status of fact and fiction. By standing as textual guarantor for his fiction, he exalts it above fact in *Sa Vie* as a bearer of truth. His freedom to rework and redefine history underlines an intense self-consciousness which is unusual for his day and age, and which stresses his important role as a daring revisionist reader, one who prefigures the modern self.

---

[9]Ricoeur, *Time and Narrative,* vol. 1, pp. 70-76.

Bibliography

PRIMARY SOURCES

Calvin, Jean. *Calvin's Commentary on Seneca,* trans. Ford Lewis Battles. Leiden: E. J. Brill, 1969.

_____. *Commentary on Genesis,* trans. the Reverend J. Anderson. Edinburgh: Calvin Translation Society, 1844-45.

_____. *Des Scandales,* ed. crit. O. Fatio. Geneva: Droz, 1984.

_____. *Institutions de la religion chrestienne,* edited by J.-P. Benoît. 5 vols. Paris: J. Vrin, 1957-63.

_____. *Institutes of the Christian Religion,* trans. Henry Beveridge. 2 vols. Grand Rapids: Eerdmans, 1962.

_____. *Lettres de Jean Calvin,* edited by J. Bonnet. 2 vols. Edinburgh: Constable, 1855-57.

Crespin, Jean. *Histoire des martyrs,* edited by D. Benoit. Toulouse: Société des livres religieux, 1885-89.

D'Aubigné, Théodore Agrippa. *Pages inédites,* edited by Pierre-Paul Plan. Geneva: Société d'histoire et d'archéologie, 1945.

_____. *Oeuvres,* edited by Eugène Réaume, and François de Caussade. 6 vols. Geneva: Slatkine Reprints, 1967.

_____. *Oeuvres,* edited by Henri Weber. Bibliothèque de la Pléiade, 206. Paris: Gallimard, NRF, 1969.

_____. *Histoire universelle,* edited by Alphonse de Ruble. 10 vols. Paris: Librairie Renouard, 1886-1909.

_____. *Mémoires,* edited by Ludovic Lalanne. Paris: Charpentier, 1854.

De Bèze, Théodore. *Abraham sacrifiant,* ed. crit. Keith Cameron. Geneva: Droz, 1967.

_____. *Chrestiennes méditations,* edited by Mario Richter. Geneva: Droz, 1964.

Des Masures, Louis. *Tragédies sainctes,* 2nd. ed. Paris: Droz, 1932.

Du Bartas, Guillaume Salluste. *La Judit,* ed. crit. André Baiche. Toulouse: Association des publications de la faculté des lettres et sciences humaines, 1971.

_____. *La Sepmaine,* edited by Yvonne Bellenger. STFM. Paris: Nizet, 1981.

Estienne, Henri. *Apologie pour Hérodote.* The Hague: Scheusler, 1735.

Goulart, Simon. *The Wise Old Man.* London: John Dawson, 1621.

Grevin, Jacques. "Bref Discours pour l'intelligence de ce théatre." *Théâtre complet,* edited by L. Pinvert. Paris: Garnier, 1922.

Marnix de Sainte-Aldegonde, Philippe de. *La Ruche de la Saincte Eglise,* trans. George Gilpin the Elder. *The BeeHive of the Romish Church.* London, 1636.

_____. "Remonstrance sérieuse sur l'estat de la Chrestienté et des moyens de la construction et salut d'iceluy." *Oeuvres.* Brussels: F. Van Meenan, 1857.

_____. "Tableau des differens de la religion." *Oeuvres.* Brussels: F. Van Meenan, 1857.

De Montenay, Georgette. *Emblesmes ou devises chrestiennes.* Lyon: Marcorelle, 1571.

Mornay, Philippe de. *De la Verité de la Religion chrestienne: Contre les Athées, Epicuriens, Paiens, Juifs, Mahumédistes et autres Infideles.* Paris: Jean Richter, 1582.

Noue, Odet de la. *Poésies chrestiennes.* Geneva, 1594.

Ramée, Pierre de la. *La Dialectique.* edited by M. Dassonville. Geneva: Droz, 1964.

Sponde, Jean de. *Méditations,* edited by Alan Boase. Geneva: Droz, 1972.

Tabourot, Estienne, Sieur des Accords. *Les Bigarrures.* Rouen: David Geoffroy, 1625.

Taille, Jean de la. *Oeuvres.* 1573. Reprinted Geneva: Slatkine, 1968.

Viret, Pierre. *The Cauteles Canon and ceremonies of the most blasphemous, abominable, monstrous, popish mass.* London: Vautrollier, 1584.

_____. *Dialogues du désordre.* Geneva, 1545.

SECONDARY SOURCES

Altizer, Alma. *Self and Symbolism in the Poetry of Michelangelo, Donne and d'Aubigné.* The Hague: Nijhoff, 1977.

Armstrong, Edward. *Robert Estienne: Royal Printer.* Cambridge: Cambridge University Press, 1954.

Allier, Robert. *Anthologie protestante française: seizième et di-septième siècles.* Geneva, 1918.

Alter, Robert. *The Art of Biblical Poetry.* New York: Basic Books, 1985.

_____. "Sacred History and the Beginnings of Prose Fiction." *Poetics Today* (1980): 143-62.

Althizer, Thomas. *Deconstruction and Theology.* New York: Crossroads Publications, 1982.

Alyn, Marc, ed. *Les Poètes du seizième siècle.* Paris: J'ai lu l'essentiel, 1962.

Arac, Jonathan, ed. *Postmodernism and Politics.* Minneapolis: University of Minnesota Press, 1986.

Aspects de la propagande religieuse. Geneva: Droz, 1957.

Auerbach, Erich. *Mimesis: The Representation of Reality in the Western World.* trans. William Trask. Garden City, New York: Doubleday, 1957.

Augustine, Saint. *Confessions,* trans. R. S. Pine-Coffin. London: Penguin Books, 1961.

Ayers, R. H. "Language, Logic and Reason in Calvin's *Institutes.*" *Religious Studies* 16 (1980): 283-97.

Aymon, Jean. *Tous les synodes nationaux des églises réformées en France.* 2 vols. La Haye, 1710.

Babelow, J.-B. "Les Débuts de la Réforme en France commémorés aux Archives nationales." *Bulletin de la société de l'histoire du protestantisme français* (1959): 145-50.

Baiche, André. "Images et baroque chez Agrippa d'Aubigné." *Actes des journées internationales du baroque.* Toulouse, 1965.

Bailbé, Jacques. "Agrippa d'Aubigné et Du Bartas." *Études seizièmistes offertes à monsieur le Professeur V.-L. Saulnier par plusieurs de ses anciens doctorants. Travaux d'humanisme et Renaissance,* 177. (Geneva: Droz, 1980).

_____. *Agrippa d'Aubigné: poète des "Tragiques."* Caen: Presse de l'université de Caen, 1968.

_____. "Rabelais et d'Aubigné." *Bibliothèque d'humanisme et Renaissance* 21 (1959): 380-419.

Barth, Karl. *Church Dogmatics,* edited by G. W. Bromley and T. F. Torrance. 4 vols. Edinburgh: T. and T. Clark, 1961.

Barthes, Roland, *S/Z.* Paris: Editions du Seuil, 1970.

Bensimon, Marc. "Essai sur Agrippa d'Aubigné Aspirations et conflits dans *les Tragiques.*" *Studi francesi* 21 (1963): 418-37.

Berthoff, Walter. "Fiction, History, Myth: Notes toward the Discrimination of Narrative Forms." *Harvard English Studies* 1 (1970): 263-87.

Bloom, Harold. *A Map of Misreading.* Oxford: Oxford University Press, 1975.

Boase, Alan, and Françoise Ruchon. *La Vie et l'oeuvre de Jean de Sponde.* Genève: Pierre Caille, 1949.

Bordier, Henri-Léonard. *Le Chansonnier huguenot du seizième siècle.* 1870. Reprinted Geneva: Slatkine, 1969.

Bossard, M. "Le Vocabulaire de la Bible française de Castellion." *Etudes lexicologiques* 2 (1959): 61-86.

Bost, Charles. *Histoire des protestants de France.* 6th ed. Carrières-sous-Poissy: La Cause, 1961.

Bouquet, Simon. *Les Imitations et traductions des cent-dix-huict emblesmes d'Alciat.* B. N. ms. fr. 19,143.

Bouwsma, William. "Calvin and the Renaissance Crisis of Knowing." *Calvin Theological Journal* (1979): 190-211.

Boyle, Marjorie. *Erasmus on Language and method in Theology.* Toronto: University of Toronto Press, 1977.

Bray, John. *Theodore Beza's Doctrine of Predestination.* Nieuwkoop: B. de Graaf, 1975.

Breen, Quirinus. "John Calvin and the Rhetorical Tradition." *Church History* 26 (1957): 3-21.

_____. *John Calvin: A Study in French Humanism.* Grand Rapids: Eerdmans, 1931.

Brunetière, Fernand. "L'Oeuvre littéraire de Calvin." *Revue des Deux Mondes* (October, 1900): 898-923.

Buffum, Imbrie. *Agrippa d'Aubigné's "Les Tragiques": Studies of the Baroque.* New Haven: Yale University Press, 1951.

Burke, Peter. *The Two Faces of Calvinism.* Oxford: Oxford University Press, 1968.

Caldwell, Patricia. *Puritan Conversion Narratives.* Cambridge: Cambridge University Press, 1983.

Calvin et la Réforme en France: Catalogue pour une exposition de la Bibliothèque nationale. Paris, 1935.

Calvin et la Réforme en France. Aix-en-Provence: Dragon, 1944.

Cameron, Keith. *Agrippa d'Aubigné.* Boston: Twayne, 1977.

Castor, Grahame. *Pléiade Poetics.* Cambridge: Cambridge University Press, 1964.

Cave, Terence. *Devotional Poetry in France: 1570-1613.* Cambridge: Cambridge University Press, 1969.

_____, and M. Jeanneret. *Métamorphoses spirituelles.* Paris: José Corti, 1972.

Celce-Murcia, Daniel. "Faeneste ou la réalisation à l'envers du héros." *Papers on Seventeenth Century French Literature* 9 (1978): 35-47.

Cerquiglini, Bernard. *La Parole médiévale: discours, syntaxe, texte.* Paris: Minuit, 1981.

Certeau, Michel de. *Heterologies: Discourse on the Other,* trans. Brian Massumi. Theory and History of Literature 17 Minneapolis: University of Minnesota Press, 1986.

Chadwick, C. "The Religion of Du Bartas." *Modern Language Notes* 69 (1954): 407-12.

Chaix, P., A. Dufour, and G. Moeckli. *Les Livres imprimés à Genève de 1550 à 1600.* Geneva: Droz, 1966.

Charbonnier, François. *La Poésie française et les guerres de religion: 1566-74.* Geneva: Slatkine, 1970.

Chatelain, Henri. "Le Style de Calvin." *Foi et Vie* (October, 1909).

Chazel, Pierre. "Y a-t-il un style réformé?" *Foi et Vie* (1947): 444-54; 588-600.

Chesneau, Augustin. *Emblesmes sacrez sur le tres saint et tres-adorable sacrement de l'eucharistie.* Bordeaux: Millanges, 1667.

Clément, Louis. *Henri Estienne et son oeuvre française.* 1899. Reprinted Geneva: Slatkine, 1967.

Clive, H. P. "The Calvinist Attitude to Music, and its Literary Aspects and Sources." *Bibliothèque d'humanisme et Renaissance* 19 (1957): 80-294.

Colish, Marcia. *The Mirror of Language: A Study in the Medieval Theory of Language.* New Haven: Yale University Press, 1968.

Colloque Calvin. Actes du Colloque Calvin à Strasbourg. Paris: Presses universitaires de France, 1965.

Coq, S. "Le Surnaturel dans *Les Tragiques.*" D.E.S. Paris: Sorbonne, 1946.

Cottrell, Robert. *Brantôme: The Writer as Portraitist of His Age.* Geneva: Droz, 1970.

_____. *The Grammar of Silence: A Reading of Marguerite de Navarre's Poetry.* Washington, D.C.: Catholic University Press, 1985.

Crosby, Virginia. "*Les Tragiques*: The Conquest of Profaned Time." Ph.D. dissertation, University of Southern California, 1969.

Culler, Jonathan. *The Pursuit of Signs: Semiotics, Literature and Deconstruction.* Ithaca: Cornell University Press, 1981.

_____. *Structuralist Poetics.* Ithaca: Cornell University Press, 1975.

Cuny, Pascal. "La *Première Sepmaine* de Du Bartas: spiritualité d'une forme." *Mélanges sur la littérature de la Renaissance à la mémoire de V.-L. Saulnier.* Geneva: Droz, 1984: 255-60.

Dagens, Jean. "La Théologie poétique au temps de Ronsard." *Le Lingue e letterature moderne nei loro rapporti con le belle arti: Atti dal Quinto Congreso Internazionale di Lingue e Letterature Moderne a Firenze* (1951): 27-31.

Davies, Rupert. *The Problem of Authority in the Continental Reformers.* London: Epworth Press, 1946.

Delumeau, Jean. *Naissance et affirmation de la Réforme.* Paris: Presses universitaires de France, 1965.

Demerson, Georges, ed. *La Notion du genre à la Renaissance.* Geneva: Slatkine, 1984.

Derrida, Jacques. *L'Ecriture et la différence.* Paris: Seuil, 1967.

_____. *Of Grammatology,* trans. G. Spivak. Baltimore: Johns Hopkins University Press, 1976.

Desonay, F. "Le Milieu de Nérac et l'inspiration baroque d'Agrippa d'Aubigné." *Actes des journées internationales de l'étude du baroque.* Toulouse, 1965.

Diehl, Huston. "Graven Images: Protestant Emblem Books in England." *Renaissance Quarterly* 39 (1986): 49-66.

Doumergue, Emile. *L'Art et le sentiment dans l'oeuvre de Calvin.* Geneva: Imprimerie Atar, 1902.

_____. *Jean Calvin, les hommes et les choses de son temps.* 7 vols. Lausanne: Bridel, 1899-1927.

Dresden, S. "La Notion d'imitation dans la littérature de la Renaissance." *Invention et Imitation,* edited by J. A. G. Tans. The Hague: Van Goor Zonen, 1968.

Droz, Eugénie. "Bibles françaises après le Concile de Trente." *Journal of the Warburg and Courtauld Institutes* 28 (1965): 210-15.

_____. *Chemins de l'hérésie: Textes et documents.* 4 vols. Genève: Slatkine Reprints, 1970-76.

Du Bois, Claude-Gilbert. *Mythe et langage au seizième siècle.* Bordeaux: Ducros, 1970.

_____. *La Conception de l'histoire en France au seizième siècle (1560-1610).* Paris: Nizet, 1977.

_____. "Les Images de parenté dans *Les Tragiques.*" *Europe* (mars, 1976): 20-51.

Du Bruck, Ernst. "Three Religious Sonneteers of the Renaissance: Sponde, Chassignet and Ceppède." *Neophilologus* 54 (1970): 235 ff.

Edwards, Michael. *Towards a Christian Poetics.* Grand Rapids: Eerdmans, 1984.

Eisenstein, Elizabeth. *The Printing Press as Agent of Change.* 2 vols. Cambridge: Cambridge University Press, 1979.

Ellul, Jacques. *L'Apocalypse: architecture en mouvement.* Brussels: Desclée, 1975.

Engels, Jean. "La Doctrine du signe chez Saint Augustin." *Studia Patristica* 6, edited by F. L. Cros. Berlin: Akademie-Verlag (1962): 366-73.

Etudes sur Calvin et le Calvinisme présentées à Paris pendant une exposition de la Bibliothèque nationale. 1935.

Fasano, G. "Per una interpretazione dei *Tragiques.*" *Saggi e richerche di letteratura francese* 24 (1965): 67-100.

Febvre, Lucien. *Au Coeur religieux du seizième siècle.* Paris: Sepven, 1957.

_____. *The Problem of Unbelief in the Sixteenth Century,* trans. B. Gottlieb. Cambridge: Harvard University Press, 1982.

_____ and H.-J. Martin. *L'Apparition du livre.* Paris: Albin Michel, 1958.

Ferguson, Margaret, Maureen Quilligan, and Nancy Vickers, eds. *Rewriting the Renaissance.* Chicago: University of Chicago Press, 1986.

Ferguson, George. *Signs and Symbols in Christian Art.* New York: Oxford University Press, 1954.

Fish, Stanley. *Self-Consuming Artifacts: The Experience of Seventeenth Century Literature.* Berkeley: University of California Press, 1972.

Fitzer, Joseph. "The Augustinian Roots of Calvin's Religious Thought." *Augustinian Studies* 7 (1976): 69-98.

Forstmann, H. J. *Word and Spirit: Calvin's Doctrine of Biblical Authority.* Stanford: Stanford University Press, 1962.

Foucault, Michel. *The Order of Things.* London: Tavistock, 1970.

Frappier, Jean. "A propos de l'esthétique de Calvin." *Bibliothèque de la Faculté de lettres de Strasbourg* 17 (1938-39): 77-85.

Frye, Northrop. *The Anatomy of Criticism.* Princeton: Princeton University Press, 1957.

_____. *The Great Code: The Bible and Literature.* New York: Harcourt, Brace, Jovanovitch, 1982.

Fumarolli, Marc. *L'Age de l'éloquence.* Geneva: Droz, 1980.

Galzy, Keith. *Agrippa d'Aubigné.* Paris: Gallimard, NRF, 1965.

Garnier, Armand. *Agrippa d'Aubigné et le parti protestant.* 3 vols. Paris: Fishbacher, 1929.

Gellrich, Jesse. "The Argument of the Book: Medieval Writing and Modern Theory." *Clio* 10 (1981): 245-63.

_____. *The Idea of the Book in the Middle Ages.* Ithaca: Cornell University Press, 1985.

Gette, Luther W. "Agrippa d'Aubigné's *Les Tragiques*: Cosmic Travail and Redemption." Ph.D. dissertation, University of Wisconsin, 1972.

Gillespie, Michael Allen. *Hegel, Heidegger and the Ground of History.* Chicago: University of Chicago Press, 1984.

Gilson, Etienne. *Painting and Reality.* New York: Pantheon Books, 1957.

Girard, René. *Violence and the Sacred.* Baltimore: Johns Hopkins University Press, 1977.

Giudici, Enzo. *Spiritualismo e carnascialismo: aspetti e problemi del Cinquecento letterario francese.* vol. 1 Napoli: Edizioni scientifiche italiane, 1968.

Goldberg, Jonathan. *Voice Terminal Echo.* Chicago: University of Chicago Press, 1986.

Gombrich, E. H. *Art and Illusion.* New York: Pantheon Books, 1960.

Gray, Floyd. "Variations on a Renaissance Theme: the Poetic Landscape and Stance of Agrippa d'Aubigné." *Philological Quarterly* 44 (1965): 433-44.

Greenberg, Mitchell. "The Poetics of Trompe-l'oeil: d'Aubigné's tableaux celestes." *Neophilologus* 53 (1979): 1-22.

Greenslade, S. L., ed. *The Cambridge History of the Bible.* 3 vols. Cambridge: Cambridge University Press, 1963-70.

Griffin, R. "Agrippa d'Aubigné: *Le Printemps* and Early French Baroque Poetry." *Symposium* 19 (1965): 197-213.

_____. "The Rebirth Motif in Agrippa d'Aubigné's *Le Printemps.*" *French Studies* 19 (1965): 227-38.

Guer, C. G. de "La Langue et le style d'Agrippa d'Aubigné étudiés dans *Les Avantures du Baron de Faeneste.*" *Le Français moderne* 9 (1941): 241-72.

Guillèn, Claudio. "Notes Toward the Study of the Renaissance Letter." In *Renaissance Genres,* edited by Barbara Lewalski. Cambridge: Harvard University Press, 1986.

Guilleroy, John. *Dalila's House.* "Rewriting the Renaissance: The Discourses of Sexual Difference in Early Modern Europe," edited by Margaret W.Ferguson, Maureen Quilligan, and Nancy J. Vickers. Chicago: University of Chicago Press, 1986.

_____. *Poetic Authority.* Chicago: Chicago University Press, 1985.

Hagiwara, M. P. *French Epic Poetry in the Sixteenth Century.* The Hague: Mouton, 1972.

Hall, Bishop Joseph. *Protestant Meditation,* edited by F. Huntley. Binghamton, N.Y.: Center for Medieval and Renaissance Studies, 1981.

Hanks, Joyce Main. *Ronsard and Biblical Tradition*. Etudes littéraires françaises, 17. Paris: Jean-Michel Place, 1982.

Harari, Josué. *Textual Strategies*. Ithaca: Cornell University Press, 1982.

Hartmann, Geoffrey. *Criticism in the Wilderness*. New Haven: Yale, 1980.

Hathaway, Baxter. *Marvels and Commonplaces: Renaissance Literary Criticism*. New York: Random House, 1968.

Hauser, Henri. *Les Débuts de l'âge moderne: la Renaissance et la Réforme*. Paris: Alcan, 1929.

Hautecoeur, Léon. "Le Concile de Trente et l'art." *La Table ronde* 190 (1963): 15-39.

Heath, J. M., and M. Payne. *Text, Interpretation, Theory*. Lewisburg, Penna.: Bucknell University Press, 1985.

Hester, Ralph. *A Protestant Baroque Poet: Pierre Poupo*. Paris: Mouton, 1970.

Higman, Francis. "The *Méditations* of Jean de Sponde: A Book for the Times." *Bibliothèque d'humanisme et Renaissance* 28 (1966): 564-82.

_____. *The Style of John Calvin in his French Polemical Treastises*. Oxford: Oxford University Press, 1967.

Hinman, Robert. "The Verser at the Temple Door." *Too Rich to Clothe the Sun*, edited by C. Summers and T. Pebworth. Pittsburgh: University of Pittsburgh Press, 1980.

Imbart de la Tour, Pierre. *Calvin*. Munich: Callwey, 1936.

Jam, A. *Agrippa d'Aubigné ou la poésie à la pointe de l'épée*. Brussels: Brepols, 1959.

Jeanneret, Michel. *Poésie et tradition biblique au seizième siècle: Recherches stylistiques sur les paraphrases des pseaumes*. Paris: Jose Corti, 1969.

_____. "Les Styles d'Agrippa d'Aubigné." *Studi francesi* 52 (1967): 246-57.

_____. "Les Tableaux spirituels d'Agrippa d'Aubigné." *Bibliothèque d'humanisme et Renaissance* 35 (1973): 232-45.

Josipovici, Gabriel. *The World and the Book*. Stanford: Stanford University Press, 1971.

Kaufmann, U. Milo. *The Pilgrim's Progress and Tradition in Puritan Meditations*. Yale Studies in English. Edited by Benjamin C. Nangle, vol. 163. New Haven: Yale University Press, 1966.

Keegstra, Peter. *"Abraham sacrifiant" de Théodore de Bèze et le théâtre calviniste de 1550 à 1566*. The Hague: Van Haeringen, 1928.

Kennedy, William J. *Rhetorical Norms in Renaissance Literature*. New Haven: Yale University Press, 1978.

Kingdon, Robert M. *Geneva and the Coming of the Wars of Religion in France*. Geneva: Droz, 1956.

_____. ed. *Registres de la compagnie des pasteurs de Genève au temps de Calvin*. Travaux d'humanisme et Renaissance, 55. Geneva: Droz, 1962.

Koenigsberger, Dorothy. *Renaissance Man and Creative Thinking: A History of Concepts of Harmony, 1400-1700*. Hassocks, Sussex: Harvester, 1979.

La Fontaine Verwey, Hervé. "Les Caractères de civilité et la propagande religieuse." *Bibliothèque d'humanisme et Renaissance* 26 (1964), 7-27.

Langer, Ulrich. *Les "Tragiques" d'Agrippa d'Aubigné: Rhétorique et intersubjectivité*. Papers of Seventeenth Century French Literature. Biblio, 17. Paris, 1983.

Lebègue, Raymond. *La Poésie française de 1560-1630.* 2 vols. Paris: S.E.D.E.S., 1951.

Le Bois, André. *La Fortune littéraire des "Tragiques" d'Agrippa d'Aubigné.* Paris: Lettres modernes, 1957.

———. "La Fortune littéraire des *Tragiques.*" *Lettres modernes* (1957): 432-38.

Lee, Rensselaer. *Ut Pictura Poesis: The Humanistic Theory of Painting.* New York: W. W. Norton, 1967.

Lefranc, Abel. *Calvin et l'éloquence française.* Paris, 1935.

Léonard, E.-G. *Calvin et la Réforme française.* Catalogue de l'exposition de la Bibliothèque nationale pour le quatrième centenaire de l'*Institution chrestienne.* Paris, 1935.

———. "Les Origines de la Réforme en France." *Calvin et la Réforme en France.* Aix-en-Provence: Dragon, 1944.

Lewalski, Barbara. *Paradise Lost and the Rhetoric of Literary Forms.* Princeton: Princeton University Press, 1985.

———. *Protestant Poetics and the Seventeenth Century Religious Lyric.* Princeton: Princeton University Press, 1979.

———, ed. *Renaissance Genres.* Cambridge: Harvard University Press, 1986.

Lowance, Mason. *The Language of Canaan: Metaphor and Symbol in New England.* Chicago: University of Chicago Press, 1980.

Macdonald, Ian. "Three Pamphlets by Agrippa d'Aubigné." *French Studies* (January, 1960): 38-51.

Mackinnon, James. *Calvin and the Reformation.* London: Longmans-Green, 1936.

Magendie, Maurice. *Le Roman français au dix-huitième siècle.* Geneva: Droz, 1932.

Martin, H.-J. "Ce qu'on lisait à Paris au seizième siècle." *Bibliothèque d'humanisme et Renaissance* 21 (1959).

Martz, Louis. *The Paradise Within.* New Haven: Yale University Press, 1964.

———. *The Poetry of Meditation.* New Haven: Yale University Press, 1962.

Mazzeo, J. A. "Augustine's Rhetoric of Silence: Truth vs. Eloquence and Things vs. Signs." *Renaissance and Seventeenth Century Studies.* New York: Columbia University Press, 1964.

McFarlane, Ian. *A Literary History of France.* New York: Barnes and Noble, 1974.

McKim, Donald, ed. *Readings in Calvin's Theology.* New York: Baker Book House, 1984.

McLuhan, Marshall. *The Gutenberg Galaxy.* Toronto: University of Toronto Press, 1964.

Ménager, Daniel. *Ronsard: le Roi, le poète, et les hommes.* Geneva: Droz, 1979.

Miller, Perry. *The New England Mind: The Seventeenth Century.* Boston: Beacon, 1951.

Minnis, A. J. *The Medieval Theory of Authorship: Scholastic Literary Attitudes in the Later Middle Ages.* London: Scolar Press, 1984.

Miquel, Pierre. *Les Guerres de religion.* Paris: Fayard, 1980.

Montaigne, Michel de. *Les Essais,* edited by P. Villey. Paris: Presses universitaires de France, 1924.

Monter, E. W. *Calvin's Geneva.* New York: Wiley, 1967.

Moore, W. G. *La Réforme allemande et la littérature française: Recherches sur la notoriété de Luther en France.* Strasbourg: Publications de la Faculté des lettres, 1930.

Morrison, Ian. "Paraître and Être: Thoughts on d'Aubigné's *Avantures du Baron de Faeneste.*" *Modern Language Review* 68 (1973): 762-70.

Nangle, Benjamin C., ed. *Yale Studies in English.* New Haven: Yale University Press, 1966.

Nelson, William. *Fact or Fiction: the Dilemma of the Renaissance Storyteller.* Cambridge: Harvard University Press, 1973.

Niesel, Wilhelm. *The Theology of Calvin,* trans. H. Knight. Philadelphia: Westminster Press, 1956.

Nothnagle, John. "Imagery in the Poetry of Agrippa d'Aubigné." Ph.D. dissertation, University of Wisconsin, 1959.

_____. "Myth in the Poetic Creation of Agrippa d'Aubigné." *Myth and Symbol* Lincoln: University of Nebraska Press, 1963. Pp. 61-70.

Ong, Walter. *Interfaces of the Word.* Ithaca: Cornell University Press, 1977.

_____. *Orality and Literacy.* London: Methuen, 1982.

_____. *The Presence of the Word.* New York: Simon and Schuster, 1970.

_____. *The Ramus Method, and the Decay of Dialogue.* Cambridge: Harvard University Press, 1958.

Parent, Annie. *Les Métiers du livre à Paris au seizième siècle: 1535-60.* Histoire et civilisation du livre, 6. Geneva: Droz, 1974.

Pelikan, Jaroslav. *The Christian Tradition: A History of the Development of Doctrine,* vol. 2. Chicago: University of Chicago Press, 1974.

Pérouse, Gabriel. *Nouvelles françaises du seizième siècle.* Geneva: Droz, 1977.

Praz, Mario. *Studies in Seventeenth Century Imagery.* 2 vols. Rome: Edizioni di storia e letteratura, 1964-75.

Preus, Robert. *The Inspiration of Scripture.* Edinburgh: Oliver and Boyd, 1955.

Peter, R. "Calvin et la traduction des *Pseaumes* de Louis Budé." *Revue d'histoire et de philosophie religieuses* 42 (1962): 188 ff.

Plattard, Jean. "Le 'beau style' de Calvin." *Bulletin de l'association Guillaume Budé* 62 (1939): 22-29.

Pybrac, Mathieu et. *Les Quatrains du Sieur Pybrac.* Paris: Robinot, 1640.

Quint, David. *Origin and Originality in Renaissance Literature: Versions of the Source.* New Haven: Yale University Press, 1983.

Raitt, Jill. *The Eucharistic Theology of Theodore Beza.* Chambersburg, Penna.: American Academy of Religion, 1972.

Raymond, Marcel. *Baroque et Renaissance poétique.* Paris, José Corti, 1955.

_____. "Réflexions sur la poésie amoureuse d'Agrippa d'Aubigné." *Mélanges en l'honneur d'Abel Lefranc.* Paris: Droz, 1936.

_____. "Calvin prosateur." *Journal de Genève* 11-12 (July, 1959): 133-52.

Regosin, Richard. *D'Aubigné's "Les Tragiques": Divine Tragedy.* Bibliothèque d'Humanisme et Renaissance: Travaux et documents, vol. 27. Geneva: Droz, 1976.

_____. "D'Aubigné's *Les Tragiques*: A Protestant Apocalypse." *PMLA* 131 (October, 1966): 363-68.

_____. *The Poetry of Inspiration: Agrippa d'Aubigné's "Les Tragiques."* Chapel Hill: University of North Carolina Press, 1970.

Reid, W. Stanford, ed. *John Calvin: His Influence on the Western World.* Grand Rapids: Zondervan, 1982.

Richter, Mario. "Aspetti et orientamenti della poetica protestante francese nel secolo XVI." *Studi francese* 2 (1967): 223-45.

_____. "Una Fonte Calvinista di J.-B. Chassignet." *Bibliothèque d'humanisme et Renaissance* 26 (1964): 341-62.

_____. *Jean de Sponde e la lingua poetica dei protestanti nel cinquecento.* Milan: Cisalpino-Goliardica, 1973.

_____. "La Poetica di Thédore de Bèze e les *Chrestiennes Méditations.*" *Aevum* 38 (1964): 574 ff.

Ricoeur, Paul. "Le Symbole donne à penser." *Esprit* (1959): 60-76.

_____. *Time and Narrative.* 2 vols., trans. K. Mclaughlin and D. Pellauer. Chicago: University of Chicago Press, 1985.

Rocheblave, S. *Agrippa d'Aubigné.* Paris: Hachette, 1910.

Rogers, Jack B., and Donald McKim. *The Authority and Interpretation of the Bible.* San Francisco: Harper and Row, 1979.

Ronsard, Pierre. *Oeuvres complètes,* ed. crit. Isidore Silver and Raymond Lebègue. 20 vols. Paris: Hachette, 1914-75.

Rousselot, Jean. *Une étude de d'Aubigné: 1552-1630.* Paris: Ecrivains d'hier et d'aujourd'hui, 1966.

Russell, Daniel. "Conception of the Self and Generic Convention." Forthcoming in *Sociocriticism.*

_____. *The Emblem and Device in Renaissance France.* Lexington, Ky.: French Forum, Publishers, 1985.

Said, Edward. *Beginnings: Intention and Method.* New York: Columbia University Press, 1982.

_____. ed. *Literature and Society: Selected Pages from the English Institute, 1978.* Baltimore: Johns Hopkins University Press, 1980.

Salmon, John. *Society in Crisis: France in the Sixteenth Century.* London: Ernest Benn, Ltd., 1975.

Sauerwein, Henry. *Agrippa d'Aubigné's "Les Tragiques": A Study in Structure and Poetic Method.* Baltimore: Johns Hopkins University Press, 1953.

Sayce, Robert. *The French Biblical Epic in the Seventeenth Century.* Oxford: Clarendon Press, 1955.

Sayous, A. *Les Ecrivains français de la Réformation.* 2 vols. Paris: Fishbacher, 1881.

Schindler, Walter. *Voice and Crisis: Invocations in Milton's Poetry.* Hamden, Conn.: Archon Books, 1984.

Schmidt, Albert-Marie. "Abel d'Argent, poète baroque et naif." *Revue de théologie et philosophie* (1959).

_____. "Calvinisme et poésie au seizième siècle en France." *Bulletin de la société de l'histoire du protestantisme français* (1935): 211-24. *Etudes sur le seizième siècle.* Paris: Albin-Michel, 1967.

_____. *Jean Calvin et la tradition calvinienne.* Paris: Editions du Seuil, 1957.

_____. "Quelques aspects de la poésie baroque protestante." *Revue des sciences humaines* 76 (October-December, 1954): 383 ff.

_____. "Remarques sur les deux derniers livres des *Tragiques*." *L'Information littéraire* 10 (1958): 47-52.

Schneidau, Herbert. *Sacred Discontent: The Bible and Western Tradition*. Berkeley: University of California Press, 1976.

Selinger, Suzanne. *Calvin Against Himself: An Inquiry in Intellectual History*. Hamden, Conn.: Archon Books, 1984.

Senebier, Jean. *Histoire littéraire de Genève*. 2 vols. Geneva: Manget et cie., 1786.

Smits, Luchesius. *Saint Augustin dans l'oeuvre de Jean Calvin*, trans. E. von Laethem. 3 vols. Assen: Van Gorcum, 1957.

Sonnenfield, A. "The Development of an Image in the Work of Agrippa d'Aubigné." *Romance Notes* 2 (1960): 42-44.

Soulié, Margeurite. *L'Inspiration biblique dans la poésie religieuse d'Agrippa d'Aubigné*. Paris: Klinckseick, 1978.

_____. "Métaphore et métamorphose chez Ronsard et d'Aubigné." *La Métamorphose dans la poésie baroque*. Actes du colloque de Valenciennes. (1979): 93-122.

_____. "L'Utilisation de la Bible dans les *Méditations* de Jean de Sponde." *Mélanges sur la littérature de la Renaissance à la mémoire de V.-L. Saulnier*. Geneva: Droz, 1984. 295-305.

Sordo, Olivia. "Agrippa d'Aubigné's *Les Tragiques* comme catharsis." Ph.D. dissertation, Indiana University, 1976.

Spitz, Lewis. *The Protestant Reformation: 1517-50*. New York: Harper and Row, 1969.

Stauffer, Richard. *Dieu, la création et la providence dans la prédication de Calvin*. Berne: Peter Lang, 1978.

_____. "Les Discours à la première personne dans les sermons de Calvin." *Revue d'histoire et de philosophie religieuses* 45 (1965): 46-78.

Steiner, Wendy. *The Colors of Rhetoric*. Chicago: University of Chicago Press, 1984.

Svoboda, K. *L'Esthétique de Saint Augustin et ses sources*. Brno, 1933.

Tarbé, Prosper. *Recueil de poésies calvinistes: 1550-66*. 2d ed. Geneva: Slatkine, 1968.

Tavard, George. *Holy Writ or Holy Church*. London: Burns and Oates, 1959.

Taylor, Edward. *The Poetical Works of Edward Taylor,* edited by T. Johson. Princeton: Princeton University Press, 1943.

TeSelle, Sally. *Speaking in Parables: A Study in Metaphor and Theology*. Philadelphia: Fortress Press, 1975.

Thierry, André. "Les Vieillards dans l'*Histoire universelle*." *Études seiziémistes* 21 (1976): 55-82.

Thomas, E. "Les Sources de l'histoire du protestantisme aux Archives Nationales." *Bulletin de la société de l'histoire du protestantisme français* (1949): 107-109.

Tieje, André. *The Theory of Characterization in Prose Fiction prior to 1740*. University of Minnesota Studies in Language and Literature, 5. Minneapolis: University of Minnesota Press, 1916.

Tinguy, Gabriel. "Agrippa d'Aubigné et le diable." *Europe* 563 (mars, 1976): 267-81.

Torrance, Thomas. *Calvin's Doctrine of Man*. London: Lutterworth, 1949.

_____. *Space, Time and Incarnation*. Oxford: Oxford University Press, 1969.

Trénel, J. *L'Elément biblique dans l'oeuvre de d'Aubigné*. Paris: Léopold Cerf, 1904.

Tricard, A. "La Propagande évangélique en France: l'imprimeur Simon du Bois." *Aspects de la propagande religieuse.* Geneva: Droz, 1957, 1-32.

Trumpi, Wesley. "The Quality of Fiction: The Rhetorical Transmission of Literary Theory." *Traditio* 30 (1974): 1-118.

Tuve, Rosamon. *Elizabethan and Metaphysical Imagery.* Chicago: University of Chicago Press, 1947.

Ullmann, Walter. *The Individual and Society in the Middle Ages.* Baltimore: Johns Hopkins University Press, 1966.

Van Veen, Otto. *Amorum emblemata.* Antwerp: C. Boel, 1608.

Vance, Eugene. "Augustine's *Confessions* and the Grammar of Selfhood." *Genre* 6 (1973): 1-28.

Varga, A. Kibédi. "La Poésie religieuse au dix-septième siècle: suggestions et cadres d'études." *Neophilologus* 46 (1962): 263.

Vianey, J. "La Bible dans la poésie française." *Revue des cours et conférences* 23 (1921-22): 31-47.

Wallace, R. S. *Calvin's Doctrine of the Work and Sacrament.* Edinburgh: Oliver and Boyd, 1953.

Warfield, Benjamin. *Calvin and Calvinism.* Oxford: Oxford University Press, 1931.

Webber, Joan. *The Eloquent "I."* Madison: University of Wisconsin Press, 1968.

Weber, Henri. *La Créations poétique au seizième siècle en France.* 2 vols. Paris: Nizet, 1956.

_____. "L'Etat présent des études sur Agrippa d'Aubigné." *Pages inédites de Théodore Agrippa d'Aubigné.* Geneva: Plon, 1945.

_____. "Structure et langage dans *Les Avantures du Baron de Faeneste.*" *Mélanges, Pierre Jourda.* Paris: Nizet, 1970.

Weitzmann, Kurt. *The Icon.* New York: Georges Braziller, 1978.

Wencelius, Léon. "Le Classicisime de Calvin." *Humanisme et Renaissance* 5 (1938): 231-46.

_____. *L'Esthétique de Calvin.* Paris: Les Belles Lettres, 1937.

Wendel, François. *Calvin et l'humanisme.* Paris: Presses universitaires de France, 1976.

White, John. *The Birth and Rebirth of Pictorial Space.* London: Faber and Faber, 1957.

Whittaker, Sir Edmund. *Space and Spirit.* Hinsdale, Ind.: Henry Regnery, 1948.

Willey, Basil. *The Seventeenth Century Background: The Thought of the The Age in Relation to Religion and Poetry.* New York: Columbia University Press, 1953.

Willis, Edward. *Calvin's Catholic Christology: the Function of the so-called "extra calvinisticum" in Calvin's Theology.* Leiden: E. J. Brill, 1966.

Wimsatt, W. K., and M. C. Beardsley. *The Verbal Icon.* New York: Noonday Press, 1965.

Wiseman, Mary Bittner. "Texts of Pleasure, Texts of Bliss." *Text, Interpretation and Theory,* edited by James M. Heath. Lewisburg, Pa.: Bucknell University Press, 1985.

Wittkower, Rudolf. "Individualism in Art and Artists: A Renaissance Perspective." *Journal of the History of Ideas* 22 (July-September, 1961): 291-302.

Yourcenar, Marguerite. "Agrippa d'Aubigné." *Nouvelle revue française* 18 (1961): 819-34.

Index